Franz-Josef Linden · Taschenlexikon der Logistik

Franz-Josef Linden

Taschenlexikon der **Logistik**

Beschaffung - Produktion - Absatz

Deutsch - Englisch – English - German

CIP-Titelaufnahme der Deutschen Bibliothek

Linden, Franz Josef:

Taschenlexikon der Logistik : Beschaffung, Produktion, Absatz ; deutsch-englisch, english-german / Franz Josef Linden. - Erstausg. - Köln : Datakontext-Verl., 1991
  ISBN 3-89209-012-2
NE: HST

ISBN 3-89209-012-2

© 1991 by DATAKONTEXT-VERLAG GmbH
Aachener Str. 1052, D-5000 Köln 40

Ohne ausdrückliche Genehmigung des Verlages ist es nicht gestattet, das Buch oder Teile daraus in irgendeiner Form zu vervielfältigen. Lizenzausgaben sind nach Vereinbarung möglich.

Druck: Raimund Roth GmbH, Solingen

Printed in Germany

Inhaltsverzeichnis - Table of Contents

1. Vorwort
   Vorbemerkung
2. Verzeichnis der Abkürzungen
3. Tabellen:
   a) Maße und Gewichte
      Deutsch - Englisch
      Englisch - Deutsch
   b) Zahlwörter
      Deutsch - Englisch
   c) Ordnungszahlen
      Deutsch - Englisch
   d) Wochentage / Monate
      Deutsch - Englisch
   e) Währungseinheit und
      Nationalitätskennzeichen
   f) Welt-Zeit-Tabelle
4. Wörterverzeichnis
   Deutsch - Englisch
   Englisch - Deutsch
5. Stichwörterverzeichnis
   Deutsch - Englisch
6. Anhang
   Anmerkungen des Autors
   Literatur und Quellen-
   nachweis

1. Foreword
   Preface Notes
2. Index of Abbreviations
3. Tables:
   a) Measures and Weights
      German - English
      English - German
   b) Numerals
      German - English
   c) Numeral Figures
      German - English
   d) Weekdays / Month
      German - English
   e) Standard Currency and
      Nationality Symbols
   f) World Time Table
4. Vocabulary
   German - English
   English - German
5. Index
   German - English
6. Appendix
   Notes of the Author
   Biographical Data-
   Reference

Vorwort

Der Entschluß, ein Fachwörterbuch der Logistik zu schaffen, entstand aufgrund der zunehmenden internationalen wirtschaftlichen Verflechtungen und insbesondere im Hinblick auf die Schaffung des "Europäischen Binnenmarktes" ab 1993 als Nachschlagewerk für die Verwendung im Bereich der Materialwirtschaft und der betrieblichen Fertigungsplanung. Die Sammlung der Wörter und Begriffe sind langjährige Erfahrungswerte und im internationalen Geschäftsverkehr praktiziert. Die Abgrenzung der Begriffe und ihre Definition gilt als vereinfachte Darstellung der Sachbezogenheit in der Materialwirtschaft. Begriffe und Begriffsinhalte werden in der deutschen und englischen Sprache nicht immer gleich gesehen, daher trägt dieses Wörterbuch zur Vereinfachung der Betrachtungsweise bei.

Die Zusammenfassung der Aufgabenstellung in der Materialwirtschaft unter der Bezeichnung "LOGISTIK" geht auf die zunehmende Bedeutung der Logistik in Wissenschaft und Industrie zurück und behandelt die betriebswirtschaftlichen Grundfunktionen: "Beschaffung - Produktion - Absatz" Ursprünglich war Logistik in der Militärsprache zusammenfassender Begriff für die Versorgung der Armee und umfaßte alle Dienste, die zur permanenten Wehrbereitschaft erforderlich waren.

Foreword

The initiative to develop a glossary of logistics is based on the increasing international trade connections particulary with regard to the "EG Free Trade Market" commencing 1993. The glossary is recommended to be used by activities of Materials Supply and Plant Production Control as reference book. The collection of words and idias are based on practical experience made during the past years. Description and definition of subjects are simplified explanation of business relation in Materials Supply. Terms and explanation of terms are not always identical in German and English language, therfore this dictionary intends to simplify the view.

The determination of Materials Supply function as "LOGISTICS" resulted from the extensive importance of logistics in science and industry and describes the basic functions of business operation: " Supply - Production - Distribution"

Original, logistics were applied to military supply actions and included all services required to maintain military preparedness.

Franz Josef Linden   Köln, im Oktober 1990

Die technische Entwicklung und Anwendung strategischer Konzepte hat in den letzten Jahren dazu geführt, daß die Disziplinen Logistik und Materialwirtschaft zunehmend in das Kosten- und Leistungsbewußtsein der Unternehmen gedrungen sind.

Vor dem Hintergrund sich weltweit öffnender Märkte und der europäischen Integration zeichnen sich für die Zukunft in den Bereichen Beschaffung, Handel, Distribution, Entsorgung sowie Transport und Verkehr neue Dimensionen ab.

Die Logistik wurde zunehmend in wettbewerbsstrategische Überlegungen einbezogen und wird in Zukunft bei globalisierenden Tendenzen noch mehr Berücksichtigung in den Strategiekonzepten der Unternehmen finden.

Der Interessenkreis, der sich mit Logistik beschäftigt und auseinandersetzt, hat sich vergrößert und wächst ständig. Logistikkonzepte und Logistikinstrumente werden komplexer und umfangreicher, wodurch der Überblick erschwert und die Verständigung über ein gemeinsames Vokabular zunehmend schwieriger wird.

Da viele Konzeptionen bereits heute grenzüberschreitend gestaltet sind, wird der Dialog zusätzlich durch sprachliche Barrieren erschwert.

Das vorliegende Taschenlexikon der Logistik versucht hier Brücken, sowohl in fachlicher als auch in sprachlicher Hinsicht, zu schlagen.

Klaus B. Bapp
Vorsitzender

Stand: Januar 1991

Vorbemerkung

Die Sortierung erfolgte beim Wörterverzeichnis in Deutsch - Englisch und Englisch - Deutsch.

Das Stichwortverzeichnis ist in Deutsch - Englisch geordnet, weil mehrheitlich bei der Suche des entsprechenden Begriffes, von der deutschen Grundbetrachtung ausgegangen wird. Um jedoch vom Englisch - Deutschen Wörterverzeichnis auf das Stichwortverzeichnis zu schließen, ist im Wörterverzeichnis jeweils die Seitenzahl als Referenz zum Stichwortverzeichnis ausgewiesen.

Technische Hinweise auf andere sachbezogene Wörter sind durch Pfeil (-►) markiert.

Die aufgeführten Abkürzungen sollen als vereinfachte Begriffserklärung dienen und die häufige Begriffsanwendung erleichtern.

Manche Grundsatzbegriffe der Logistik sind im komplexen Zusammenhang der angrenzenden Funktionen aufgeführt, um hierdurch auf die besondere Bedeutung des Sachverhaltes hinzuweisen. (-►Just in Time, -►Materialreserve u.a.)

Preface Notes

The vocabulary is listed in German - English and in English - German order.

The Index is in German - English order, as in majority the relation from German to English is required. For reason of cross reference from vocabulary to Index, there is an appropriate page numbering mentioned in the vocabulary.

Technical references to other Index are marked by (-►) arrow.

The abbreviations mentioned are understood as simplified explanation and to be used in case of repeated use as easy definition of subjects.

Some principles of logistics are specified in complex order of associate functions to draw special attention to the importance of subject items. (-►just in time, -►production material float etc.)

Abkürzungen, die im Wörterbuch Anwendung finden
Abbreviations used in this Glossary

ATR	: All-Time Requirement
BDV	: Budget Development Volume
BSK	: Bedarfsstammkarte
BUB	: Bewegungs und Bestands-Bericht
CAD	: Computer Aided Design
CAM	: Computer Aided Manufacturing
CAP	: Computer Aided Planning and Manufacturing Method
CIB	: Capital Investment Budget
CIM	: Computer Integrated Manufacturing Systems
COMECON	: Council for Mutual Economic Assistance
CPV	: Capacity Planning Volume
DC	: Departmental Communication
DPV	: Daily Planning Volume
ECU	: European Currency Unit
EDV	: Elektronische Datenverarbeitung
EG	: Europäische Gemeinschaft
EP	: External Purchase
FPV	: Financial Planning Volume
FPV	: Finanzplanungsvolumen
ICC	: International Chamber of Commerce
INCOTERMS	: International Commercial Terms
IR	: Industrial Relation
JIT	: Just-In-Time
OPT	: Optimize Production Timing
PC	: Personal Computer
PC	: Personnel Computer

PCR	:	Parts Control Record
PMR	:	Parts Movement Report
PSO	:	Parts Supply Operation
RGW	:	Rat für Gegenseitige Wirtschaftshilfe
WO	:	Work Order

Maße und Gewichte / Measures and Weights
Metrische und Englische / USA Längenmaße
Metrical and English / USA Linear Measures

Millimeter	(mm)	0,001	m	=	0,03937	inch	(in)
Zentimeter	(cm)	0,010	m	=	0,39370	inch	(in)
Dezimeter	(dm)	0,100	m	=	3,93701	inch	(in)
Meter	(m)	1,000	m	=	3,28084	feet	(ft)
Kilometer	(km)	1000	m	=	0,62137	mile	(mi)
Landmeile		7,532	km	=	4,6802	mile	(mi)
geogr. Meile		7,420	km	=	4,6115	mile	(mi)
Seemeile	(sm)	1,852	km	=	international nautical		mile	(sm)
line				=	2,539	mm	
inch	(in)	10	lines	=	25,399	mm	
foot	(ft)	12	in	=	30,480	cm	
yard	(yd)	3	ft	=	91,440	cm	
pole, rod	(rd)	5,5	yd	=	5,03	m	
chain	(ch)	4	poles	=	20,12	m	
furlong	(fur)	10	chains	=	201,17	m	
mile	(mi)	8	furlong	=	1,6093	km	
imperial nautical mile				=	1,853	km	

Metrische und Englische / USA Flächenmaße
Metrical and English / USA Square Measures

Quadratmillimeter	(mm^2)	0,01	cm^2	= 0,01550	square	inch	(sq.in)
Quadratzentimeter	(cm^2)	0,01	dm^2	= 0,1500	square	inch	(sq.in)
Quadratdezimeter	(dm^2)	0,01	m^2	= 0,10764	square	feet	(sq.ft)
Quadratmeter	(m^2)	1,00	m	= 10,76390	square	feet	(sq.ft)
Quadratkilometer	(km^2)	1000000	m^2	= 0,3861	square	miles	(sq.mi)
Land-Quadratmeile		56,73	km^2	= 21,9034	square	miles	(sq.mi)
geogr.Quadratmeile		55,06	km	= 21,2587	square	miles	(sq.mi)
Ar	(a)	100	m^2	= 119,599	square	yards	(sq.yd)
Hektar	(ha)	100	a	= 2,4711	acres		
	(ha)	10000	m^2				

square line	(sq.line)			=	6,452 mm^2	
square inch	(sq.in)	100	sq.lines	=	6,452 cm^2	
square foot	(sq.ft)	144	sq.in	=	9,290 dm^2	
square yard	(sq.yd)	9	sq.ft	=	0,836 m^2	
rod, pole, perch		30 1/4	sq.yd	=	25,289 m^2	
rood		40	rods	=	1012 m^2	= 10,12 a
acre		4	roods	=	4048 m^2	= 0,4048 ha
mile of land		640	acres	=	2,589 km^2	

Metrische und Englische/USA Raum- u. Hohlmaße
Metrical and English/USA Cubic and Capacity Measures

Kubikmillimeter	(mm³)	0,001	cm³				
Kubikzentimeter	(cm³)	0,001	dm³	=	0,0610	cubic inch	(cu. in)
Kubikdezimeter	(dm³)	0,001	m³	=	61,02	cubic inch	(cu. in)
Kubikmeter	(m³)	1,000	m³	=	35,315	cubic feet	(cu. ft)
Liter	(l)	1,000	dm³	=	1,760	imp. pints	(imp. pt)
					2,144	US-pints	(US pt)
Hektoliter	(hl)	100	l	=	21,997	imp. gallons	(imp. gal)
					20,417	US-gallons	(US gal)

cubic line	(cu. line)			=	16,39	mm³
cubic inch	(cu. inch)	1000	cu. line =	16,39	cm³
cubic foot	(cu. ft)	1728	cu. in =	28,32	dm³
cubic yard	(cu. yd)	27	cu. ft =	0,765	m³

gill			=	0,142 l	(imp.)
				0,118 l	(US)
pint	(pt)	4 gills	=	0,568 l	(imp.)
				0,473 l	(US)
quart	(qt)	2 pints	=	1,136 l	(imp.)
				0,946 l	(US)
gallon	(gal)	4 quarts	=	4,546 l	(imp.)
				3,785 l	(US)
bushel	(bu)	8 gallons	=	36,370 l	(imp.)
				35,240 l	(US)
barrel	(petroleum)	42 gallons	=	190,900 l	(imp.)
				158,800 l	(US)
barrel	(bbl)	31 gallons	=	143,200 l	(imp)
				119,200 l	(US)

Metrische und Englische / USA Gewichte
Metrical and English / USA Weights

Milligramm	(mg)	0,001 g			
Gramm	(g)	1,000 g	=	15,3846 grains	(gr)
Dekagramm	(dg)	10,000 g	=	5,6433 dram	(dr)
Hektogramm	(hg)	100,000 g	=	3,5273 ounce	(oz)
Kilogramm	(kg)	1000,000 g	=	2,2046 pounds	(lb)
Doppelzentner	(dz)	100,000 kg	=	15,7480 stone	(st)
Tonne	(t)	1000,000 kg	=	0,9842 long ton	
				1,1023 short ton	
grain	(gr)		=	0,065 g	
dram	(dr)	27,34 gr	=	1,772 g	
ounce	(oz)	16,00 dr	=	28,350 g	
pound	(lb)	16,00 oz	=	453,590 g	
stone	(st)	14,00 lb	=	6,350 kg	
quarter	(gr.)	2,00 st	=	12,700 kg	(Engl.)
				11,339 kg	(US)
hundredweight	(cwt)	4,00 gr.	=	50,802 kg	(Engl.)
				45,359 kg	(US)
long ton		20,00 cwt	=	1016,050 kg	
short cwt		100,00 lb	=	45,359 kg	
short ton		20,00 Short cwt	=	907,185 kg	

Edelmetallgewichte
Troy - Weights

grain	(gr)	0,065	g		
penyweight	(dwt)	24,00	gr	=	1,555 g
ounce	(oz)	20,00	dwt	=	31,104 g
pound	(lb)	12,00	oz	=	373,240 g

Zahlwörter / Numerals

null	0	zero	fünfzehn	15	fifteen	
eins	1	one	sechzehn	16	sixteen	
zwei	2	two	siebzehn	17	seventeen	
drei	3	three	achtzehn	18	eighteen	
vier	4	four	neunzehn	19	nineteen	
fünf	5	five	zwanzig	2o	twenty	
sechs	6	six				
sieben	7	seven	einundzwanzig	21	twenty-one	
acht	8	eight	zweiundzwanzig	22	twenty-two	
neun	9	nine	dreiundzwanzig	23	twenty-three	
zehn	10	ten				
elf	11	eleven	dreißig	30	thirty	
zwölf	12	twelve	vierzig	40	fourty	
dreizehn	13	thirteen	fünfzig	50	fifty	
vierzehn	14	fourteen	sechzig	60	sixty	
			siebzig	70	seventy	
			achtzig	80	eighty	
			neunzig	90	ninety	
			hundert	100	one hundred	
			tausend	1000	one thousand	

Ordnungszahlen / Numeral Figures

erster	:	1st first	dreizehnte	:	13th thirteenth
zweiter	:	2nd second	vierzehente	:	14th fourteenth
dritter	:	3rd third	zwanzigster	:	20th twentieth
vierter	:	4th fourth	einundzwanzigster	:	21st twenty-first
fünfter	:	5th fifth	dreißigster	:	30th thirtieth
sechster	:	6th sixth	vierzigster	:	40th fortieth
siebter	:	7th seventh	fünfzigster	:	50th fiftieth
achter	:	8th eight	sechzigste	:	60th sixtieth
neunter	:	9th ninth	siebzigster	:	70th seventieth
zehnter	:	10th tenth	achtzigster	:	80th eightieth
elfter	:	11th eleventh	neunzigster	:	90th ninetieth
zwölfte	:	12th twelfth	hundertste	:	100th one hundredth

tausendster	:	1000th	one thousandth
millionster	:	1000000th	one millionth

einfach	=	single		zweifach	=	double
dreifach	=	treble, triple		vierfach	=	fourfold
				fünffach	=	fivefold
einmal	=	once		zweimal	=	twice
dreimal	=	three times		viermal	=	four times
erstens	=	firstly		zweitens	=	secondly
drittens	=	thirdly		viertens	=	fourthly

Wochentage / Weekdays

Montag	:	Monday
Dienstag	:	Tuesday
Mittwoch	:	Wednesday
Donnerstag	:	Thursday
Freitag	:	Friday
Samstag	:	Saturday
Sonntag	:	Sunday

Monate / Months.

Januar	:	January	Juli	:	July
Februar	:	February	August	:	August
März	:	March	September	:	September
April	:	April	Oktober	:	October
Mai	:	May	November	:	November
Juni	:	June	Dezember	:	December

Währungseinheit und Nationalitätskennzeichen einiger Handelsländer
Standard Currency and Nationality Symbols of some Trading Nations

Land	Währungseinheit	Kurz-zeichen	ISO Code	Nationali-tätskenn-zeichen
Country	Standard Currency	Abbr.	ISO Code	Nationality Symbols
Ägypten	1 ägypt. Pfund	ägypt	EGP	ET
Egypt	100 Piastres			
Algerien	1 algr. Dinar	DA	DZD	DZ
Algeria	100 Centimes			
Argentinien	1 Austral		ARA	RA
Argentina	100 Centavos			
Australien	1 austral. Dollar	A	AUD	AUS
Australian	100 Cents			
Belgien	1 bel.Franc	bfr	BEC	B
Belgium	100 Centimes			
Brasilien	1 Neuer Cruzado	NC 2 $	BRN	BR
Brazil	100 Centavos			
BR Deutschland	1 Deutsche Mark	DM	DEM	D
Fed. Rep. Germany	100 Pfennig			
Bulgarien	1 Lew	Lw	BGL	BG
Bulgarian	100 Stotinki			
Chile	1 chil. Peso	Chil	CLP	RCH
Chilian	100 Centavos			
China Volksrep.	1 Ren mimbi Yuan	RMBY	CNY	VRC/TJ
China Rep.	10 Jiao			
Dänemark	1 dänische Krone	Dkr	DKK	DK
Denmark	100 Ore			
Finnland	1 Finnmark	Fmk	FIM	SF
Finland	100 Penniä			

Land	Währungseinheit	Kurz-zeichen	ISO Code	Nationali-tätskenn-zeichen
Country	Standard Currency	Abbr.	ISO	Nationality Symbols
Frankreich	1 Franc	FF	FRF	F
France	100 Centimes			
Griechenland	1 Drachme	Dr	GRD	GR
Greece	100 Lepta			
Großbritannien	1 Pfund Sterling	£	GBP	GB / UK
Great Britain	100 New Pence			
Hongkong	1 Hongk. Dollar	HK $	HKD	HK
Hongkong	100 Cents			
Indien	1 indische Rupie	iR	INR	IND
India	100 Paise			
Irak	1 Irak-Dinar	ID	IQD	IRQ
Iraquia	1000 Fils			
Iran	1 Rial	RI	IRR	IR
Iran	100 Dinars			
Irland	1 irisches Pfund	Ir £	IEP	IRL
Eire	100 New Pence			
Island	1 isländ. Krone	ikr	ISK	IS
Iceland	100 Aurar			
Italien	1 Lira	Lit	ITL	I
Italy	100 Centesimi			
Japan	1 Yen	Y	JPY	J
Japan	100 Sen			
Jugoslawien	1 jugosl.Dinar	Din	YUD	YU
Yugoslavia	100 Para			
Kanada	1 kanad. Dollar	kan	CAD	CDN
Canada	100 Cents			
Luxemburg	1 lux. Franc	lfr	LUC	L
Luxembourg	100 Centime			
Marokko	1 Dirham	DH	MAD	Ma
Morocco	100 Centimes			
Mexiko	1 mexik. Peso	mex	MXP	MEX
Mexico	100 Centavos			

Land	Währungseinheit	Kurz-zeichen	ISO Code	Nationalitätskennzeichen
Country	Standard Currency	Abbr.	ISO	Nationality Symbols
Neuseeland	1 Neus.-Dollar	NZ	NZD	NZ
New Zealand	100 Cents			
Niederlande	1 holl. Gulden	hfl	NLG	NL
Netherlands	100 Cents			
Norwegen	1 norweg.Krone	nkr	NOK	N
Norway	100 ore			
Österreich	1 Schilling	S	AIS	A
Austria	100 Groschen			
Polen	1 Zloty	Zl	PLZ	PL
Poland	100 Groszy			
Portugal	1 Escudo	Esc	PTE	P
Portuguese	100 Centavos			
Rumänien	1 Leu	l	ROL	RO
Rumanian	100 Bani			
Schweden	1 schwed. Krone	skr	SEK	S
Sweden	100 re			
Schweiz	1 Schweiz.Franke	sfr	CHF	CH
Switzerland	100 Rappen			
Spanien	1 Peseta	Pta	ESB	E
Spain	100 Centimos			
Tschechoslowakei	1 tsch. Krone	Kcs	CSK	CSFR
Czechoslovakia	100 Haleru lovakia			
Türkei	1 türk. Pfund	TL	TRL	TR
Turkey	100 Kurus			
U d S S R	1 Rubel	Rbl	SUR	UdSSR SU
Soviet Russia	100 Kopeken			
Ungarn	1 Forint	Ft	HUF	H
Hungary	100 Filler			
U S A	1 US Dollar	US	USD	USA
American	100 Cents			
Venezuela	1 Bolivar	Bs	VEB	YV
Venezuelan	100 Centimos			

Land	Währungseinheit	Kurz-zeichen	ISO Code	Nationali-tätskenn-zeichen
Country	Standard Currency	Abbr.	ISO	Nationality Symbols
Europäische Gemeinschaft	ECU Europ. Verrechnungs-Einheit	ECU a/b		EG
Common Market	ECU European Currency Unit			

a) Durchschnittswert Jan. 1990/Avarage value Jan. 1990

Amerikanische Dollar	$	1,20
Belgische Francs	bfr	42,60
Britische Pfund	£	0,73
Dänische Kronen	Dkr	7,88
Deutsche Mark	DM	2,03
Französische Francs	FF	6,92
Griechische Drachmen	Dr	189,42
Holländische Gulden	hfl	2,29
Irisches Pfund	ir £	0,77
Italienische Lire	Lit	1517,71
Japanische Yen	Y	174,60
Österreichische Schilling	S	14,26
Spanische Peseten	Pta	132,31
Portugiesische Escudo	Esc	179,29
Japanische Yen	Y	174,60
Österreichische Schilling	S	14,26
Spanische Peseten	Pta	132,31
Portugiesische Escudo	Esc	179,29

(Werte nach Börsen-Notierung Jan.90 Tageszeitung DIE WELT)

b) Der Wert einer ECU setzt sich aus der Wirtschaftskraft der EG-Länder zusammen und wird mindestens alle 5 Jahre überprüft und gegebenenfalls neu festgestellt. Der gegenwärtige Wert wurde 1989 festgestellt und erstmals Portugal und Spanien mit einbezogen.

ECU value consist of the economical position of the EG-countries and will be verified and if necessary new rated, at least every 5 years. The current value position were rated 1989 and for the first time Portuguese and Spain have been considered.

3,301 Belgische Francs	bfr	7,60 %
0,08784 Britische Pfund	£	13,00 %
0,1976 Dänische Kronen	Dkr	2,45 %
0,6242 Deutsche Mark	DM	30,10 %
1,332 Französische Francs	FF	19,00 %
1,440 Griechische Drachmen	Dr	0,80 %
0,2198 Holländische Gulden	hfl	9,40 %
0,008552 Irische Pfund	ir £	1,10 %
151,8 Italienische Lire	Lit	10,15 %
0,130 Luxemburgische Francs	lfr	0,30 %
1,393 Portugiesische Escudo	Esc	0,80 %
6,885 Spanische Peseta	Pta	5,30 %

(Werte: Handelsblatt 20.06.1989 und BMF Nr.51/89 22.09 1989)

WELT - ZEIT - TABELLE
World - Time - Table

Westliche Zeitzone

-12	-11	-10	-09	-08	-07	-06
0:00	01:00	02:00	03:00	04:00	05:00	06:00
	Wales (Alaska) Aleuten	Honolulu (Hawaii) Fairbanks Muruoa Polynesien		Los Angeles San Diego San Francisco Vancouver	Colorado Denver La-Paz (Mexico) Phoenix	Acapulco Chicago Dallas Guatemala Housten Kansas City Managua Mexico-City Milwaukee Oklahoma Sanjose Winnipeg

West-Time Zone

- 05	- 04	- 03	- 02	- 01	- 00
07:00	08:00	09:00	10:00	11:00	12:00
Atlanta	Caracas	Brasilia	Kapverdische	Azoren	Accra
Baltimore	Halifax	Buenos-Aires	Inseln	Bissau	Cassablanca
Bogota	La-Paz	Recife			Conakry
Boston	Santiago	Rio de Janeiro			Dakar
Detroit		Salvador			Dublin
Haiti		Santa Cruz			Glasgow
Havanna		Sao Paulo			Greenwich
Lima					Las Palmas
Miami					Lissabon
Montreal					London
New York					Rabat
Ottawa					Reykjavik
Philadelphia					
Quebec					
Toronto					
Washington					

WELT - ZEIT - TABELLE
World - Time - Table

Östliche Zeitzone

+ 01	+ 02	+ 03	+ 04	+ 05	+ 06
13:00	14:00	15:00	16:00	17:00	18:00
Algier	Alexandria	Addis-Abeda	Abu-Dhabi	Karatschi	Alma-Ata
Amsterdam	Amman	Aden	Eriwan	Perm	Dhaka
Barcelona	Athen	Ankara	Gorki	Swerdlowsk	Lasa
Belgrad	Bukarest	Bagdad	Kazan		Omsk
Bern	Damaskus	Daressalam	Maskat	Bombay	Taschkent
Berlin	Helsinki	Istambul	Mouritius	Neu Delhi	
Bonn	Jerusalem	Kiew		Kalkutta	
Brüssel	Johannesburg	Kuweit	Kabul	(5,5)	
Budapest	Kairo	Leningrad	(4,5)		
Koppenhagen	Kappstadt	Madagaskar			
Lagos	Khartum	Minsk			
Luanda	Lusaka	Moskau			
Luxemburg	Nairobi				
Madrid	Pretoria	Odessa			
Oslo	Sofia	Riga			
Paris	Windhuk				
Prag					
Rom					
Stockholm		Teheran			
Tripoli		(3,5)			
Tunis					
Warschau					
Wien					

27

East-Time Zone

+07	+08	+09	+10	+11	+12
19:00	20:00	21:00	22:00	23:00	24:00
Bangkok	Danton	Osaka	Brisbane	Kurilen	Auckland
Djakarta	Honkong	Pusan	Canberra	Magedan	Fidschi-
Hanoi	Kuala-Lumpur	Pyongyang	Melburne	Salomonen-	Inseln
Novosibirsk	Manila	Seoul	Sidney	Inseln	Petropawlosk
	Peking	Tokio	Wladiwostock		Wellington
	Perth				
	Shanghai	Darwin			
	Singapur	Adelaide			
	Taipeh	(9,5)			
	Wuhan				
	Xian				

Die Zeitdarstellung ist " + **oder** – " ausgehend von der West-Europäischen Zeit - WEZ (Greenwich Time).
Zeitabweichungen durch Umstellung auf Sommerzeit sind nicht immer berücksichtigt.

Explanation of time is " + **oder** – " from Greenwich Time.
Variance from standard time due to alteration of time to the summer are not always considered.

WELTZEITINDEX, bezogen auf 12h°° WEZ Greenwich-Zeit
World Time Index Relative to 12h°° WEZ Greenwich-Time

Area / Town	Acutal Time	Variance +/— to Greenwich
Abu-Dhabi	16 h°°	+ 04 h°°
Acapulco	06 h°°	— 06 h°°
Accra	12 h°°	00 h°°
Addis-Abeba	15 h°°	+ 03 h°°
Adelaide	21 h°°	+ 09 h³⁰
Aden	15 h°°	+ 03 h°°
Aleuten	01 h°°	— 11 h°°
Alexandria	14 h°°	+ 02 h°°
Algier	13 h°°	+ 01 h°°
Alma-Ata	18 h°°	+ 06 h°°
Amman	14 h°°	+ 02 h°°
Amsterdam	13 h°°	+ 01 h°°
Ankara	15 h°°	+ 03 h°°
Athen	14 h°°	+ 02 h°°
Atlanta	07 h°°	— 05 h°°
Auckland	24 h°°	+ 12 h°°
Azoren	11 h°°	— 01 h°°
Bagdad	15 h°°	+ 03 h°°
Baltimore	07 h°°	— 05 h°°
Bangkok	19 h°°	+ 07 h°°
Barcelona	13 h°°	+ 01 h°°
Belgrad	13 h°°	+ 01 h°°
Berlin	13 h°°	+ 01 h°°
Bern	13 h°°	+ 01 h°°
Bogota	07 h°°	— 05 h°°
Bombay	17 h°°	+ 05 h³⁰
Bonn	13 h°°	+ 01 h°°
Boston	07 h°°	— 05 h°°
Brasilia	09 h°°	— 03 h°°
Brisbane	22 h°°	+ 10 h°°
Brüssel	13 h°°	+ 01 h°°
Budapest	13 h°°	+ 01 h°°
Buenos-Aires	09 h°°	— 03 h°°

Bukarest	14 h°°	+ 02 h°°
Canberra	22 h°°	+ 10 h°°
Canton	20 h°°	+ 08 h°°
Caracas	08 h°°	− 04 h°°
Casablanca	12 h°°	00 h°°
Chicago	06 h°°	− 06 h°°
Colorado	05 h°°	− 07 h°°
Conakry	12 h°°	00 h°°
Dakar	12 h°°	00 h°°
Dallas	06 h°°	− 06 h°°
Damaskus	14 h°°	+ 02 h°°
Daressalam	15 h°°	+ 03 h°°
Darwin	21 h°°	+ 09 h³⁰
Denver	05 h°°	− 07 h°°
Detroit	07 h°°	− 05 h°°
Dhaka	18 h°°	+ 06 h°°
Djakarta	19 h°°	+ 07 h°°
Dublin	12 h°°	00 h°°
Eriwan	16 h°°	+ 04 h°°
Fairbanks	02 h°°	− 10 h°°
Fidschi-Inseln	24 h°°	+ 12 h°°
Glasgow	12 h°°	00 h°°
Gorki	16 h°°	+ 04 h°°
GREENWICH	**12 h°°**	**00 h°°**
Guatemala	06 h°°	− 06 h°°
Haiti	07 h°°	− 05 h°°
Halifax	08 h°°	− 04 h°°
Hanoi	19 h°°	+ 07 h°°
Havanna	07 h°°	− 05 h°°
Helsinki	14 h°°	+ 02 h°°
Hongkong	20 h°°	+ 08 h°°
Honolulu	02 h°°	− 10 h°°
Houston	06 h°°	− 06 h°°
Istanbul	15 h°°	+ 03 h°°
Jerusalem	14 h°°	+ 02 h°°
Johannesburg	14 h°°	+ 02 h°°
Kabul	16 h°°	+ 04 h³⁰
Kairo	14 h°°	+ 02 h°°
Kalkutta	17 h°°	+ 05 h³⁰
Kansas-City	06 h°°	− 06 h°°
Kapstadt	14 h°°	+ 02 h°°

Kapverdische Inseln	10 h°°	− 02 h°°
Karatschi	17 h°°	+ 05 h°°
Kazan	16 h°°	+ 04 h°°
Khartum	14 h°°	+ 02 h°°
Kiew	15 h°°	+ 03 h°°
Kopenhagen	13 h°°	+ 01 h°°
Kuala-Lumpur	20 h°°	+ 08 h°°
Kurilen	23 h°°	+ 11 h°°
Kuwait	15 h°°	+ 03 h°°
La Paz (Mexico)	05 h°°	− 07 h°°
La Paz (Bolivien)	08 h°°	− 04 h°°
Lagos	13 h°°	+ 01 h°°
Las Palmas	12 h°°	00 h°°
Lasa	18 h°°	+ 06 h°°
Leningrad	15 h°°	+ 03 h°°
Lima	07 h°°	− 05 h°°
Lissabon	12 h°°	00 h°°
London	12 h°°	00 h°°
Los Angeles	04 h°°	− 08 h°°
Luanda	13 h°°	+ 01 h°°
Lusaka	14 h°°	+ 02 h°°
Luxemburg	13 h°°	+ 01 h°°
Madagaskar	15 h°°	+ 03 h°°
Madrid	13 h°°	+ 01 h°°
Magedan	23 h°°	+ 11 h°°
Managua	06 h°°	− 06 h°°
Manila	20 h°°	+ 08 h°°
Maskat	16 h°°	+ 04 h°°
Melbourne	22 h°°	+ 10 h°°
Mexico-City	06 h°°	− 06 h°°
Miami	07 h°°	− 05 h°°
Milwaukee	06 h°°	− 06 h°°
Minsk	15 h°°	+ 03 h°°
Montreal	07 h°°	− 05 h°°
Moskau	15 h°°	+ 03 h°°
Mauritius	16 h°°	+ 04 h°°
Mururoa	02 h°°	− 10 h°°
Nairobi	15 h°°	+ 03 h°°
Neu Delhi	17 h°°	+ 05 h^{30}
New York	07 h°°	− 05 h°°
Novosibirsk	19 h°°	+ 07 h°°

Odessa	15 h°°	+ 03 h°°
Oklahoma	06 h°°	− 06 h°°
Omsk	18 h°°	+ 06 h°°
Osaka	21 h°°	+ 09 h°°
Oslo	13 h°°	+ 01 h°°
Ottawa	07 h°°	− 05 h°°
Paris	13 h°°	+ 01 h°°
Peking	20 h°°	+ 08 h°°
Perm	17 h°°	+ 05 h°°
Perth	20 h°°	+ 08 h°°
Petropawlowsk	24 h°°	+ 12 h°°
Philadelphia	07 h°°	− 05 h°°
Phoenix	05 h°°	− 07 h°°
Polynesien	02 h°°	− 10 h°°
Prag	13 h°°	+ 01 h°°
Pretoria	14 h°°	+ 02 h°°
Pusan	21 h°°	+ 09 h°°
Pyongyang	21 h°°	+ 09 h°°
Quebec	07 h°°	− 05 h°°
Rabat	12 h°°	00 h°°
Recife	09 h°°	− 03 h°°
Reykjavik	12 h°°	00 h°°
Riga	15 h°°	+ 03 h°°
Rio de Janeiro	09 h°°	− 03 h°°
Rom	13 h°°	+ 01 h°°
Salomonen	23 h°°	+ 11 h°°
Salvador	09 h°°	− 03 h°°
San Diego	04 h°°	− 08 h°°
San Francisco	04 h°°	− 08 h°°
San José	06 h°°	− 06 h°°
Santa Cruz	09 h°°	− 03 h°°
Santiago	08 h°°	− 04 h°°
Sao Paulo	09 h°°	− 03 h°°
Seoul	21 h°°	+ 09 h°°
Shanghai	20 h°°	+ 08 h°°
Sidney	22 h°°	+ 10 h°°
Singapur	20 h°°	+ 08 h°°
Sofia	14 h°°	+ 02 h°°
Stockholm	13 h°°	+ 01 h°°
Swerdlowsk	17 h°°	+ 05 h°°
Taipeh	20 h°°	+ 08 h°°

Taschkent	18 h^{oo}	+ 06 h^{oo}
Teheran	15 h^{oo}	+ 03 h^{30}
Tokio	21 h^{oo}	+ 09 h^{oo}
Toronto	07 h^{oo}	− 05 h^{oo}
Tripoli	13 h^{oo}	+ 01 h^{oo}
Tunis	13 h^{oo}	+ 01 h^{oo}
Vancouver	04 h^{oo}	− 08 h^{oo}
Wales	01 h^{oo}	− 11 h^{oo}
Warschau	13 h^{oo}	+ 01 h^{oo}
Washington	07 h^{oo}	− 05 h^{oo}
Wellington	24 h^{oo}	+ 12 h^{oo}
Wien	13 h^{oo}	+ 01 h^{oo}
Windhuk	14 h^{oo}	+ 02 h^{oo}
Winnipeg	06 h^{oo}	− 06 h^{oo}
Wladiwostock	22 h^{oo}	+ 10 h^{oo}
Wuhan	20 h^{oo}	+ 08 h^{oo}
Xian	20 h^{oo}	+ 08 h^{oo}

Zeitabweichungen durch Umstellung auf Sommerzeit sind nicht immer berücksichtigt.
UDSSR: Dekretzeit (Normalzeit plus 1 Stunde).

Variance from Standard time due to alteration of time to the summer are not always considered.
UDSSR: Decree Time (Standard time plus 1 hour).

DEUTSCH

ENGLISCH

A

Abfall	offal / waste
Abladen	unload
Abladeplatz	unloading place
Abladeschlüssel	unloading code
Ablage	file
Ablaufpunkt	off line-/buy off point
Abnahmeverpflichtung	commitment
Abrufprogramm	master schedule formula
Abschreibung f.Anlagewerte	depreciation
Abweichungsgenehmigungsantrag	deviation request
Abweichungsgrund	reason for variance
Agenturkraft/Aushilfskraft	agency labour
Aggregat	aggregate/assembly/end item
Aggregatauflösung	assembly break-down
Akkumulative	cumulative
Akkumulative-Bedarfserrechnung	cumulative req. calculation
Allzeitbedarf / ATR	ATR all-time requirement
Amortisationskosten	amortization costs
Änderung	change
Änderungsanzeige	change notice
Anfangsbestand	starting inventory
Angebot	offer/quotation
Anlauf/Produktion	start initial produktion
Anlaufkosten	launching cost
Anlieferschlüssel	delivery frequency code
Anlieferungsfreigabe	shipment authorization
Anliefertage	delivery days
Antrag	application
Anzahl	number/quantity
Arbeit	labour / work
Arbeiter	labourer
Arbeitsablaufplan	flow chart
Arbeitsanweisung	operating procedure

Arbeitsauftrag	WO, work-order
Arbeitsbedingungen	employment condition
Arbeitsfluß	work-flow
Arbeitsfolge	process sheet
Arbeitskampf/Streik	industrial dispute/strike
Arbeitskräfte	operating personnel
Arbeitslohn	wage/labour expense
Arbeitsplatz / Funktion	job position
Arbeitsplatzbeschreibung	job description
Arbeitsplatzbewertung	job evaluation
Arbeitstage	working days
Arbeitstageeinteilung	work-day-allocation
Arbeitsvorgang	working process
Arbeitszeitvorgabe/Norm	work standard
Auflage/Kürzung	task
Auflöseband	assembly break-down tape
Aufnahme / Bestand	inventory taking
Aufnahmeintervall	stocktaking frequency
Aufteilungsplan	allocation scheme
Auftrag / Bestellung	order / commission
Auftragsabwicklung	execution of order
Auftragsbestand	order bank
Auftragseinplanung/Abwicklung	respond time of order proc
ausbalancieren	balance-out
Ausbesserung/Nacharbeit	repairs rework
Ausbildung am Arbeitsplatz	on-the-job training
auseinandernehmen	dismantle/strip down
Ausfallzeit	down-time
Ausgabe/Material-Lager	crib/store
Ausgabedatum	issue date
Ausgaben	expenditure
ausgelaufenes Material	obsolete material
ausgelegte Kapazität	rated capacity
Auslauf/Fertigungsabschluß	production run-/phase out
Auslaufmaterial/zukünftiges	potential obsolescence
Auslaufschein	notice of no-requirement
Auslaufstatus	balance-out report
Auslaufteil	discontinued part

Ausschreibung	quotation
Ausschußmaterial	waste / rejects
Ausstattung/Anlagen/Einrichtung	equipment/facilities
Aussteller/Dokumente	initiator
austauschbar	interchangeable
Austauschmaterial/Teile	reconditoned-mat./parts
Austauschteilelager	recondition material store
auswählen	select
Auswertungskarte	evaluation card

B

Bauzahl	job number
Beanstandung	objection
Bedarf / Verbrauch	requirement usage
Begleitpapier	transmittal
Bedarfsänderung	requirement change
Bedarfserrechnung	requirement calculation
Bedarfsnachweis	audit trail
Bedienung	handling
Bedienungsanleitung	operation instruction
Begründung	justification
Behälter	case/casket/bin/container
Behälterkennzeichen	bin-identification
Beladung	load
Belastung/Kosten	charges
Benutzung	utilization
Bereitstellung/Verfügbarkeit	availability
Berichtigung	adjustment
Beschädigung	damage
Bestandsabstimmung	consolidated stock report
Bestandsaufnahme	cycle count / stocktaking
Bestandsaufnahmedifferenz	cycle count discrepancy
Bestandsaufnahmehäufigkeit	cycle count frequency
Bestandsbericht	stock status report
Bestandsberichtigung	inventory adjustment
Bestandsmeldung	stock report
Bestandsprüfer	cycle checker/stock chaser

Bestandsprüfung	inventory audit
Bestandssituation	stock position
Bestellbedingungen	order condition
Bestellformular	order requisition
Bestellung/Einkauf	purchase order
bestücken	feeding
Betrag/Wert	amount / value
Betrieb/Fertigung	operation / shopfloor
Betriebsausgaben	manufacturing expense
Betriebsrat	workers council
Betriebsbuchhaltung	cost accounting
Betriebshilfsmittel	non prod.items/operating supplies
Betriebskosten/Fertigung	operating cost
Beurlaubung	lay off
Bevorratung	stock pile
Bewertung/Wertbestimmung	evaluation
Bezugsmengeneinheit	unit of measure
Bezugsquelle	source
Bezugsschein	material requisition slip
Bildschirmarbeitsplatz	screen working place
Bildschirm-Masken	screen masks
Brutto-Aufwand	gross expense
Brutto-Gewinn	gross profit
BSK Bedarfsstammkarte	PCR, part control record
BUB Bewegungs-u.Best.-Bericht	PMR, part movement report
Buchnummer	book number
Buchbestand	book balance
Buchbestandsanfrage	request for book balance
Buchbestandserrechnung	book balance calculation
Buchungsvermerk	booking remark
Budget	budget
Budgetentwicklungsvolumen/BDV	BDV, budget development volume
Budgetgenehmigung	budget authorization

C

CAD Computer Aided Design	CAD computer aided design
CAM Computer Aided Manuf.	CAM computer aided manufacturing

CAP Computer Aided Planning	CAP, computer aided planning and manufacturing method
Carryover - Effect	carry over effect
Cash - Flow	cash - flow
Charakteristik	characterization
chartern	charter
CIM Computer Integrated Manufacturing Systems	CIM computer integrated manufacturing systems
Codeverzeichnis	schedule formula index
Container	container
Controller	controller
Cross - Shipping	cross - shipping
Cross - Check	cross - check

D

Datenauflistung	data file
Datenbank	data bank
Datenerstellung	data file generation
Datenübertragung	data transmission
Datenverarbeitung	data processing
Dauerverpackung	duarable packing
Dauerversuch	duarability test
De-Integration	de-intregation/outsourcing
demontieren	dismantle
Diebstahl	pilferage
Dienstanweisung	procedure
direkter Lohn	direct labour
Disponent	parts analyst
Disposition	scheduling and parts control
Dispositionskarte	scheduling card/record
Dispositionskennzeichen	record status indicator
Durchführung	realization
Durchlaufplan	sequence chart
Durchlaufzeit	respond time
Durchschnitt	average
durchzählen	count-up

E

ECU Europ. Rechnungseinheit	ECU, European Currency Unit
EDV Elektr.Datenverarbeitung	electronical data processing/EDV
effektiv	effective
EG Europäische Gemeinschaften	Common Market / EG
Eigenfertigungsteile	manufactured parts
Einbauprobe / Funktionsbau	functional build
Einfuhr / Import	importation
Einführungsdatum	introduction date
Eingabe	input
Eingang	receival / receipt
Eingangsbericht	receiving report
Eingangsdatum	receival date
Eingangsschein	delivery document
Einheit	unit
Einkauf	purchase
Einkäufer	buyer
Einkaufskostenanalyse	purchasing cost analysis
Einkaufspreis	prime cost
Einkaufsrechnung	purchase invoice
Einkaufsteil / EP	EP, external purchase
Einkaufsverbindlichkeiten	purchase commitments
Einrichtung	facility
Einrichtungsabnahme/Maschinen	acceptance of equipments / machines
Einrichtungsplan/Fabrik	layout / plant
Einsatzgewicht	rough weight
Einsatzmeldung	notification of effective date
Einsatzmenge	initial quantity
Einwegpackung	one-way package
Einzelpreis	piece price
Elektr.Bedarfserrechnung	mechanical requ.calculation
Elektr.Bestandsführung	mechanical stock control
Elektr.Warenidentifizierung	bar code reading
Empfehlung	recommendation
Endkontrolle	final inspection
Endkostenstelle	main cost center/buy off centre

Endlosformular	continous stationery
Endmontage	final assembly line
Endprodukt / Fertigprodukt	end item/finished product
Energie/Strom/Wasser	utilities/electricity/water
Energieverbrauchswerte	utility consumption data
Engpaß	bottleneck
Entladestelle	unloading area
Entwicklung	development
Entwicklungsbüro	engineering office
Entwicklungskosten/techn.	engineering costs
Entwurf/Konstruktion	design/construction
Entwurf/Projekt/Plan	project plan
Erfassungsliste	holding list/transaction register
Erfolg	efficiency
Erfolglosigkeit	inefficiency
Erfordernisse/Auflagen	legal aspects
Ersatz	replacement
Ersatzbeleg	substitute document
Ersatzteil	service part/spare part
Ersatzteile und Zubehör	parts and accessories
Ersatzteilfertigung	service part manufacturing
Ersatzteillager	spare/service parts depot
Ersatzteillager-Verwaltung/PSO	PSO, parts supply operation
Ersatzteilliste/Katalog	spare parts catalogue
ersetzen	replace
Ersparnisse/Einsparungen	savings / economics
Erstattung	refund/reimbursement
Erstfertigung	job number one/initial production
Erstmuster	initial sample
Erstmusterkontrolle	initial sample inspection
Erstmustertermin	initial sample date
Ertrag	income earned
Erweiterung	expansion
Etatkontrolle	budget control
Exportversand	export shipping
Expressendung	express shipment/1st class mail

F

Fabrik	plant/factory
Fabrik-Direktion	manufacturing staff
Fabrikation	production/manufacture
Fabrikationsplanung	manufacturing planning
Fabrikationstechnik	manufacturing engineering
Fabrikleiter	plant manager
Fabrikmarke/Zeichen	trade-mark
Facharbeiter	skilled worker/specialist
Fähre	ferry boat
Falschverbrauch	incorrect usage/misusage
Farblager	paint store
Fehlanzeige	nil return
Fehler-Analyse	error inquiry
fehlerhaft	incorrect
Fehlmeldung	failure report
Fehlmenge	missing quantity
Fertigkaufteile	purchase finished parts
Fertigungsabweichung	out of specification
Fertigungsauslastung	capacity utilization
Fertigungsauslauf	production phase out
Fertigungsausschuß	scrap/waste/rejects
Fertigungsbedingungen	in-process condition
Fertigungsdauer	manufacturing period
Fertigungsdurchlauf	manufacturing process
Fertigungsengpaß	capacity bottleneck
Fertigungserweiterung	capacity expansion
Fertigungsfreigabe	manufacturing release
Fertigungsfrequenz	manufacturing frequency
Fertigungsgemeinkosten	manufacturing overhead
Fertigungsgröße	manufacturing lot
Fertigungsinspektion	in-process inspection
Fertigungskapazität	manufacturing capacity
Fertigungskontrolle	production control
Fertigungskosten	manufacturing cost/expense
Fertigungskostenstellen	manufacturing cost centre
Fertigungsleiter	superintendent

Fertigungslenkung	manufacturing coordination
Fertigungsmeldung/Bericht	production report
Fertigungsmöglichkeit	manufacturing feasibility
Fertigungsmuster	production sample
Fertigungsplan	manufacturing plan
Fertigungsplaner	scheduling analyst
Fertigungsprogrammsteuerung	manuf.programme coordination
Fertigungsreserve	material in process
Fertigungsschlüssel	manufacturing frequency code
Fertigungssteuerung	production coordination
Fertigungstiefe	range of company produced assets
Fertigungsüberschuß	excess material
Fertigungsumstellung	machine change over
Fertigungsunterbrechung	process interruption
Fertigungsverlust	manufacturing losses
Fertigungszahl	production quantity
Fertigungszyklus	cyclic production
Festabruf	fixed order
Festpreis	fixed price
Feuerschutz	fire protection
Filiale	subsidiary
Finanz	finance
first in - first out	first in - first out
Fixmenge/ Materialreserve	fix float
Flexibilität	flexibility
Forderungen	receivables
Formaländerung	record change
FPV, Finanzplanungsvolumen	FPV, financial planning volume
Frachtbrief	consignment note
frachtfrei	free freight
Freigabe	release
Freigabenummer	release number
Fremdleistung	outside services
Frequenz	frequency
Frist/Zeitraum	lead time
Fuhrpark	transport and supply unit
Führungskräfte	supervisory personnel

Funktion	function
funktionieren	operate
Funktionsbeschreibung	statement of function
Funktionsprüfung	functional test
Funktionsüberprüfung	audit of function performance

G

Gabelstabler	fork truck
Garantie/Gewährleistung	warranty
Gebrauchsanweisung	operational instruction
gebrauchsfähig	usable/serviceable
gebrauchsfertig	ready for use
Gebühren	fees/taxes
gebührenfrei	free of charge
Gebührenordnung	tariff
Gegenstand/Sache	item
Gegenstück	counterpart
gegenwärtiger Stand	current status
Gehaltsabzüge	salary deductions
Gehaltsempfänger	salaried employee
Gehaltserhöhung	salary increase
Geldfluß	cash flow
Geldfreigabe	funds release
Geldmittel	funds on hand
Geltungsbereich	scope of validity
Gemeinkosten	overheads
Gemeinsamer Markt	Common Market
Genehmigung	approval
geplanter Verbrauch vor-	planned usage prior
geplanter Verfügbarkeit	planned availability
geringfügig	insignificant
Gesamtansicht	general view
Gesamtbedarf	total requirement
Gesamtertrag	total profit/return
Gesamtforderung	total charges
Gesamtleistung	overall efficiency
Gesamtübersicht	general survey

Gesamtwert	aggregate value
Gesamtzahl	total number
Geschäftsbericht	company report
Geschäftsgrundsatz	policy letter
Geschäftsjahr	business/trading year
Geschäftskenntnis	business experience
Geschäftsordnung	standing orders
Geschäftsreisender	commercial traveler
Geschäftssprache	commercial language
Geschäftsverbindung	business connexion
Geschäftsverkehr	commercial intercourse
geschätzt	estimate
Gesellschaft	company
Gesenkedisposition	die scheduling
Gesenkelager	die store
gesetzliche Vorschriften	legal requirements
gesetzlicher Feiertag	legal holiday
Gewerbeaufsichtamt	trade control office
Gewerbeordnung	trade regulations
Gewerkschaften	trade unions
Gewinn	profit
Gewinn nach Steuern	profit after tax
Gewinn vor Steuern	profit before tax
Gewinnprognose	profit forecast
grenzüberschreitender Verkehr	border- crossing traffic
Großraumbehälter	high cube container
Großversuch	large quantity trial
Grundlohn	base rate/base wage
Grundrißplan	layout
Gruppe	section / group
Gruppenleiter	supervisor
Gruppenstab	group staff
Gültigkeitsdauer	validity
Gültigkeitsverlängerung	extension of validity
Gutachten	appraisal
Güter	goods
Güterbeförderung	forwarding of goods
Gutschrift	crediting

H

Haftung	liability
Halbfabrikate	semi finished production goods
Halle/Fabrik	plant/building
Handbuch	manual
Handel	trade
Handelsangelegenheit	trade matter
Handelsgesellschaft	trading company
Handelsgesetz	commercial law
handelsübliches Material	general supplies
Händler	dealer
Handlung	transaction
Handlungsregister	transaction register
Harmonisierung	harmonization
Häufigkeit	frequency
Hauptlager	main store
Hauptmerkmal	main feature
Haushaltsplan	budget
Hausmitteilung/DC	DC, departmental communication
Heizmaterial	fuel
Heizwert	calorific value
Herstellungskosten	expense of production
Hilfsarbeiter	unskilled worker
Hilfsmaterial	non production material
Hilfsmaterialanforderung	non prod.mat.requisition
Hilfswerkzeug	auxiliary tool
Hochbaulager	high-bay warehouse
Hochbauregal	high-bay shelf
Höchstarbeitszeit	maximum working time
Höchstgrenze	limit
Höchstleistung	best performance/max.output
Höchstpreis	maximum price
Humanisierung der Arbeit	humanization of work

I

I.O.Teile	o.k. parts
Import	importation
Importware	articles of import
inaktives Material	inactive material
Inanspruchnahme öffentl. Mittel	utilization of public money recources
Inbetriebnahme	starting / opening
INCOTERMS / Internat. Comm. Terms	INCOTERMS / intern. commercial terms
Index	index
indirekter Lohn	indirect labour
individuelle Disposition	as required scheduling
Industrieausstellung	industrial exhibition
Industriestreik	industrial strike
Inhalt	content
Inhaltsverzeichnis	table of contents
inländische Transportzeit	inbound time
Inlandversand	inland shipping
Innenrevision	internal audit
innerbetrieblich	intra-plant
innerbetriebliche Zuordnung	internal allocation
innerbetrieblicher Versand	intra-plant shipment
inoffiziell	unofficial
Inspection	inspection
Installation	installation
Instandhaltung/vorbeugend	preventive maintenance
Instanz	instance
Instanzenweg	normal chanel
Instruktion	instruction
Integration	integration
Interimsmaßnahme	provisional measure
Internationale Handelskammer	ICC- Internat. Chamber of Commerce
Inventur	inventory/stock-taking
Inventurstichtag	annual inventory day
Investition	investment
Investitionsantrag	appropriation request

Investitionsausgaben	capital phasing/expenditure
Investitionsbudget	capital investment budget
Irrtum	error
Ist-Kosten	actual costs

J

Jahresabschluß	annual account
Jahresabschlußprüfung	year-end audit
Jahresbericht	annual report
Jahresdurchschnitt	year average
Jahresergebnis	annual return
jahresproduktion	annual production output
Jahresvertrag	contract for one year
Jahreswechselroutine	year-end routine
Jahreszahlen	year-to-date figure
jährlich	annual
Joint Venture	joint venture
Just in Time /JIT	JIT just in time

K

Kapazität	capacity
Kapazitätsausdehnung	capacity extension
Kapazitätsengpaß	capacity bottleneck
Kapazitätsgrenze	capacity limitation
Kapazitätsnutzung	work to capacity
Kapazitätsplanungsvolumen/CPV	CPV, capacity planning volume
Kapital	capital
Kapitalanlage	capital investment
Kapitalbindung	capital binding
Kapitaldienst	annual capital charge
Kapitalinvestierungsbudget/CIB	CIB, capital investment budget
Karton	cardboard box
Kasten	box
Katalog	catalogue
kaufen	purchase/buy
Kaufpreis	purchase price
Kaufteil	purchase part
Kaufvertrag	purchase contract

Kenn-Nummerung	code number
Kennwort	pass word
Kennzeichnung	identification
Kennziffer	reference number
Kettenförder-Anlage	overhead conveyor
Kilometerzähler	mileometer
klären einer Sache	clear-up a matter
Klassifizierung	classification
Knappheit	shortage
Kombination	combination
Komplexität	complexity
Konferenz	conference
Konjunktur	market condition
Konjunkturverlauf	economic trend
Konkurrent	competitor
Konkurs	bankruptcy
Konsignation	consignment
konsolidieren	consolidate
Konsolidierungsort	consolidation point
Konstrukteur	designer
Konstruktion	construction
Konsum	consumption
Konsument	user/consumer
Konten	accounts
Kontierung	allocation of accounting
Kontingent	contingent
Kontingentierung	fixing quota
Kontinuität	continuity
Kontoauszug	statement of account
Kontokorrent	current account
Kontrollabschnitt	control tag
Kontrolleur	checker
kontrollieren	checking
Kontrollpunkt	check point
konvertierbar	convertible
Konvertierbarkeit	convertibility
Konzeption	concept
Konzern	group of companies

Konzession	allowance/licence
Kooperation	cooperation
Koordination	coordination
Kopfzahl	head count
Kopie	copy
kopieren	duplicate/imitate
Korb	basket
Korrektur	correction
Korrekturmaßnahmen	corrective action
Korrespondenz	correspondence
Kosten	costs
Kostenanalyse	cost analysis
Kostenbewertung	cost evaluation
Kostenermittlung	cost finding
Kostenersparnis	cost savings
Kostenklassen	cost classification
Kostenkontrolle	cost control
Kostenrechnung	account of charges
Kostenstelle	cost centre
Kostenstellenplan	cost centre plan
Kostenumlage	cost allocation
Kostenvergleich	cost comparison
Kraftanlage	power station
Krafteinheit	unit of work
kraftlos	powerless
Kraftquelle	source of power/energy
Kraftstoff	fuel/petrol
kraftvoll	powerful
Kriterium	criterion
Kritik	critique
Küchengüter	cantine supplies
Kumulative	accumulative
Kunde	customer
Kundendienst	customer service
Kündigung	termination
Kündigungsfrist	period of notice
Kurs	exchange rate
Kursbericht	market report

Kursbuch	time table
Kursfestsetzung	rate-fixing
Kurswert	market value
Kurzarbeit	short-time work
Kurzbericht	shortage report
Kurzform	abbreviation
kurzfristig	short-dated
Kürzungs-Auflage	task

L

Laboratorium	laboratory
Lackiererei	paint shop
Ladebrief	bill of loading
Ladeeinheit	unit-load
Ladeliste	freight list
laden	freight
Laderampe	loading dock
Ladestation	loading station
Ladung	load/freight
Lageplan	layout
Lager	store/warehouse/depot
Lagerbestand	stocks inventory
Lagergebühren	charge for storage
Lagerkosten	cost of storage
lagerlose Fertigung	out of stock production
Lagerplatz	storage location
Lagerreserve	inventory reserve
Lagerumschlag	inventory turnover
Lagerverwalter	store-keeper
Länge	length
langfristig	long-term
lastenfrei	free of taxes/charges
Lastkraftwagen	truck/lorry
Lastschrift	debit
laufender Monat	current month
Laufkarte	pallet tag
Laufzeit / Lebensdauer	time span/life time

Leasing	leasing
Leergut	empties
Leergutlagerreserve	empties stock reserve
Leergutprüfer	empties checker
Lehrling	apprentice
Lehrvertrag	indenture of apprenticeship
Lehrwerkstatt	training department
Leiharbeitskraft	agency clerk
Leihverpackung	returnable packing
Leistung	performance
Leistungsbericht	performance report
Leistungseinstufung	merit rating
Leistungsfähigkeit	commercial efficiency
Leistungslohn	incentive wage
Leistungsverlust	inefficiency/off standard
Leistungszulage	merit/salary increase
Leiter	manager
Leute-Anzahl	number of people
Lieferant	supplier/vendor
Lieferanten-Informationssystem	supplier communication system
Lieferanten-Situationsbericht	supplier performance report
Lieferantenanpassung	supplier adjustment
Lieferantenfehler	supplier error
Lieferantenkartei	supplier card file
Lieferantenkontonummer	supplier account number
Lieferantenschlüssel	supplier identification code
lieferbar	available for delivery
Lieferbedingungen	delivery conditions
Lieferdifferenzen	delivery discrepancies
Liefereingang	receiving/receipt
Lieferfrequenz	delivery frequency
Liefermenge	quantity delivered
Lieferprozentsatz	delivery percentage
Lieferreserve	supply protection
Lieferschein	bill of delivery
Lieferscheinberichtigung	discrepancy note
Liefertermin	time of delivery
Liefervertrag	delivery contract

Lieferzeit	delivery time
Lieferzusage	delivery promise
Linie/Produktionsstraße	production line
Linienbestückung	line feeding
Linienverteiler	line feeder
Liste	bill
Lizenz	licence
Lochkarte	punch card
Logistik / Material Management	logistic/ material management
Lohn	wage
Lohnempfänger	hourly employee
Lohnerhöhung	wage increase
Lohnkosten	labour cost
Lohnnebenkosten	incidental wage cost
lokalisieren	determine the position
Löschkennzeichen	cancellation indicator
Losgrößen-Produktion	batch production
Luftfracht	air-freight

M

machen	make/manufacture/produce
Magazin	magazine
mangelhaft	defective
Manufaktur	manufacturing
Marke	label/brand/identification mark
Markenartikel	branded article
Markenschutz	protection of trademarks
Markt	market
Marktanteil	market share
Marktbericht	market letters
marktfähig	marketable/saleable
Marktordnung	market regulation
Maß	measurement
Maschinenausfallzeit	machine down-time
Maschinenauslastung	machine utilization
Maschinenbelegungsplan	machine sequencing

Maßeinheit	work unit
Massengüter	bulk articles
Massenverbrauch	bulk consumption
massenweise	large quantities
Materialart	type of material
Materialbestand	stock on hand
Materialbestandswert	material stock value
Materialbewegung	material movement
Materialdisponent	disposal clerk
Materialdisposition	material scheduling
Materialentnahmeschein	material requisition
Materialfluß	material flow
Materialfreigabe	material authorization
Materiallager	store/depot
Materiallieferung	material delivery
Materialplanung und Kontrolle	material planning & control
Materialreserve	production material float
Materialreserve-Wert	production material float value
Materialschaden	material damage
Materialwirtschaft	materials supply
Maximalbelastung	maximal load
Maximalbestand	maximum stock
Maximalleistung	maximum output
Mehrarbeit	overtime work
Mehrfachsatz	multi-page document
Mehrfachversand	multiple shipping
Mehrkosten	excess costs
Meister	foreman
Meldestelle	reporting point
Mengeneinheit	unit of quantity
Methodenverbesserung	method of improvement
methodisch	methodical
Mindestbestand	minimum stock
Mindestfertigungsmenge	minimum production-run
Mindestliefermenge	minimum delivery quantity
Minus-Buchbestand	minus stock balance
Modellanlauf	model launch
Modifikation	modification

monatliche Akkumulative	month-to-date figure
Monatsrate	monthly installments
Montage	assembly
Montageline	assembly line
Montagesytem/Materialbindung	assembly line float
Montagewerk	assembly plant
Mußänderung	mandatory change
Muster	sample
Musterbefund	sample report

N

Nacharbeit	rework
Nacharbeitskosten	rework expense
Nachbestellung	re-order
Nachbezahlung	subsequent payment
Nachfrage	demand/ request
Nachholtag	make-up day
Nachlieferung	additional delivery
Nachnahme	collection on-delivery
Nachricht	message
Nachtschicht	night shift
Nachtschichtzulage	night shift premium
Nachweis	supporting record
nachzählen	recount
Nebenwirkung	secondary effect
Nennbelastung	nominal load
Nettoeinkünfte	net earnings
Nettogewicht	net weight
Nettogewinn	net profit
Nettopreis	net price
Neuanschaffung	re-tool
Neueinstellungen	new hirings
Neugestaltung	inovations
Neugruppierung	re-classification
Neuordnung	re-arrangement
nicht auffindbares Material	missing material
Nicht-Produktionsmaterial	non production supplies

Niederlassung	business location
Nivellierungsprozeß	leveling process
Norm	standard
Normalarbeitszeit	normal operating hours
Notmaßnahmen	emergency actions
nutzbar	useful
Nutzen	utilization

O

Obergrenze	border line
Obermeister	general foreman
Objekt	object
Obliegenheit	obligation
offener Posten	unpaid item
Öffentlichkeitsarbeit	public relation work
offerieren	offer
offiziell	official
ökonomisch	economical
Operationsreserve	operational reserve
optimale Losgröße	optimized production rate
optimale Produktionsgestaltung	OPT optimized prod.timing
ordnungsgemäß	properly
Ordnungsstrafe	administrative fine
Organisationsgrundsätze	principles of organization
Organisationsplan	organization chart
organisieren	organize
Ortsbehörde	local authority
Ortsbesichtigung	local inspection
Ortsbezeichnung	indication of place
Ortsverkehr	local traffic
Ortszuschlag	local allowance
Output	output
Overhead	fix cost

P

Pacht	tenancy
Pachtbedingungen	terms of tenancy
Packzettel	packing slip
Paginierstempel	pagination stamp
Paket	parcel
Palette	palette
PC Personal Computer	PC, personnel computer
periodische Fertigung	periodical manufacturing
Personalbedarf	manpower requirements
Personalkosten	personnel expenses
Personallohnliste	payroll
Personalstärke	head count
Personalverwaltung/IR	IR, industrial relation
Personalvorschätzung	head count forecast
Planbestand	target inventory
planmäßig	according to plan
Planung	planning
Planzahl	target figure
Platz/Stelle/Ort	location / place
Platzmangel	short of space
Plombe	seal
plombieren	lead
Positionsbeschreibung	position description
Posten	lot
Postzeichen	mailing symbol
Preis	price
Preisabweichung	price variance
Preisangabe	quotation of price
Pressmenge	press load
Pressteile	stampings/press parts
Presswerk	press shop
Presswerkzeuge	dies/press tools
Prinzipien z. Best.d.Mat.Reserve	prinziples of float allocation
Probe	pattern
Produktentwicklung	product design development
produktionsabhängig	production related

Produktionsänderungsanzeige	product change notice
Produktionsänderungstermin	break point
Produktionsauslauf	phase out of production
Produktionsausschuß	rejects
Produktionsbeginn	start of production
Produktionsbericht	production account
Produktionserhöhung	increase in output
Produktionsfähigkeit	productive capacity
Produktionsgefahr	production risk
Produktionskontrolle	production control
Produktionskosten	production expense
Produktionsleistung	manufacturing efficiency
Produktionslenkung	production allocation programme
Produktionsmaterial	production material
Produktionsmeldung	production rate report
Produktionsprogramm	production schedule
Produktionssteigerungsrate	production rate of climb
Produktionsteil	production part
Produktionsüberschuß	excess to schedule
Produktionsunterbrechung	production interruption
Produktionsverzögerung	production delay
Prognose	forecasting
Projekt	project
Projektvorschlag	project proposal
Protokollabfassung	minute writing
Protokolländerung	alteration of the minutes
Prototyp/Musterbau	prototype/pilot build
Prüfeinrichtung	test facility
Prüfer	auditor
Prüfergebnis	check result
Prüfungshäufigkeit	checking frequency
Prüfveranlassung	query notice
Puffermenge	buffer stock
Punkt der absol. Kostendeckung	break even point

Q

Qualifikation	qualification
Qualität	quality

Qualitätsabnahmeschein	certificate of inspection
Qualitätsabweichung	deviation in quality
Qualitätskontrolle	quality control
Qualitätsnorm	standards of quality
Quantität	quantity
Quartal	quarter
Quelle/Ursprung	source of supply
quittieren	acknowledge of receipt
Quittung	receipt
Quote	share/contingent

R

Rabatt	discount
Rahmen	scope
Rang	grade
Rangordnung	ranking order
Rate	installment
Rationalisierung	rationalization
rationell	rational
Raum/Platz	room/space
Raumeinheit	unit of space
Raummangel	lack of space
Raumplanung	area planning
Raumverschwendung	waste of space
Reaktionszeit	reaction time
Rechenzentrum	data processing center
Rechnung	invoice
Rechnungseinheit	unit of account
Rechnungsjahr	financial year
Rechnungsnummer	invoice number
Rechnungsprüfung	auditing
Rechnungsstelle	accounting office
Recht	law
Rechtfertigung	justification
Rechtsanspruch	claim
Regal	shelf

Regelfall	normal case
regeln	regulate
Register	register
Reihenfolge	sequence
Reinertrag	clean profit
Reinverlust	net loss
Reisespesenabrechnung	billing of travel expenses
Reklame	publicity
reklamieren	complain
Reparaturkosten	expenditure on repairs
Reparaturwerkstatt	repair workshop
Restbestand	remainder of stocks
Restmaterialwert	scrap value
Restposten	remaining stock
Restsumme	balance
Revision	revision
RGW-Rat für gegenseitige Wirtschaftshilfe / COMECON	COMECON, Council for Mutual Economic Assistance / RGW
Richtlinien	directives
Richtwert für die Fertigung	production standards
Rohling	rough part
Rohmaterial	raw material
Rückgängigmachung	cancellation
Rückgewinnung	salvage/recovery
Rückrufaktion	recall campaign
Rückstand	arrears
Rückständig	old-fashioned
Rückversand	return shipment

S

Sachverhalt	facts of the case
Sammelladung	mixed cargo
Sammelstützpunkt	collecting point
Schaden	loss
Schadenersatz	compensation for damage
Schalterdienst	counter service
Schichteinteilung	shift pattern

Schichtwechsel	shift change
Schichtzuschlag	shift premium
Schienenverkehr	rail transport
Schiffahrt	navigation /shipping
Schmiede	forge
Schmiederohling	forging
Schrott	scrap
Schrottmeldung	scrap report
Schrottprozentsatz	scrap percentage
Schrottwert	salvage value
Schutt	rubbish
Schutzbestimmung	safety regulation
Schutzmarke	brand
Schutzzoll	protective tariff
Schwerpunkt	keypoint
Schwund	deficit
Seetransport	carriage by sea
Seeverpackung	seaproof packing
Selbstanfertigung	own make
Serienfertigung	serial production
Sicherheitseinrichtungen	safety facilities
Sicherheitsfaktor	safety factor
Skonto	discount allowance
Sollarbeitsstunden	nominal manhours
Sollbestand	target inventory
Sonderbestellung	special order
Sonderteile	options/accessories
Sonderverpackung	special wrapping
sortieren	sort
Sortiment	collection
Sparprodukt	economy product
Sparprogramm	cost reduction programme
Spediteur	carrier
Speditionsabteilung	forwarding department
Speicher	storehouse
Sperrgut	measurement cargo / goods
Sperrlager	storage area for unapproved parts
Spesen	expenses

Spezialist	specialist
Spezifikation	specification
Spitzenleistung	outstanding performance
Spitzenlohn	maximum wages
staatliche Zuschüsse	govermental grants
Stammdaten-File	parts master file
Stammkarte	master card
Standardteile	standard parts
Standort einer Industrie	location of an industry
Standzeiten für Werkzeuge	tool-life time
Stangenmaterial	bar material
Stapelplätze	staple locations
statistische Angaben	statistical data
statistische Qualitätskontrolle	statistical quality control
Steigerung	progression
Stellfläche	shelf space
Stellung	position
Stellungnahme	statement
Steuer	tax
Stichprobe	spot check
Stichtag	key date
Stillegung	shutdown
Stillstand	standstill
Störung	disturbance
Streik	strike/dispute
Stück	piece
Stückliste	bill of material
Stückzahl	piece number
Stundenlohn	wage per hour
Summe	amount
System-Menge	system float
Systemfüllung	system fill

T

Tabelle	table
Tagesordnung	agenda
Tagesplanungsvolumen/DPV	DPV, daily planning volume

Tagesrate	daily rate
Tagessatz	daily travel allowance
Tagesverbrauchswert	daily usage value
Tagung	conference
Taktzeiten	process tact time
Tarifabkommen	wage settlement
Tarifgebiet	tariff area
Tätigkeitsbereich	field of business activity
technische Änderung	technical change
technische Einrichtung	engineering facilities
technische Unterlagen	technical data
technische Verbesserung	technical improvement
Teilbezeichnung	part description
Teilefertigung	manufacturing of components
Teileklassifizierung	parts classification
Teileliste	parts list
Teilnummer	part number
Termin	stated time
termingemäß	on the agreed time
Terminplan	time schedule
Terminüberwachung	follow-up of orders
Terminverfolgungsplan	follow-up chart
Terminzahlung	payment in due time
Toleranz	tolerance
Toleranzüberschreitung	out of tolerance
Transit	transit
Transitzeiten	transit times
Transport	transport
Transportabteilung	traffic department
Transportanweisungen	shipping instructions
Transportkosten	transport charges
Transportschaden	transport damage
Typ	type

U

Überbestände	excess stocks
Überbrückung	bridge-over

Übereinkommen	agreement
überfällig	overdue
Überholung	overhaul
Überkapazität	excess capacity
Überlastung der Fertigung	overload production
Überproduktion	overproduction
Überprüfung	examination
Überschreitung des Budgets	exceeding the budget
Überstunden	extra work
Überstundenzuschlag	overtime premium
Überwachung - innerbetrieblich	in-house control
Umänderung	alteration
Umbau	rebuilding
umbuchen	rebook
Umklassifizierung	reclassification
Umrechnungskurs	conversion rate
Umsatz	overturn
Umschlaghäufigkeit	turn-over ratio
Umweltschutz	environmental safety
unbrauchbar	useless
unfertig	unfinished
ungültig	invalid
unpaarige Bewegungen	mismatched items
Unteraggregat	subassembly
Unterbeschäftigung	underemployment
Unterbrechung	interruption
Unterhalt	maintenance
Unterlieferant	subcontructor
Unternehmen	concern
Urlaubsplan	vacation schedule
Ursache	cause
Ursprungsangabe	indication of origin
Ursprungsland	country of origin

V

Vakanz	vacancy

Validierung	validity
Value added	value added
Valuta	foreign exchange
Veranschlagung	estimation
Verantwortung	responsibility
Verarbeitung	processing
Verbesserung	improvement
Verbesserungsvorschlag	suggestion scheme
Verbindlichkeiten	obligations
Verbrauch	usage
Verbraucher	consumer
Verbrauchsabweichung	usage variance
Verbrauchsbestimmung	usage determination
Verdienstausfall	loss of wages
Veredelung	finishing
Veredelungsstufe	processing stage
Veredelungsverkehr	improvement trade
Vereinheitlichung	standardization
Verfahrensplanung	planning of operation method
Verfügbarkeit	disposibility
Vergütung	compensation
Verkaufsbedingungen	sales conditions
Verkaufsorganisation	sales organization
Verkehr	traffic
Verlagerung aus Fremdbezug	integration from outside source
Verlagerung nach Fremdbezug	outsourcing of make parts
Verlustquellen	deficiencies
Verpachtung	letting on lease
Verpackungsart	type of packing
Versand	shipping
Versandabfertigung	customs clearance
Versandanzeige	advice note
Versandart	method of shipping
Versandbedingungen	forwarding terms
Versandbericht	shipping report
Versanddatum	date of dispatch
Versandkosten	shipping costs
Versandlager	shipping storage

Versandland	country of shipment
Versandliste	shipping bill
Versandpapiere	shipping documents
Versandplan	forwarding schedule
Versandreserve	shipping bank
Versandschein	clearance paper
Versandstation	shipping point
Versandveranlassung	shipping request
Versandverzögerung	delay in dispatch
Versandzeit	shipping time
verschicken	send off
verschieben	postpone
verschiedene Abgänge	miscellaneous disbursement
Verschiffung	water carriage
Verschlußlager	locked store
Verschrottung	scrapping
Verschrottungsantrag	scrapping request
versenden	deliver
Versicherung	insurance
Versuchsabteilung	pilot plant
Versuchsmaterial	tryout material
Verteiler	distributor
Verteilung	distribution
Vertrag	contract
Vertragsablauf	determination of a contract
Vertragsänderung	alteration of a contract
Vertragsannullierung	avoidance of a contract
Vertragsform	form of a contract
Vertrieb	sales
Vertriebskosten	sales cost
Vertriebsleiter	sales manager
Verwaltung	administration
Verwerfung	rejection
Verwertung	disposal
Verzeichnis	register
Verzinsung	payment of interest
Verzollung	customshouse entry
Verzug	delay

Vollbeschäftigung	full employment
vorbeugende Instandhaltung	preventive repair keeping
Vorgabezeit	standard time
Vorlaufmenge	advanced stock
Vorrat	material holding
vorrätig	carried in stock
Vorratsabbau	inventory cutting
Vorratsproduktion	stockpiling in advance
Vorschlagswesen	suggestion programme
Vorschrift	direction
Vorserie	pilot run
Vorstand	executive board
Vorteil	advantage
vorziehen von Bestellungen	predate of orders

W

Wahlgruppe	alternative parts group
Währung	currency
Waren	articles
Warenabsatz	sale of goods
Warenannahme	receiving location
Warenausgang	outgoing goods
Warenbedarf	demand of goods
Warenbestand	material in stock
Wareneingangsprüfer	receiving checker
Warengruppen	commodity pattern
Warenidentifizierungsmerkmal	bar coding of goods
Warenlager	warehouse
Warenpreis	price of goods
Warenprobe	trade pattern
Warensendung	shipment of goods
Warenumsatz	sales turnover
Warenzeichen	trade name
Wartung	servicing
Wegfall	omission
Weisung	direction
Werbung	advertising

Werk	factory
Werkhalle	shopfloor
Werksanlagen	operating facilities
Werksleistung	operating performance
Werksleitung	plant management
Werksschutz	plant security
Werkstoff	material
Werktag	weekday
werktäglich	daily
Werktechnik	plant engineering
Werkzeugausgabe	tool store
Werkzeugbau	tool shop
Wertsteigerung	increased value
Wettbewerb	competition
Wiederausfuhr	reexport
Wiedereinfuhr	reimport
Wiederverwertung	recycling
wirtschaftliche Fertigungsgröße	economical production rate
wirtschaftliche Lagerhaltung	economical stock control
Wirtschaftlichkeitsuntersuchung	profitability study
Wirtschaftsplan	economic plan
Woche	week
wöchentlich	weekly

Z

Zahl	number
zahlbar	payable
zahlen	make payment
Zahlenfolge	numerical order
Zahlenreihe	column of figures
Zählhäufigkeit	counting frequency
Zahltag	day of payment
Zählung	counting
Zahlung	payment
Zahlenübersicht	statistical table
Zahlungsbedingungen	terms of payment
Zählwaage	counting scale

Zeichnung	drawing
Zeitablauf	expiration of time
zeitgerecht	in time
Zeitplan	timing plan
Zeitpunkt	point of time
Zeitraum	period of time
Zeittafel	time indicator board
zeitverzug	loss of time
Zeitvorgabe	time allowance
zeitweilig	temporary
zerlegen	knock down
Zettel	slip
Zielvorgabe	objective
Ziffer	figure
Zinsen	interest
Zoll	customs
Zoll und Verkehrsdienste	customs and traffic
Zollabfertigung	customs examination
Zollabfertigungsamt	customs claringhouse
Zollager	bonded store
Zollbehörde	customs authorities
zollfrei	free of customs duty
zollpflichtig	liable to pay customs duty
Zolltarif	customs tariff
Zubehör	accessory
Zukunftsplanung	forward planning
Zulieferer	component supplier
Zuordnung	allocation
zurückschicken	send back
Zurückzahlung	repayment
zusammenklappbare Verpackung	collapsible package
zusätzliche Operationsreserve	add. operational reserve
Zusatzlieferung	supplementary delivery
Zuschuß/Subvention	grants/investment
Zustellung/Lieferung	delivery
Zweigbetrieb	affiliated organization
Zwischenlösung	interims solution
Zwischenprodukt	semi finished product

ENGLISH

GERMAN

A

abbreviation, 167
acceptance of equipments/
machines, 123
accessory, 232
according to plan, 191
account of charges, 165
accounting office, 199
accounts, 162
accumulative, 166
acknowledge of receipt, 197
actual costs, 155
add. operational reserve, 232
additional delivery, 185
adjustment, 112
administration, 224
administrative fine, 189
advanced stock, 225
advantage, 225
advertising, 227
advice note, 220
affilitated organization, 233
agency clerk, 171
agency labour, 106
agenda, 210
aggregate value, 142
aggregate/assembly/
end-item, 106
agreement, 213
air-freight, 176
allocation, 232
allocation of accounting, 162
allocation scheme, 109
allowance/licence, 163
alteration, 214

Kurzform
Einrichtungsabnahme/Maschinen

Zubehör
planmäßig
Kostenrechnung
Rechnungsstelle
Konten
Kumulative
quittieren
Ist-Kosten
zusätzliche Operationsreserve
Nachlieferung
Berichtigung
Verwaltung
Ordnungsstrafe
Vorlaufmenge
Vorteil
Werbung
Versandanzeige
Zweigbetrieb
Leiharbeitskraft
Agenturkraft/Aushilfskraft
Tagesordnung
Gesamtwert
Aggregat

Übereinkommen
Luftfracht
Zuordnung
Kontierung
Aufteilungsplan
Konzession
Umänderung

alteration of a contract, 223	Vertragsänderung
alteration of the minutes, 195	Protokolländerung
alternative parts group, 236	Wahlgruppe
amortization cost, 106	Amortisationskosten
amount, 114/209	Summe
amount / value, 114	Betrag/Wert
annual, 156	jährlich
annual account, 155	Jahresabschluß
annual capital charge, 158	Kapitaldienst
annual inventory day, 154	Inventurstichtag
annual production output, 155	jahresproduktion
annual report, 155	Jahresbericht
annual return, 155	Jahresergebnis
application, 107	Antrag
appraisal, 145	Gutachten
apprentice, 171	Lehrling
appropriation request, 154	Investitionsantrag
approval, 141	Genehmigung
area planning, 198	Raumplanung
arrears, 202	Rückstand
articles, 226	Waren
articles of import, 149	Importware
as required scheduling, 151	individuelle Disposition
assembly, 183	Montage
assembly break-down, 106	Aggregatauflösung
assembly break-down tape, 109	Auflöseband
assembly line, 184	Montageline
assembly line float, 184	Montagesystem/Materialbindung
assembly plant, 184	Montagewerk
ATR all-time requirement, 106	Allzeitbedarf / ATR
audit of function performance, 139	Funktionsüberprüfung
audit trail, 111	Bedarfsnachweis
auditing, 198	Rechnungsprüfung
auditor, 195	Prüfer
auxiliary tool, 148	Hilfswerkzeug
availability, 112	Bereitstellung/Verfügbarkeit
available for delivery, 173	lieferbar
average, 121	Durchschnitt

avoidance of a contract, 223	Vertragsannullierung

B

balance, 200	Restsumme
balance-out, 109	ausbalancieren
balance-out report, 110	Auslaufstatus
bankruptcy, 160	Konkurs
bar code reading, 124	Elektr. Warenidentifizierung
bar coding of goods, 227	Warenidentifizierungsmerkmal
bar material, 208	Stangenmaterial
base rate/base wage, 145	Grundlohn
basket, 164	Korb
batch production, 176	Losgrößen-Produktion
BDV budget development volume, 117	Budgetentwicklungsvolumen/BDV
best performance/max. output, 149	Höchstleistung
bill, 175	Liste
bill of delivery, 174	Lieferschein
bill of loading, 168	Ladebrief
bill of material, 209	Stückliste
billing of travel expenses, 199	Reisespesenabrechnung
bin- identification, 112	Behälterkennzeichen
bonded store, 231	Zollager
book balance, 116	Buchbestand
book balance calculation, 116	Buchbestandserrechnung
book number, 116	Buchnummer
booking remark, 117	Buchungsvermerk
border line, 187	Obergrenze
border- crossing traffic, 144	grenzüberschreitender Verkehr
bottleneck, 125	Engpaß
box, 158	Kasten
brand, 204	Schutzmarke
branded article, 177	Markenartikel
break even point, 196	Punkt der abs. Kostendeckung
break point, 193	Produktionsänderungstermin
bridge- over, 213	Überbrückung
budget, 117	Budget

budget, 147	Haushaltsplan
budget authorization, 117	Budgetgenehmigung
budget control, 128	Etatkontrolle
buffer stock, 196	Puffermenge
bulk articles, 179	Massengüter
bulk consumption, 179	Massenverbrauch
business connexion, 143	Geschäftsverbindung
business experience, 142	Geschäftskenntnis
business location, 187	Niederlassung
business/trading year, 142	Geschäftsjahr
buyer, 122	Einkäufer

C

CAD computer aided design, 117	CAD Computer Aided Design
calorific value, 148	Heizwert
CAM computer aided manufacturing, 117	CAM Computer Aided Manuf.
cancellation, 201	Rückgängigmachung
cancellation indicator, 176	Löschkennzeichen
cantine supplies, 166	Küchengüter
CAP computer aided planning and manufacturing method, 117	CAP Computer Aided Planning Manufacturing Method
capacity, 157	Kapazität
capacity bottleneck, 131	Fertigungsengpaß
capacity bottleneck, 157	Kapazitätsengpaß
capacity expansion, 131	Fertigungserweiterung
capacity extension, 157	Kapazitätsausdehnung
capacity limitation, 157	Kapazitätsgrenze
capacity utilization, 131	Fertigungsauslastung
capital, 157	Kapital
capital binding, 158	Kapitalbindung
capital investment, 157	Kapitalanlage
capital investment budget, 155	Investitionsbudget
capital phasing/expenditure, 155	Investitionsausgaben
cardboard box, 158	Karton
carriage by sea, 205	Seetransport
carried in stock, 225	vorrätig

carrier, 206	Spediteur
carry over effect, 118	Carryover - Effect
case/casket/bin/container, 112	Behälter
cash - flow, 118	Cash - Flow
cash flow, 140/180	Geldfluß
catalogue, 158	Katalog
cause, 216	Ursache
certificate of inspection, 196	Qualitätsabnahmeschein
change, 106	Änderung
change notice, 106	Änderungsanzeige
characterization, 118	Charakteristik
charge for storage, 168	Lagergebühren
charges, 112	Belastung/Kosten
charter, 118	chartern
check point, 163	Kontrollpunkt
check result, 195	Prüfergebnis
checker, 163	Kontrolleur
checking, 163	kontrollieren
checking frequency, 195	Prüfungshäufigkeit
CIB-capital investment budget, 158	Kapitalinvestierungsbudget/CIB
CIM computer integrated manufacturing systems, 118	CIM Computer Integrated Manufacturing Systems
claim, 199	Rechtsanspruch
classification, 159	Klassifizierung
clean profit, 199	Reinertrag
clear up a matter, 159	klären einer Sache
clearance paper, 221	Versandschein
code number, 159	Kenn-Nummerung
collapsible package, 232	zusammenklappbare Verpackung
collecting point, 202	Sammelstützpunkt
collection, 206	Sortiment
collection on-delivery, 185	Nachnahme
column of figures, 230	Zahlenreihe
combination, 160	Kombination
COMECON - Council for Mutual Economic Assistance / RGW, 200	RGW-Rat für gegenseitige Wirtschaftshilfe / COMMECON
commercial efficiency, 172	Leistungsfähigkeit

commercial intercourse, 143	Geschäftsverkehr
commercial language, 142	Geschäftssprache
commercial law, 146	Handelsgesetz
commercial traveler, 142	Geschäftsreisender
commitment, 105	Abnahmeverpflichtung
commodity pattern, 226	Warengruppen
Common Market, 141	Gemeinsamer Markt
Common Market / EG, 121	EG Europäische Gemeinschaften
company, 143	Gesellschaft
company report, 142	Geschäftsbericht
compensation, 219	Vergütung
compensation for damage, 202	Schadenersatz
competition, 228	Wettbewerb
competitor, 160	Konkurrent
complain, 200	reklamieren
complexity, 160	Komplexität
component supplier, 232	Zulieferer
concept, 163	Konzeption
concern, 216	Unternehmen
conference, 160	Konferenz
conference, 210	Tagung
consignment, 161	Konsignation
consignment note, 138	Frachtbrief
consolidate, 161	konsolidieren
consolidated stock report, 112	Bestandsabstimmung
consolidation point, 161	Konsolidierungsort
construction, 161	Konstruktion
consumer, 218	Verbraucher
consumption, 161	Konsum
container, 118	Container
content, 152	Inhalt
contingent, 162	Kontingent
continous stationery, 125	Endlosformular
continuity, 162	Kontinuität
contract, 223	Vertrag
contract for one year, 155	Jahresvertrag
control tag, 163	Kontrollabschnitt
controller, 118	Controller

conversion rate, 215	Umrechnungskurs
convertibility, 163	Konvertierbarkeit
convertible, 163	konvertierbar
cooperation, 163	Kooperation
coordination, 163	Koordination
copy, 164	Kopie
correction, 164	Korrektur
corrective action, 164	Korrekturmaßnahmen
correspondence, 164	Korrespondenz
cost accounting, 114	Betriebsbuchhaltung
cost allocation, 166	Kostenumlage
cost analysis, 164	Kostenanalyse
cost centre, 165	Kostenstelle
cost centre plan, 165	Kostenstellenplan
cost classification, 165	Kostenklassen
cost comparison, 166	Kostenvergleich
cost control, 165	Kostenkontrolle
cost evaluation, 164	Kostenbewertung
cost finding, 164	Kostenermittlung
cost of storage, 169	Lagerkosten
cost reduction programme, 206	Sparprogramm
cost savings, 164	Kostenersparnis
costs, 164	Kosten
count-up, 121	Durchzählen
counter service, 202	Schalterdienst
counterpart, 140	Gegenstück
counting, 230	Zählung
counting frequency, 230	Zählhäufigkeit
counting scale, 230	Zählwaage
country of origin, 217	Ursprungsland
country of shipment, 220	Versandland
CPV capacity planning volume, 157	Kapazitätsplanungsvolumen/CPV
crediting, 146	Gutschrift
crib/store, 109	Ausgabe/Material-Lager
criterion, 166	Kriterium
critique, 166	Kritik
cross - check, 118	Cross - Check

cross - shipping, 118	Cross - Shipping
cumulative, 106	Akkumulative
cumulative req. calculation, 106	Akkumulative-Bedarfserrechnung
currency, 226	Währung
current account, 162	Kontokorrent
current month, 170	laufender Monat
current status, 140	gegenwärtiger Stand
custome, 166	Kunde
customer service, 166	Kundendienst
customs, 231	Zoll
customs and traffic, 231	Zoll und Verkehrsdienste
customs authorities, 232	Zollbehörde
customs claringhouse, 231	Zollabfertigungsamt
customs clearance, 220	Versandabfertigung
customs examination, 231	Zollabfertigung
customs tariff, 232	Zolltarif
customshouse entry, 224	Verzollung
cycle checker/stock chaser, 113	Bestandsprüfer
cycle count / stocktaking, 112	Bestandsaufnahme
cycle count discrepancy, 113	Bestandsaufnahmedifferenz
cycle count frequency, 113	Bestandsaufnahmehäufigkeit
cyclic production, 135	Fertigungszyklus

D

daily, 228	werktäglich
daily rate, 210	Tagesrate
daily travel allowance, 210	Tagessatz
daily usage value, 210	Tagesverbrauchswert
damage, 112	Beschädigung
data bank, 119	Datenbank
data file, 119	Datenauflistung
data file generation, 119	Datenerstellung
data processing, 119	Datenverarbeitung
data processing center, 198	Rechenzentrum
data transmission, 119	Datenübertragung
date of dispatch, 220	Versanddatum
day of payment, 230	Zahltag

DC departmental communication, 147	Hausmitteilung/DC
de-intregation/outsourcing, 119	De-Integration
dealer, 147	Händler
debit, 170	Lastschrift
defective, 177	mangelhaft
deficiencies, 219	Verlustquellen
deficit, 204	Schwund
delay, 224	Verzug
delay in dispatch, 221	Versandverzögerung
deliver, 222	versenden
delivery, 233	Zustellung/Lieferung
delivery conditions, 173	Lieferbedingungen
delivery contract, 174	Liefervertrag
delivery days, 107	Anliefertage
delivery discrepancies, 173	Lieferdifferenzen
delivery document, 122	Eingangsschein
delivery frequency, 173	Lieferfrequenz
delivery frequency code, 107	Anlieferschlüssel
delivery percentage, 174	Lieferprozentsatz
delivery promise, 174	Lieferzusage
delivery time, 174	Lieferzeit
demand of goods, 226	Warenbedarf
demand/request, 185	Nachfrage
depreciation, 105	Abschreibung f.Anlagewerte
design/construction, 126	Entwurf/Konstruktion
designer, 161	Konstrukteur
determination of a contract, 223	Vertragsablauf
determine the position, 176	lokalisieren
development, 125	Entwicklung
deviation in quality, 196	Qualitätsabweichung
deviation request, 105	Abweichungsgenehmigungsantrag
die scheduling, 143	Gesenkedisposition
die store, 143	Gesenkelager
dies/press tools, 192	Presswerkzeuge
direct labour, 120	direkter Lohn
direction, 225	Vorschrift

direction, 227	Weisung
directives, 201	Richtlinien
discontinued part, 110	Auslaufteil
discount, 197	Rabatt
discount allowance, 205	Skonto
discrepancy note, 174	Lieferscheinberichtigung
dismantle, 119	demontieren
dismantle/strip down, 109	auseinandernehmen
disposal, 224	Verwertung
disposal clerk, 179	Materialdisponent
disposibility, 219	Verfügbarkeit
distribution, 223	Verteilung
distributor, 223	Verteiler
disturbance, 209	Störung
down-time, 109	Ausfallzeit
DPV- daily planning volume, 210	Tagesplanungsvolumen/DPV
drawing, 230	Zeichnung
duarability test, 119	Dauerversuch
duarable packing, 119	Dauerverpackung
duplicate/imitate, 164	kopieren

E

economic plan, 229	Wirtschaftsplan
economic trend, 160	Konjunkturverlauf
economical, 188	ökonomisch
economical production rate, 229	wirtschaftliche Fertigungsgröße
economical stock control, 229	wirtschaftliche Lagerhaltung
economy product, 206	Sparprodukt
ECU European Currency Unit, 121	ECU Europ. Rechnungseinheit
effective, 121	effektiv
efficiency, 126	Erfolg
electronical data processing/ EDV, 121	EDV Elektr.Datenverarbeitung
emergency actions, 187	Notmaßnahmen
employment condition, 107	Arbeitsbedingungen
empties, 170	Leergut

empties checker, 171	Leergutprüfer
empties stock reserve, 170	Leergutlagerreserve
end item/finished product, 125	Endprodukt / Fertigprodukt
engineering costs, 126	Entwicklungskosten/techn.
engineering facility, 211	technische Einrichtung
engineering office, 125	Entwicklungsbüro
environmental safety, 215	Umweltschutz
EP external purchase, 123	Einkaufsteil / EP
equipment/facilities, 110	Ausstattung/Anlagen/Einrichtung
error, 155	Irrtum
error inquery, 130	Fehler-Analyse
estimate, 143	geschätzt
estimation, 217	Veranschlagung
evaluation, 115	Bewertung/Wertbestimmung
evaluation card, 111	Auswertungskarte
examination, 214	Überprüfung
exceeding the budget, 214	Überschreitung des Budgets
excess capacity, 214	Überkapazität
excess costs, 182	Mehrkosten
excess material, 135	Fertigungsüberschuß
excess stocks, 213	Überbestände
excess to schedule, 194	Produktionsüberschuß
exchange rate, 167	Kurs
execution of order, 109	Auftragsabwicklung
executive board, 225	Vorstand
expansion, 128	Erweiterung
expenditure, 109	Ausgaben
expenditure on repairs, 200	Reparaturkosten
expense of production, 148	Herstellungskosten
expenses, 206	Spesen
expiration of time, 230	Zeitablauf
export shipping, 128	Exportversand
express shipment/1st class mail, 129	Expressendung
extension of validity, 145	Gültigkeitsverlängerung
extra work, 214	Überstunden

F

factory, 227	Werk
facts of the case, 202	Sachverhalt
failure report, 130	Fehlmeldung
facility, 123	Einrichtung
feeding, 114	bestücken
fees/taxes, 139	Gebühren
ferry boat, 130	Fähre
field of business activity, 211	Tätigkeitsbereich
figure, 231	Ziffer
file, 105	Ablage
final assembly line, 125	Endmontage
final inspection, 124	Endkontrolle
finance, 136	Finanz
financial year, 198	Rechnungsjahr
finishing, 218	Veredelung
fire protection, 136	Feuerschutz
first in - first out, 136	first in - first out
fix cost, 189	Overhead
fix float, 137	Fixmenge
fixed order, 135	Festabruf
fixed price, 136	Festpreis
fixing quota, 162	Kontingentierung
flexibility, 137	Flexibilität
flow chart, 107	Arbeitsablaufplan
follow-up chart, 212	Terminverfolgungsplan
follow-up of orders, 212	Terminüberwachung
forecasting, 195	Prognose
foreign exchange, 217	Valuta
foreman, 182	Meister
forge, 203	Schmiede
forging, 203	Schmiederohling
fork truck, 139	Gabelstabler
form of a contract, 223	Vertragsform
forward planning, 232	Zukunftsplanung
forwarding department, 206	Speditionsabteilung
forwarding of goods, 145	Güterbeförderung

forwarding schedule, 221	Versandplan
forwarding terms, 220	Versandbedingungen
FPV- financial planning volume, 137	FPV- Finanzplanungsvolumen
free freight, 138	frachtfrei
free of charge, 139	gebührenfrei
free of customs duty, 232	zollfrei
free of taxes/charges, 170	lastenfrei
freight, 168	laden
freight list, 168	Ladeliste
frequency, 138	Frequenz
frequency, 147	Häufigkeit
fuel, 147	Heizmaterial
fuel/petrol, 166	Kraftstoff
full employment, 224	Vollbeschäftigung
function, 138	Funktion
functional test, 139	Funktionsprüfung
functional build, 122	Einbauprobe / Funktionsbau
funds on hand, 140	Geldmittel
funds release, 140	Geldfreigabe

G

general foreman, 187	Obermeister
general supplies, 146	handelsübliches Material
general survey, 142	Gesamtübersicht
general view, 141	Gesamtansicht
goods, 145	Güter
govermental grants, 207	staatliche Zuschüsse
grade, 197	Rang
grants/investment, 233	Zuschuß/Subvention
gross expense, 116	Brutto-Aufwand
gross profit, 116	Brutto-Gewinn
group of companies, 163	Konzern
group staff, 145	Gruppenstab

H

handling, 112	Bedienung
harmonization, 147	Harmonisierung

head count, 164	Kopfzahl
head count, 190	Personalstärke
head count forecast, 191	Personalvorschätzung
high bay shelf, 148	Hochbauregal
high bay warehouse, 148	Hochbaulager
high cube container, 144	Großraumbehälter
holding list/transaction register, 126	Erfassungsliste
hourly employee, 176	Lohnempfänger
humanization of work, 149	Humanisierung der Arbeit

I

ICC Internat. Chamber of Commerce, 154	Internationale Handelskammer/
identification, 59	Kennzeichnung
import, 149	Import
importation, 122	Einfuhr / Import
improvement, 217	Verbesserung
improvement trade, 219	Veredelungsverkehr
in time, 230	zeitgerecht
in-house control, 214	Überwachung - innerbetrieblich
in-process condition, 131	Fertigungsbedingungen
in-process inspection, 132	Fertigungsinspektion
inactive material, 149	inaktives Material
inbound time, 152	inländische Transportzeit
incentive wage, 172	Leistungslohn
incidental wage cost, 176	Lohnnebenkosten
income earned, 128	Ertrag
incorrect, 130	fehlerhaft
incorrect usage/misusage, 130	Falschverbrauch
INCOTERMS-int. commercial terms, 150	INCOTERMS /Internat. Comm. Terms
increase in output, 193	Produktionserhöhung
increased value, 228	Wertsteigerung
indenture of apprenticeship, 171	Lehrvertrag
index, 151	Index
indication of origin, 216	Ursprungsangabe
indication of place, 189	Ortsbezeichnung

indirect labour, 151	indirekter Lohn
industrial dispute/strike, 108	Arbeitskampf/Streik
industrial exhibition, 152	Industrieausstellung
industrial strike, 152	Industriestreik
inefficiency, 126	Erfolglosigkeit
inefficiency/off standard, 172	Leistungsverlust
initial quantity, 124	Einsatzmenge
initial sample, 128	Erstmuster
initial sample date, 128	Erstmustertermin
initial sample inspection, 128	Erstmusterkontrolle
initiator, 110	Aussteller/Dokumente
inland shipping, 152	Inlandversand
inovations, 186	Neugestaltung
input, 122	Eingabe
insignificant, 141	geringfügig
inspection, 153	Inspektion
installation, 153	Installation
installment, 197	Rate
instance, 153	Instanz
instruction, 153	Instruktion
insurance, 222	Versicherung
integration, 153	Integration
integration from outside source, 219	Verlagerung aus Fremdbezug
interchangeable, 111	austauschbar
interest, 231	Zinsen
interims solution, 233	Zwischenlösung
internal allocation, 152	innerbetriebliche Zuordnung
internal audit, 152	Innenrevision
interruption, 216	Unterbrechung
intra-lant, 152	innerbetrieblich
intra-plant shipment, 153	innerbetrieblicher Versand
introduction date, 122	Einführungsdatum
invalid, 215	ungültig
inventory adjustment, 113	Bestandsberichtigung
inventory audit, 113	Bestandsprüfung
inventory cutting, 225	Vorratsabbau
inventory reserve, 169	Lagerreserve

inventory/stock-taking, 154	Inventur
inventory taking, 109	Aufnahme / Bestand
inventory turnover, 169	Lagerumschlag
investment, 154	Investition
invoice, 198	Rechnung
invoice number, 198	Rechnungsnummer
IR industrial relation, 190	Personalverwaltung/IR
issue date, 109	Ausgabedatum
item, 140	Gegenstand/Sache

J

JIT, just in time, 156	Just in Time /JIT
job description, 108	Arbeitsplatzbeschreibung
job evaluation, 108	Arbeitsplatzbewertung
job number, 111	Bauzahl
job number one/initial production, 128	Erstfertigung
job position, 108	Arbeitsplatz / Funktion
joint venture, 156	Joint Venture
justification, 112	Begründung
justification, 199	Rechtfertigung

K

key date, 209	Stichtag
keypoint, 204	Schwerpunkt
knock down, 231	zerlegen

L

label/brand/identification mark, 177	Marke
laboratory, 168	Laboratorium
labour / work, 107	Arbeit
labour cost, 176	Lohnkosten
labourer, 107	Arbeiter
lack of space, 198	Raummangel
large quantities, 179	massenweise
large quantity trial, 145	Großversuch
launching cost, 107	Anlaufkosten
law, 199	Recht

lay off, 115	Beurlaubung
layout / plant, 123	Einrichtungsplan/Fabrik
layout, 145/168	Lageplan/Grundrißplan
lead, 191	plombieren
lead time, 138	Frist/Zeitraum
leasing, 170	Leasing
legal aspects, 126	Erfordernisse/Auflagen
legal holiday, 143	gesetzlicher Feiertag
legal requirements, 143	gesetzliche Vorschriften
length, 170	Länge
letting on lease, 219	Verpachtung
leveling process, 187	Nivellierungsprozeß
liability, 146	Haftung
liable to pay customs duty, 232	zollpflichtig
licence, 175	Lizenz
limit, 149	Höchstgrenze
line feeder, 175	Linienverteiler
line feeding, 175	Linienbestückung
load, 112	Beladung
load/freight, 168	Ladung
loading dock, 168	Laderampe
loading station, 168	Ladestation
local allowance, 189	Ortszuschlag
local authority, 189	Ortsbehörde
local inspection, 189	Ortsbesichtigung
local traffic, 189	Ortsverkehr
location / place, 191	Platz/Stelle/Ort
location of an industry, 207	Standort einer Industrie
locked store, 222	Verschlußlager
logistic/ material management, 175	Logistik / Material Management
long-term, 170	langfristig
loss, 202	Schaden
loss of time, 231	Zeitverzug
loss of wages, 218	Verdienstausfall
lot, 191	Posten

M

machine change over, 135	Fertigungsumstellung
machine down-time, 178	Maschinenausfallzeit

machine sequencing, 178	Maschinenbelegungsplan
machine utilization, 178	Maschinenauslastung
magazine, 177	Magazin
mailing symbol, 192	Postzeichen
main cost center/buy off centre, 125	Endkostenstelle
main feature, 147	Hauptmerkmal
main store, 147	Hauptlager
maintenance, 216	Unterhalt
make payment, 230	zahlen
make-up day, 185	Nachholtag
make/manufacture/produce, 177	machen
manager, 172	Leiter
mandatory change, 184	Mußänderung
manpower requirements, 190	Personalbedarf
manual, 146	Handbuch
manuf.programm coordination, 134	Fertigungsprogrammsteuerung
manufactured parts, 122	Eigenfertigungsteile
manufacturing, 177	Manufaktur
manufacturing capacity, 132	Fertigungskapazität
manufacturing coordination, 133	Fertigungslenkung
manufacturing cost centre, 133	Fertigungskostenstellen
manufacturing cost/expense, 133	Fertigungskosten
manufacturing efficiency, 194	Produktionsleistung
manufacturing engineering, 129	Fabrikationstechnik
manufacturing expense, 114	Betriebsausgaben
manufacturing feasibility, 133	Fertigungsmöglichkeit
manufacturing frequency, 131	Fertigungsfrequenz
manufacturing frequency code, 134	Fertigungsschlüssel
manufacturing losses, 135	Fertigungsverlust
manufacturing lot, 132	Fertigungsgröße
manufacturing of components, 211	Teilefertigung
manufacturing overhead, 132	Fertigungsgemeinkosten
manufacturing period, 131	Fertigungsdauer
manufacturing plan, 134	Fertigungsplan

manufacturing planning, 129	Fabrikationsplanung
manufacturing process, 131	Fertigungsdurchlauf
manufacturing release, 131	Fertigungsfreigabe
manufacturing staff, 129	Fabrik-Direktion
market, 177	Markt
market condition, 160	Konjunktur
market letters, 177	Marktbericht
market report, 167	Kursbericht
market share, 177	Marktanteil
market value, 167	Kurswert
market regulation, 178	Marktordnung
marketable/saleable, 177	marktfähig
master card, 207	Stammkarte
master schedule formula, 105	Abrufprogramm
material, 228	Werkstoff
material authorization, 179	Materialfreigabe
material damage, 181	Materialschaden
material delivery, 179	Materiallieferung
material flow, 179	Materialfluß
material holding, 225	Vorrat
material in process, 134	Fertigungsreserve
material in stock, 226	Warenbestand
material movement, 179	Materialbewegung
material planning & control, 180	Materialplanung und Kontrolle
material requisition, 179	Materialentnahmeschein
material requisition slip, 115	Bezugsschein
material scheduling, 179	Materialdisposition
material stock value, 179	Materialbestandswert
materials supply, 181	Materialwirtschaft
maximal load, 181	Maximalbelastung
maximum output, 181	Maximalleistung
maximum price, 149	Höchstpreis
maximum stock, 181	Maximalbestand
maximum wages, 207	Spitzenlohn
maximum working time, 149	Höchstarbeitszeit
measurement, 178	Maß
measurement cargo / goods, 206	Sperrgut
mechanical requ.calculation, 124	Elektr.Bedarfserrechnung

mechanical stock control, 124	Elektr.Bestandsführung
merit rating, 171	Leistungseinstufung
merit/ salary increase, 172	Leistungszulage
message, 185	Nachricht
method of improvement, 182	Methodenverbesserung
method of shipping, 220	Versandart
methodical, 182	methodisch
mileometer, 159	Kilometerzähler
minimum delivery quantity, 183	Mindestliefermenge
minimum production-run, 182	Mindestfertigungsmenge
minimum stock, 182	Mindestbestand
minus stock balance, 183	Minus-Buchbestand
minute writing, 195	Protokollabfassung
miscellaneous disbursement, 222	verschiedene Abgänge
mismatched items, 215	unpaarige Bewegungen
missing material, 186	nicht auffindbares Material
missing quantity, 130	Fehlmenge
mixed cargo, 202	Sammelladung
model launch, 183	Modellanlauf
modification, 183	Modifikation
month-to-date figure, 183	monatliche Akkumulative
monthly installments, 183	Monatsrate
multi-page document, 182	Mehrfachsatz
multiple shipping, 182	Mehrfachversand

N

navigation /shipping, 203	Schiffahrt
net earnings, 186	Nettoeinkünfte
net loss, 199	Reinverlust
net price, 186	Nettopreis
net profit, 186	Nettogewinn
net weight, 186	Nettogewicht
new hirings, 186	Neueinstellungen
night shift, 185	Nachtschicht
night shift premium, 185	Nachtschichtzulage
nil return, 130	Fehlanzeige
nominal load, 186	Nennbelastung
nominal manhours, 205	Sollarbeitsstunden

non prod.items/operating suppl., 115	Betriebshilfsmittel
non prod.mat.requisition, 148	Hilfsmaterialanforderung
non production material, 148	Hilfsmaterial
non production supplies, 186	Nicht-Produktionsmaterial
normal case, 199	Regelfall
normal chanel, 153	Instanzenweg
normal operating hours, 187	Normalarbeitszeit
notice of no-requirement, 110	Auslaufschein
notification of effective date, 124	Einsatzmeldung
number, 229	Zahl
number of people, 172	Leute-Anzahl
number/quantity, 107	Anzahl
numerical order, 230	Zahlenfolge

O

o.k. parts, 149	I.O. Teile
object, 187	Objekt
objection, 111	Beanstandung
objective, 231	Zielvorgabe
obligation, 187	Obliegenheit
obligations, 218	Verbindlichkeiten
obsolete material, 110	ausgelaufenes Material
off line-/buy off point, 105	Ablaufpunkt
offal / waste, 105	Abfall
offer, 188	offerieren
offer/quotation, 107	Angebot
official, 188	offiziell
old-fashioned, 202	Rückständig
omission, 227	Wegfall
on the agreed time, 212	termingemäß
on-the-job training, 109	Ausbildung am Arbeitsplatz
one-way package, 124	Einwegpackung
operate, 139	funktionieren
operating cost, 115	Betriebskosten/Fertigung
operating facilities, 228	Werksanlagen
operating performance, 228	Werksleistung
operating personnel, 108	Arbeitskräfte

operating procedure, 107	Arbeitsanweisung
operation / shopfloor, 114	Betrieb/Fertigung
operation instruction, 112	Bedienungsanleitung
operational instruction, 139	Gebrauchsanweisung
operational reserve, 188	Operationsreserve
OPT optimized prod.timing, 188	optimale Produktionsgestaltung
optimized production rate, 188	optimale Losgröße
options/accessories, 205	Sonderteile
order / commission, 109	Auftrag / Bestellung
order bank, 109	Auftragsbestand
order condition, 113	Bestellbedingungen
order requisition, 114	Bestellformular
organization chart, 189	Organisationsplan
organize, 189	organisieren
out of specification, 131	Fertigungsabweichung
out of stock production, 169	lagerlose Fertigung
out of tolerance, 212	Toleranzüberschreitung
outgoing goods, 226	Warenausgang
output, 189	Output
outside services, 138	Fremdleistung
outsourcing of make parts, 219	Verlagerung nach Fremdbezug
outstanding performance, 207	Spitzenleistung
overall efficiency, 141	Gesamtleistung
overdue, 214	überfällig
overhaul, 214	Überholung
overhead conveyor, 159	Kettenförder-Anlage
overheads, 141	Gemeinkosten
overload production, 214	Überlastung der Fertigung
overproduction, 214	Überproduktion
overtime premium, 214	Überstundenzuschlag
overtime work, 181	Mehrarbeit
overturn, 215	Umsatz
own make, 205	Selbstanfertigung

P

packing slip, 190	Packzettel
pagination stamp, 190	Paginierstempel
paint shop, 168	Lackiererei

paint store, 130	Farblager
palette, 190	Palette
pallet tag, 170	Laufkarte
parcel, 190	Paket
part description, 211	Teilbezeichnung
part number, 212	Teilnummer
parts analyst, 120	Disponent
parts and accessories, 127	Ersatzteile und Zubehör
parts classification, 211	Teileklassifizierung
parts list, 212	Teileliste
parts master file, 207	Stammdaten-File
pass word, 159	Kennwort
pattern, 193	Probe
payable, 229	zahlbar
payment, 230	Zahlung
payment in due time, 212	Terminzahlung
payment of interest, 224	Verzinsung
payroll, 190	Personallohnliste
PC, personnel computer, 190	PC Personal Computer
PCR, part control record, 116	BSK Bedarfsstammkarte
performance, 171	Leistung
performance report, 171	Leistungsbericht
period of notice, 166	Kündigungsfrist
period of time, 231	Zeitraum
periodical manufacturing, 190	periodische Fertigung
personnel expenses, 190	Personalkosten
phase out of production, 193	Produktionsauslauf
piece, 209	Stück
piece number, 209	Stückzahl
piece price, 124	Einzelpreis
pilferage, 120	Diebstahl
pilot plant, 222	Versuchsabteilung
pilot run, 225	Vorserie
planned usage prior -	geplanter Verbrauch vor-
planned availability, 141	geplante Verfügbarkeit
planning, 191	Planung
planning of operation method, 219	Verfahrensplanung
plant engineering, 228	Werktechnik

plant management, 228	Werksleitung
plant manager, 129	Fabrikleiter
plant security, 228	Werksschutz
plant/building, 146	Halle/Fabrik
plant/factory, 129	Fabrik
PMR part movement report, 116	BUB Bewegungs-u.Best.-Bericht
point of time, 230	Zeitpunkt
policy letter, 142	Geschäftsgrundsatz
position, 208	Stellung
position description, 191	Positionsbeschreibung
postpone, 222	verschieben
potential obsolescence, 110	Auslaufmaterial/zukünftiges
power station, 166	Kraftanlage
powerful, 166	kraftvoll
powerless, 166	kraftlos
predate of orders, 226	vorziehen von Bestellungen
press load, 192	Pressmenge
press shop, 192	Presswerk
preventive maintenance, 153	Instandhaltung/vorbeugend
preventive repair keeping, 224	Vorbeugende Instandhaltung
price, 192	Preis
price of goods, 227	Warenpreis
price variance, 192	Preisabweichung
prime cost, 123	Einkaufspreis
principles of organization, 189	Organisationsgrundsätze
prinziples of float allocation, 192	Prinzipien z. Best. d. Mat. Reserve
procedure, 120	Dienstanweisung
process interruption, 135	Fertigungsunterbrechung
process sheet, 108	Arbeitsfolge
process tact time, 211	Taktzeiten
processing, 217	Verarbeitung
processing stage, 218	Veredelungsstufe
product change notice, 193	Produktionsänderungsanzeige
product design development, 193	Produktentwicklung
production account, 193	Produktionsbericht
production allocation programme, 194	Produktionslenkung

production control, 132	Fertigungskontrolle
production control, 194	Produktionskontrolle
production coordination, 134	Fertigungssteuerung
production delay, 195	Produktionsverzögerung
production expense, 194	Produktionskosten
production interruption, 195	Produktionsunterbrechung
production line, 174	Linie/Produktionsstraße
production material, 194	Produktionsmaterial
production material float, 180	Materialreserve
production material float value, 181	Materialreserve-Wert
production part, 194	Produktionsteil
production phase out, 131	Fertigungsauslauf
production quantity, 135	Fertigungszahl
production rate of climb, 194	Produktionssteigerungsrate
production rate report, 194	Produktionsmeldung
production related, 193	produktionsabhängig
production report, 133	Fertigungsmeldung/Bericht
production risk, 193	Produktionsgefahr
production run-/phase out, 110	Auslauf/Fertigungsabschluß
production sample, 133	Fertigungsmuster
production schedule, 194	Produktionsprogramm
production standards, 201	Richtwert für die Fertigung
production/manufacture, 129	Fabrikation
productive capacity, 193	Produktionsfähigkeit
profit, 144	Gewinn
profit after tax, 144	Gewinn nach Steuern
profit before tax, 144	Gewinn vor Steuern
profit forecast, 144	Gewinnprognose
profitability study, 229	Wirtschaftlichkeitsuntersuchung
progression, 208	Steigerung
project, 195	Projekt
project plan, 126	Entwurf/Projekt/Plan
project proposal, 195	Projektvorschlag
properly, 188	ordnungsgemäß
protection of trademarks, 177	Markenschutz
protective tariff, 204	Schutzzoll
prototype/pilot build, 195	Prototyp/Musterbau
provisional measure, 154	Interimsmaßnahme

PSO parts supply operation, 127	Ersatzteillager-Verwaltung/PSO
public relation work, 188	Öffentlichkeitsarbeit
publicity, 200	Reklame
punch card, 175	Lochkarte
purchase, 122	Einkauf
purchase commitments, 123	Einkaufsverbindlichkeiten
purchase contract, 158	Kaufvertrag
purchase finished parts, 130	Fertigkaufteile
purchase invoice, 123	Einkaufsrechnung
purchase order, 114	Bestellung/Einkauf
purchase part, 158	Kaufteil
purchase price, 158	Kaufpreis
purchase/buy, 158	kaufen
purchasing cost analysis, 123	Einkaufskostenanalyse

Q

qualification, 196	Qualifikation
quality, 196	Qualität
quality control, 196	Qualitätskontrolle
quantity, 197	Quantität
quantity delivered, 174	Liefermenge
quarter, 197	Quartal
query notice, 196	Prüfveranlassung
quotaion, 110	Ausschreibung
quotation of price, 192	Preisangabe

R

rail transport, 203	Schienenverkehr
range of company produced assets, 134	Fertigungstiefe
ranking order, 197	Rangordnung
rate-fixing, 167	Kursfestsetzung
rated capacity, 110	ausgelegte Kapazität
rational, 198	rationell
rationalization, 197	Rationalisierung
raw material, 201	Rohmaterial
re-arrangement, 186	Neuordnung
re-classification, 186	Neugruppierung

re-order, 184	Nachbestellung
reaction time, 198	Reaktionszeit
ready for use, 139	gebrauchsfertig
realization, 120	Durchführung
reason for variance, 105	Abweichungsgrund
rebook, 215	umbuchen
rebuilding, 215	Umbau
recall campaign, 202	Rückrufaktion
receipt, 197	Quittung
receivables, 137	Forderungen
receival, 122	Eingang
receival date, 122	Eingangsdatum
receiving checker, 226	Wareneingangsprüfer
receiving location, 226	Warenannahme
receiving report, 122	Eingangsbericht
receiving/receipt, 173	Liefereingang
reclassification, 215	Umklassifizierung
recommendation, 124	Empfehlung
recondition material store, 111	Austauschteilelager
reconditoned-mat./parts, 111	Austauschmaterial/Teile
record change, 137	Formaländerung
record status indicator, 120	Dispositionskennzeichen
recount, 185	nachzählen
recycling, 229	Wiederverwertung
reexport, 228	Wiederausfuhr
reference number, 159	Kennziffer
refund/reimbursement, 128	Erstattung
register, 199	Register
register, 224	Verzeichnis
regulate, 199	regeln
reimport, 229	Wiedereinfuhr
rejection, 224	Verwerfung
rejects, 193	Produktionsausschuß
release, 138	Freigabe
release number, 138	Freigabenummer
remainder of stocks, 200	Restbestand
remaining stock, 200	Restposten
repair workshop, 200	Reparaturwerkstatt

repairs / rework, 109	Ausbesserung/Nacharbeit
repayment, 232	Zurückzahlung
replace, 127	ersetzen
replacement, 126	Ersatz
reporting point, 182	Meldestelle
request for book balance, 116	Buchbestandsanfrage
requirement / usage, 111	Bedarf / Verbrauch
requirement calculation, 111	Bedarfserrechnung
requirement change, 111	Bedarfsänderung
respond time, 121	Durchlaufzeit
respond time of order proc, 109	Auftragseinplanung/Abwicklung
responsibility, 217	Verantwortung
retool, 186	Neuanschaffung
return shipment, 202	Rückversand
returnable packing, 171	Leihverpackung
revision, 200	Revision
rework, 184	Nacharbeit
rework expense, 184	Nacharbeitskosten
room/space, 198	Raum/Platz
rough part, 201	Rohling
rough weight, 123	Einsatzgewicht
rubbish	Schutt

S

safety factor, 205	Sicherheitsfaktor
safety facilities, 205	Sicherheitseinrichtungen
safety regulation, 204	Schutzbestimmung
salaried employee, 140	Gehaltsempfänger
salary deductions, 140	Gehaltsabzüge
salary increase, 140	Gehaltserhöhung
sale of goods, 226	Warenabsatz
sales, 223	Vertrieb
sales conditions, 219	Verkaufsbedingungen
sales cost, 223	Vertriebskosten
sales manager, 223	Vertriebsleiter
sales organization, 219	Verkaufsorganisation
sales turnover, 227	Warenumsatz
salvage value, 204	Schrottwert

salvage/recovery, 202	Rückgewinnung
sample, 184	Muster
sample report, 184	Musterbefund
savings / economics, 128	Ersparnisse/Einsparungen
schedule formula index, 118	Codeverzeichnis
scheduling analyst, 134	Fertigungsplaner
scheduling and parts control, 120	Disposition
scheduling card/record, 120	Dispositionskarte
scope, 197	Rahmen
scope of validity, 140	Geltungsbereich
scrap, 203	Schrott
scrap percentage, 204	Schrottprozentsatz
scrap report, 204	Schrottmeldung
scrap value, 200	Restmaterialwert
scrap/waste/rejects, 131	Fertigungsausschuß
scrapping, 222	Verschrottung
scrapping request, 222	Verschrottungsantrag
screen masks, 116	Bildschirm-Masken
screen working place, 116	Bildschirmarbeitsplatz
seal, 191	Plombe
seaproof packing, 205	Seeverpackung
secondary effect, 185	Nebenwirkung
section / group, 145	Gruppe
select, 111	auswählen
semi finished product, 233	Zwischenprodukt
semi finished production goods, 146	Halbfabrikate
send back, 232	zurückschicken
send off, 222	verschicken
sequence, 199	Reihenfolge
sequence chart, 121	Durchlaufplan
serial production, 205	Serienfertigung
service part manufacturing, 127	Ersatzteilfertigung
service part/spare part, 127	Ersatzteil
servicing, 227	Wartung
share/contingent, 197	Quote
shelf, 199	Regal
shelf space, 208	Stellfläche

terms of payment, 230	Zahlungsbedingungen
terms of tenancy, 189	Pachtbedingungen
test facility, 195	Prüfeinrichtung
time allowance, 231	Zeitvorgabe
time indicator board, 231	Zeittafel
time of delivery, 174	Liefertermin
time schedule, 212	Terminplan
time span/lifetime, 170	Laufzeit / Lebensdauer
time table, 167	Kursbuch
timing plan, 230	Zeitplan
tolerance, 212	Toleranz
tool store, 228	Werkzeugausgabe
tool shop, 228	Werkzeugbau
tool-life time, 207	Standzeiten für Werkzeuge
total charges, 141	Gesamtforderung
total number, 142	Gesamtzahl
total profit/return, 141	Gesamtertrag
total requirement, 141	Gesamtbedarf
trade, 146	Handel
trade control office, 143	Gewerbeaufsichtamt
trade matter, 146	Handelsangelegenheit
trade name, 227	Warenzeichen
trade pattern, 227	Warenprobe
trade regulations, 144	Gewerbeordnung
trade unions, 144	Gewerkschaften
trade-mark, 129	Fabrikmarke/Zeichen
trading company, 146	Handelsgesellschaft
traffic, 219	Verkehr
traffic department, 213	Transportabteilung
training department, 171	Lehrwerkstatt
transaction, 147	Handlung
transaction register, 147	Handlungsregister
transit, 212	Transit
transit times, 212	Transitzeiten
transmittal, 112	Begleitpapier
transport, 213	Transport
transport and supply unit, 138	Fuhrpark
transport charges, 213	Transportkosten

standard parts, 207	Standardteile
standard time, 224	Vorgabezeit
standardization, 219	Vereinheitlichung
standards of quality, 197	Qualitätsnorm
standing orders, 142	Geschäftsordnung
standstill, 209	Stillstand
staple locations, 208	Stapelplätze
start initial produktion, 107	Anlauf/Produktion
start of production, 193	Produktionsbeginn
starting / opening, 150	Inbetriebnahme
starting inventory, 106	Anfangsbestand
stated time, 212	Termin
statement, 208	Stellungnahme
statement of account, 162	Kontoauszug
statement of function, 139	Funktionsbeschreibung
statistical data, 208	statistische Angaben
statistical quality control, 208	statistische Qualitätskontrolle
statistical table, 230	Zahlenübersicht
stock on hand, 179	Materialbestand
stock position, 113	Bestandssituation
stock report, 113	Bestandsmeldung
stock status report, 113	Bestandsbericht
stockpile, 115	Bevorratung
stockpiling in advance, 225	Vorratsproduktion
stocks inventory, 168	Lagerbestand
stocktaking frequency, 109	Aufnahmeintervall
storage area for unapproved parts, 206	Sperrlager
storage location, 169	Lagerplatz
store-keeper, 169	Lagerverwalter
store/depot, 179	Materiallager
store/warehouse/depot, 168	Lager
storehouse, 206	Speicher
strike/dispute, 209	Streik
subassembly, 216	Unteraggregat
subcontructor, 216	Unterlieferant
subsequent payment, 185	Nachbezahlung
subsidiary, 136	Filiale

substitute document, 126	Ersatzbeleg
suggestion programme, 225	Vorschlagswesen
suggestion scheme, 217	Verbesserungsvorschlag
superintendent, 133	Fertigungsleiter
supervisor, 145	Gruppenleiter
supervisory personnel, 138	Führungskräfte
supplementary delivery, 233	Zusatzlieferung
supplier account number, 173	Lieferantenkontonummer
supplier adjustment, 173	Lieferantenanpassung
supplier card file, 173	Lieferantenkartei
supplier communication system, 172	Lieferanten-Informationssystem
supplier error, 173	Lieferantenfehler
supplier identification code, 173	Lieferantenschlüssel
supplier performance report, 172	Lieferanten-Situationsbericht
supplier/vendor, 172	Lieferant
supply protection, 174	Lieferreserve
supporting record, 185	Nachweis
system fill, 209	Systemfüllung
system float, 209	System-Menge

T

table, 210	Tabelle
table of contents, 152	Inhaltsverzeichnis
target figure, 191	Planzahl
target inventory, 191	Planbestand
target inventory, 205	Sollbestand
tariff, 139	Gebührenordnung
tariff area, 211	Tarifgebiet
task, 109	Auflage/Kürzung
task, 167	Kürzungs-Auflage
tax, 208	Steuer
technical change, 211	technische Änderung
technical data, 211	technische Unterlagen
technical improvement, 211	technische Verbesserung
temporary, 231	zeitweilig
tenancy, 189	Pacht
termination, 166	Kündigung

shift change, 203	Schichtwechsel
shift pattern, 203	Schichteinteilung
shift premium, 203	Schichtzuschlag
shipment authorization, 107	Auslieferungsfreigabe
shipment of goods, 227	Warensendung
shipping, 220	Versand
shipping bank, 221	Versandreserve
shipping bill, 221	Versandliste
shipping costs, 220	Versandkosten
shipping documents, 221	Versandpapiere
shipping instructions, 213	Transportanweisungen
shipping point, 221	Versandstation
shipping report, 220	Versandbericht
shipping request, 221	Versandveranlassung
shipping storage, 220	Versandlager
shipping time, 221	Versandzeit
shopfloor, 227	Werkhalle
short of space, 191	Platzmangel
short-dated, 167	kurzfristig
short-time work, 167	Kurzarbeit
shortage, 160	Knappheit
shortage report, 167	Kurzbericht
shutdown, 209	Stillegung
skilled worker/specialist, 129	Facharbeiter
slip, 231	Zettel
sort, 206	sortieren
source, 115	Bezugsquelle
source of supply, 197	Quelle/Ursprung
source of power/energy, 166	Kraftquelle
spare parts catalogue, 127	Ersatzteilliste/Katalog
spare/service parts depot, 127	Ersatzteillager
special order, 205	Sonderbestellung
special wrapping, 206	Sonderverpackung
specialist, 207	Spezialist
specification, 207	Spezifikation
spot check, 209	Stichprobe
stampings/press parts, 192	Pressteile
standard, 187	Norm

transport damage, 213	Transportschaden
truck/lorry, 170	Lastkraftwagen
tryout material, 223	Versuchsmaterial
turn-over ratio, 215	Umschlaghäufigkeit
type, 213	Typ
type of material, 179	Materialart
type of packing, 220	Verpackungsart

U

underemployment, 216	Unterbeschäftigung
unfinished, 215	unfertig
unit, 122	Einheit
unit of account, 198	Rechnungseinheit
unit of measure, 115	Bezugsmengeneinheit
unit of quantity, 182	Mengeneinheit
unit of space, 198	Raumeinheit
unit of work, 166	Krafteinheit
unit-load, 168	Ladeeinheit
unload, 105	Abladen
unloading area, 125	Entladestelle
unloading code, 105	Abladeschlüssel
unloading place, 105	Abladeplatz
unofficial, 153	inoffiziell
unpaid item, 188	offener Posten
unskilled worker, 148	Hilfsarbeiter
usable/serviceable, 139	gebrauchsfähig
usage, 218	Verbrauch
usage determination, 218	Verbrauchsbestimmung
usage variance, 218	Verbrauchsabweichung
useful, 187	nutzbar
useless, 215	unbrauchbar
user/consumer, 161	Konsument
utilities/electricity/water, 125	Energie/Strom/Wasser
utility consumption data, 125	Energieverbrauchswerte
utilization, 112	Benutzung
utilization, 187	Nutzen
utilization of public money resources, 150	Inanspruchnahme öffentl.Mittel

V

vacancy, 217	Vakanz
vacation schedule, 216	Urlaubsplan
validity, 145	Gültigkeitsdauer
validity, 217	Validierung
value added, 217	Value added

W

wage, 176	Lohn
wage increase, 176	Lohnerhöhung
wage per hour, 209	Stundenlohn
wage settlement, 211	Tarifabkommen
wage/labour expense, 108	Arbeitslohn
warehouse, 227	Warenlager
warranty, 139	Garantie/Gewährleistung
waste / rejects, 110	Ausschußmaterial
waste of space, 198	Raumverschwendung
water carriage, 222	Verschiffung
week, 229	Woche
weekday, 228	Werktag
weekly, 229	wöchentlich
WO work-order, 107	Arbeitsauftrag
work standard, 108	Arbeitszeitvorgabe/Norm
work to capacity, 157	Kapazitätsnutzung
work unit, 178	Maßeinheit
work-day-allocation, 108	Arbeitstageeinteilung
work-flow, 108	Arbeitsfluß
workers council, 114	Betriebsrat
working days, 108	Arbeitstage
working process, 108	Arbeitsvorgang

Y

year average, 155	Jahresdurchschnitt
year-end audit, 155	Jahresabschlußprüfung
year-end routine, 156	Jahreswechselroutine
year-to-date figure, 156	Jahreszahlen

A

Abfall Anfallende Materialreste bei der Werkstoffbearbeitung.

offal / waste Remaining material as waste from manufacturing process.

Abladen

unload

Abladeplatz Ort der Anlieferung.

unloading place Location of delivery.

Abladeschlüssel Index zur Bestimmung des Entladeortes.

unloading code Code-index indicating place of receiving.

Ablage Registratur von Dokumenten.

file Document register.

Ablaufpunkt Meldepunkt des Fertigproduktes.

off line-/buy off point Final production reporting of end-item.

Abnahmeverpflichtung Anerkennung der vertragsmäßigen Herstellung und Übernahme einer Ware.

commitment Acceptance of manufacturing and delivery for scheduled material.

Abrufprogramm Tabellarische Auflistung von zukünftigen Produktionsvorhaben nach Zeit und Stückzahl zur Planung und Bestellung von Produktionsmaterial.

master schedule formula Content of future programme figures for the purpose of planning and scheduling production material.

Abschreibung für Anlagewerte Verfahren um Anschaffungs- oder Herstellungskosten nach einer bestimmten Methode auf Zeit oder Leistungseinheiten zu verteilen. (Steuerrecht)

depreciation Method to distribute installation- and manufacturing cost to products produced within a given period. (tax law)

Abweichungsgenehmigungsantrag Antrag zur zeitlichen oder mengenmäßigen Genehmigung einer Abweichung von den technischen Spezifikationen.

deviation request Request to obtain approval for usage out of tolerance material for a limited quantity or a certain period.

Abweichungsgrund Aufgliederung der Möglichkeiten die zur außerordentlichen Bestandsminderung führen.

reason for variance Index indicating possibilities for exceptional usage.

Agenturkraft / Aushilfskraft Arbeitskräfte die über eine Agentur vermittelt werden.

Aggregat Aus Einzelteilen zusammengebautes Produkt.

Aggregatauflösung Auflistung der zu einer Montagestufe führenden Einzelteile.

Akkumulative Fortlaufende Summenbildung einer Bestandsgröße entsprechend Materialbewegungen.

Akkumulative-Bedarfserrechnung Fortschreibung der Bestellmengen im Rahmen eines Kalender- oder Produktionsjahres.

Allzeitbedarf / ATR Letzte Bestellmöglichkeit für ausgelaufenes oder zum Auslauf vorgesehenes Material, bevor die Fertigungseinrichtungen abgebaut werden. In die Bedarfsfindung muß die Kalkulation des Kundendienstbedarfes für die Lebensdauer der Produkte einfließen.

Amortisationskosten Rückfluß der Investitionsbeträge im Rahmen der Wirtschaftlichkeitsrechnung.

Änderung Produktmodifizierung

Änderungsanzeige Hinweis auf Produktionsänderungsvorhaben.

Anfangsbestand Am Jahresanfang vorhandener Warenbestand, aus vorheriger Abrechnungsperiode.

agency labour Labour offered by an agency office.

aggregate / assembly / enditem Production unit consist of detail parts.

assembly break-down Breakdown of assembly part content.

cumulative Accumulating of endfigures according movements.

cumulative requirement calculation Adding-up of schedule figure during calender- or production year.

ATR all-time requirement Last posibility to schedule discontinued material or material assigned for discontinuation, prior disposal of manufacturing equipments. ATR calculation must include customer demand to support life-time service.

amortization cost Pay back-period of investments during phase of profitability calculation.

change Product modification

change notice Notification of product change.

starting inventory Stock on hand at the beginning of production year. Carry over from previous business year.

Angebot Sondierung der Marktlage bezüglich kostengünstiger Bezugsquellen.

Anlauf / Produktion Fertigungsbeginn eines neuen Produktes.

Anlaufkosten Mit der Fertigungsaufnahme verbundenen Kosten.

Anlieferschlüssel Index für die systemmäßige Erfassung der - ▶Lieferfrequenz von Produktionsmaterial.

Anlieferungsfreigabe Autorisierung zur Lieferung von Bestellgrößen nach erfolgter Musterabnahme.

Anliefertage Vorgegebene Tage zur Anlieferung von Material.

Antrag Dokument zur Einleitung eines Genehmigungsverfahrens.

Anzahl / Menge

Arbeit Wertschaffende Tätigkeit, die durch Entgelt honoriert wird.

Arbeiter Lohnarbeiter.
-▶Lohnempfänger

Arbeitsablaufplan Kronologische Zusammenfassung von Vorgängen.

Arbeitsanweisung Detaillierte Darstellung des Arbeitsverfahrens.

Arbeitsauftrag Durchführung einer Arbeit im Rahmen von festen Bedingungen.

Arbeitsbedingungen Betriebsvereinbarung zwischen Betriebsrat und Arbeitgeber, über die Durchführung der Beschäftigung.

offer / quotation Analysis of market condition to establish economical source.

start initial produktion Manufacturing start of new product.

launching cost New product related manufacturing costs.

delivery frequency code Index for -▶delivery frequency of production material for systematical processing.

shipment authorization Shipment authorization for bulk supply after sample approval.

delivery days Pre-determinated days for material deliveries.

application Request to obtain approval.

number / quantity

labour / work Work accomplished and paid for.

labourer Wage earner. -▶hourly employee

flow chart Sequence of related functions.

operating procedure Detailed description of work process.

WO Workorder, work performed under fix conditions

employment condition Factory agreement between shop commitee and employer for execution of employment.

Arbeitsfluß Kontinuität der Arbeitsvorgänge.

Arbeitsfolge Beschreibung und Darstellung der zu verrichtenden Tätigkeit.

Arbeitskampf / Streik Störung des geordneten Arbeitsablaufes zum Zweck der Durchsetzung von Vertragsänderungen der Beschäftigten.

Arbeitskräfte Anzahl der Arbeiter / Belegschaft.

Arbeitslohn -▶Lohn

Arbeitsplatz /Funktion Der mit der Funktion verbundene Titel / Position in der Beschäftigungsordnung.

Arbeitsplatzbeschreibung Beschreibung der auszuführenden Tätigkeiten nach Richtlinien der Arbeitsplatzbewertung.

Arbeitsplatzbewertung Bewertung der Arbeitsplätze nach einem Punktsystem zur Erfassung der Arbeitsbedingungen und die Leistungen als Grundlage für Entlohnung.

Arbeitstage Festlegung der jährlichen Arbeitstage. (Arbeitstagekalender)

Arbeitstageeinteilung Zeitliche Festlegung oder Aufgliederung der Arbeitstage in Schichten.

Arbeitsvorgang Fertigungsverlauf.

Arbeitszeitvorgabe Zeiteinheit für die Durchführung einer bestimmten Arbeit.

work-flow Continuity of processing steps.

process sheet Description and presentation of work performance.

industrial dispute/strike Interruption of work to improve contract conditions of employee.

operating personnel Number of labours/crew.

wage / labour expense -▶wage

job position Titel of job related function / position within organizational structure.

job description Statement of functions based on instruction of the job evaluation office.

job evaluation Job evaluation based on criterias to determ working rules and performance.

working days Determination of yearly working days. (Work day calender)

work-day-allocation Time or shift pattern according to allocation of working days.

working process Production flow.

work standard Calculated period for work in process.

Auflage / Kürzung (s.Kürzungs-Auflage)

Auflöseband Datenträger mit Speicherung aller Einzelteile der nächst höheren Fertigungsstufe.

Aufnahme / Bestand -▶Bestandsaufnahme

Aufnahmeintervall -▶Bestandsaufnahmehäufigkeit

Aufteilungsplan Kalendarisierung

Auftrag / Bestellung -▶Kaufvertrag

Auftragsabwicklung Durchführung / Plazierung.

Auftragsbestand Anzahl der fixen Bestellungen.

Auftragseinplanung / Abwicklung Zeitraum der Abwicklung.

ausbalancieren Koordination für auslaufendes Produktionsmaterial.

Ausbesserung / Nacharbeit Korrekturmaßnahmen an fehlerhaftem Material.

Ausbildung am Arbeitsplatz Praktische Ausbildung.

auseinandernehmen Ein Aggregat in Einzelteile zerlegen.

Ausfallzeiten Nicht nutzbare Maschinenkapazität.

Ausgabe / Material-Lager Ort der Materiallagerung. -▶Lager

Ausgabedatum Termin der Veröffentlichung.

Ausgaben Kosten

task

assembly break-down tape Computer tape containing all details of next assembly.

inventory taking -▶cycle count/ stocktaking

stocktaking frequency -▶cycle count frequency

allocation scheme calendarization

order / commission -▶purchase order

execution of order Processing of order/ order commitment.

order bank Number of fix orders.

respond time of order processing Time span of execution.

balance-out Coordination of discontinued production material.

repairs / rework Corrective action on defective material.

on-the-job training Practical training.

dismantle / strip down Breakdown of an assembly.

down-time Non-utilized machine capacity.

crib / store Material storage place. -▶store/warehouse/depot

issue date Date of publishing.

expenditure Costs

ausgelaufenes Material Durch Produktänderung verbliebener Materialrestbestand, der in seiner ursprünglichen Zweckbestimmung nicht mehr zu verwenden ist.

ausgelegte Kapazität Auslastungsgrad der Kapazität / Planerische Wertgröße.

Auslauf / Fertigungsabschluß Abschluß einer Serienfertigung.

Auslaufmaterial / zukünftiges Ab einem bestimmten Zeitpunkt nicht mehr benötigtes Produktionsmaterial.

Auslaufschein Dokument zur Erfassung von auslaufendem Produktionsmaterial zum Zwecke der kostenbewußten Verwertung.

Auslaufstatus Auflistung der vorgesehenen und effektiven Auslaufpositionen.

Auslaufteil Nicht länger benötigtes Produktionsteil.

Ausschreibung Anfrage bei Lieferanten zur Angebotsabgabe.

Ausschuß - Material Erzeugnisse die für den vorgesehenen Zweck nicht mehr verwendbar sind. Herstellungsfehler - maßliche oder Materialabweichungen.

Ausstattung / Anlagen / Einrichtungen Erforderliche Ausstattung zur Herstellung von Produkten. (Maschinen/ Werkzeuge / Lehren / Hilfsgüter)

Aussteller Antragsteller für Genehmigungsverfahren.

obsolete material Stock on discontinued material as a result of product change, which can't be used anymore as originally intended.

rated capacity Capacity utilization/ Planning figure.

production run-out Balance-out of mass production.

potential absolescence Production material not required anymore from a certain cut off date.

notice of no-requirement Record for deleting production material to control disposal action.

balance out report Status of proposed and actual deleted items.

discontinued part Production part not longer required.

quotation Negotiation for estimates at suppliers.

waste / rejects Products which can't be used as intended. Items out of tolerance - deviating from specification.

equipment / facilities Required equipment for product manufacturing. (machines / tools / gauges / non production items)

initiator Person who requests the approval routine.

austauschbar Ersetzen von Produktionsteilen in gleicher Funktion durch Neuentwicklungen.

Austauschmaterial / Teile Wieder aufgearbeitete oder reparierte Teile / Aggregate.

Austauschteilelager Ersatzteillager für Austauschaggregate.

auswählen Aussuchen von verworfenem Material.

Auswertungskarte Kontrollkarte mit den Ergebnissen der Bestandsaufnahmen.

interchangeable Replacement of production parts by new designed components, performing same function.

reconditioning-material/ parts Repaired or reworked parts /assemblies.

reconditioned- material storage Parts depot for reconditioned material.

select Select rejected material.

evalution card Control record for cycle count results.

B

Bauzahl Akkumulative einer Produktionsserie.

Beanstandung Fehleranzeige-Abweichung von den Vorgaben.

Bedarf / Verbrauch Vorgegebener Materialverbrauch in Mengeneinheit.

Bedarfsänderung Verbrauchsmengenänderung aufgrund Produktänderungen.

Bedarfserrechnung Ermittlung der Verbrauchsmengen für zukünftige Produktionszeiträume auf Basis der Programmplanung.
-►Abrufprogramm

Bedarfsnachweis Netto Bedarfsmengen für Produktionssegmente,ohne Zuschläge für -►Materialreserve.

job number Accumulative number of product series.

objection Error-deviation from planned objective.

reqirement / usage Pre-determined usage of material expressed in unit of measurement.

requirement change Usage amendment based on product modifications.

requirement calculation Calculation of usage requirement for planned production build phases.
-►master schedule formula.

audit trail Net material requirement segmented according production programme, excluding additional material for -►production material float.

Bedienung Versorgung der Fertigung mit Material. -▶Linienbestückung

Bedienungsanleitung Beschreibung der zur Bedienung einer Einrichtung erforderlichen Funktion.

Begleitpapier Begleitdokument zur Identifizierung der Lieferung.

Begründung Rechtfertigung einer Antragstellung.

Behälter

Behälterkennzeichen Symbolmerkmal.

Beladung Verladung von Material auf Transportmittel.

Belastung/ Kosten In Verbindung mit der Produktherstellung entstehende Kosten.

Benutzung Gebrauch oder Verwendung von Gegenständen.

Bereitstellung / Verfügbarkeit Termin- und mengengerechte Materialversorgung.

Berichtigung Anpassung bei Bestandsabweichungen.

Beschädigung Deformierung von Gegenständen.

Bestandsabstimmung Zusammenfassung von Bestandspositionen gleicher- oder Wahlgruppen Teile.

Bestandsaufnahme Körperliche Erfassung von Materialvorräten nach Mengen und Mengeneinheit.

handling Provide production line with material. -▶line feeding

operating instruction Function description of equiment.

transmittal Document for identification of supplies.

justification Arguments to support request.

case /casket/bin/container

bin - identification/marks Bin -symbolization.

load To put material into transportation equipments.

charges Manufacturing and process related costs.

utilization Use or utilize of objects.

availability Material delivery in quantity and time as appropriate.

adjustment Adjust stock discrepancy.

damage Deformation of goods.

consolidated stock report Listing of different stock positions of same design or alternative parts groups.

cycle count/stocktaking Physical count on stock on hand according quantity and unit of measure.

Bestandsaufnahme-Differenz Unterschied zwischen physischer Bestandsaufnahme und buchmäßiger Bestandsgröße.

Bestandsaufnahme-Häufigkeit Kalendarisierung der während des Jahres vorgesehenen körperlichen Bestandsaufnahmen.

Bestandsbericht Zeigt den Materialbestand vom Einang bis zur Auslieferung in den jeweiligen Fertigungsstufen einer Abrechnungsstelle.

Bestandsberichtigung Anpassung der theoretischen Bestandsakkumulative an die physische Bestandsgröße.
Vorgang löst die Materialabrufkorrektur aus.
Berichtigungsmaßnahmen sind nur im Rahmen der Finanzrichtlinien erlaubt.

Bestandsmeldung Bericht der täglichen Bestandssituation, zeigt Materialbestand vor Fertigungsbeginn.

Bestandsprüfer Verantwortlicher Sachbearbeiter für die Bestandskontrolle.

Bestandsprüfung Überprüfung der Bestände. Soll - Ist - Vergleich.

Bestandssituation Ausweisung der verfügbaren Materialbestände zu einem bestimmten Zeitpunkt.

Bestellbedingungen Richtlinien unter denen der Materialbezug und die Warenherstellung erfolgt.

cycle count discrepancy Difference between physical count and book balance.

cycle count frequency Calendarization of cycle counts to be performed during year of business.

stock status report Shows wall to wall stock position in various steps of progress according production points.

inventory adjustment Adjust book cum to physical cum. Action initiates revised schedules.
Inv. adjustm. are only allowed in line with finance procedures.

stock report Stock position prior start of production.

cycle checker/stock chaser Analyst responsible for physical stock control.

inventory audit Check stock on hand. Presumed and actual.

stock position Report of stock on hand at a certain point in time.

order condition Conditions to organize the supply of products.

Bestellformular Vertrag über Lieferung von Waren zu bestimmten Bedingungen, die vielfach auf der Rückseite des Formulars ausgedruckt sind.

Bestellung / Einkauf Verbindliche Aufforderung des Bestellers an einen Lieferanten, eine bestimmte Ware zu vereinbarten Bedingungen zu liefern.
-▶INCOTERMS

bestücken Versorgung einer Fertigungseinrichtung mit Material, um eine kontinuierliche Produktion zu gewährleisten.
(Erstfüllmenge)

Betrag/Wert Die Gesamtsumme.

Betrieb / Fertigung Arbeitsstätte des Unternehmens / Ort der Produkterzeugung.

Betriebsausgaben Aufwendungen durch den Bertieb.
Mindern den steuerpflichtigen Gewinn. (Spesen / Bewirtung)

Betriebsrat Gewählte Vertretung der Arbeitnehmer zur Wahrnehmung des Rechts auf Basis der gesetzlichen Grundlagen.

Betriebsbuchhaltung Die Betriebsbuchhaltung umfaßt die Kosten- und Leistungsrechnung und schließt Material-, Lohn- und Anlagenbuchhaltung ein. Als Resultat wird das Betriebsergebnis auf Basis der Kosten und Erträge ermittelt.

order requisition Order-form outlining conditions for delivery and timing of supplies. Conditions sometimes are printed on the backside of the form.

purchase order Supply contract to order products from a vendor according specific delivery conditions. -▶INCOTERMS

feeding Equipment releted number on material to support continiously production flow. (Initial fill)

amount/value Total amount.

operation / shopfloor Factory workshop / place of manufacturing.

manufacturing expense Expenditure coused by company. Depreciating tax on profit.(Travel expense/ accommodation of guests)

workers council Elected representatives of company workers who look after their interests based on legal requirements.

cost accounting Cost accounting controls operating costs and performance and includes wage - material and installation - cost.
Based on loss and profit the overall gain is calculated.

Betriebshilfsmittel Produkte die nicht Bestandteil des Endproduktes sind. (Reinigungsmittel, Instandhaltungseinrichtungen)

Betriebskosten Aufgliederung der in einem Rechnungszeitraum entstehenden Kosten, getrennt nach Herstellungsaufwand einschließlich Material und Vertriebskosten.

Beurlaubung Unfreiwillige Freistellung von der Arbeit durch den Arbeitgeber, wenn infolge fehlenden Absatzes oder Materialmangel, die Herstellung von Produkten nicht mehr sinnvoll oder möglich ist.

Bevorratung Vorbestellung einer angenommenen Material-Fehlmenge zur Sicherstellung der kontinuierlichen Fertigung, aufgrund zu erwartender Störungen der Materialversorgung oder zur Überbrückung einer Fertigungs-Ruhephase beim Lieferanten. (Unterschiedliche Arbeitstage)

Bewertung / Wertbestimmung Produktbezogene Geldgrößen-Zuordnung.

Bezugsmengeneinheit Normeinheit für den Umgang mit Waren, in Stück, Liter, Kilo oder andere Maßeinheiten.

Bezugsquelle Lieferant / Hersteller.

Bezugsschein Autorisation für die Warenentnahme aus dem Lager.

non production items / operating supplies Not end-item related products. (Maintenance requirements)

operating cost Structure of company costs into manufacturing costs including material and distribution costs.

lay off Plant closing on decision of Company Management in case of lack of sales or missing material.

stock pile Protection against expected material losses due to supply problems or to bridge cessation of production at a supplier. (Different working pattern)

evaluation Product related value allocation.

unit of measure Specification to handle material as piece, pint, kilo or other measuring units.

source Supplier / Vendor.

material requisition slip Autorization for material receipt from store.

Bildschirmarbeitsplatz Funktionsausübung mittels Computerterminal.

Bildschirm-Masken Eingabeformate für Vorgänge der Datenerstellung.

Brutto-Aufwand Zusammenfassung der Kontenumsätze eines Geschäftsjahres oder kürzeren Rechnungsabschnittes.

Brutto-Gewinn Differenz aus den Verkaufspreisen und den Einkaufspreisen einer Abrechnungsperiode.

BSK - Bedarfsstammkarte Dokumentation der Stammdaten für die Bestellung und Kontrolle von Produktionsmaterial.

BUB - Bewegungs- u. Bestands-Bericht Verbrauchsnachweis des angelieferten oder in Eigenfertigung hergestellten Produktionsteils. Zeigt die verschiedenen Abgänge und losen Bestand.
-▶Bestandsbericht

Buchnummer Numerische Identifizierung des Disponenten für bestimmte Materialumfänge.

Buchbestand Materialbestand auf Basis der Ein- und Abgänge.

Buchbestandsanfrage Anforderung eines Berichtes mit Angabe der Bestandssituation.
(Computer-Bericht)

Buchbestandserrechnung Errechnung des theoretischen Mate-

screen working place Performance of function via visual display unit.

screen masks Form/masks for data input.

gross expense Accumulation of accounts from a business year or a shorter period.

gross profit Difference between selling-price and purchase costs of a business period.

PCR, part control record Parts record containing production material specification for scheduling and controlling of production material.

PMR, parts movement report Declaration of production material - Miscellaneous disbursement and stock on hand. -▶ stock status report

book number Numerical identification of parts analyst for certain categories of material.

book balance Calculated stock on hand based on receipts and shippings.

request for book balance Request for stock on hand record. (Computer record)

book balance calculation Calculation of theoretically stock on hand

rialbestandes auf Basis der Ein- und verschiedenen Abgänge. -▶Buchbestand

Buchungsvermerk Buchungsbeleg über Stornobuchung aufgrund von Fehlbuchung.

Budget Kernstück der betrieblichen Planungsrechnung. Zeitraumbezogene Zusammenfassung aller zu erwartender Einnahmen und Ausgaben zur Ermittlung des Kapital- und Geldbedarfes.

Budgetentwicklungsvolumen/ BDV - Zeitraumbezogene Vorschätzung der Umsatzerlöse auf Basis der Verkaufserwartungen. Ergebnis dient als Grundlage für die Budgetplanung.

Budgetgenehmigung Überprüfung, ob die zur Budgeterstellung angewandten Werte mit den planerischen Grundsätzen des Unternehmens übereinstimmen.

figure based on receipts and miscellaneous disbursement -▶Book balance

booking remark Verification of booking cancellation resulting from booking-error.

budget Business year related major planning element estimating all expected costs of sales and expenses for the calculation of investments and cash requirements.

BDV, budget development volume Time-span related estimation of costs of sales based on programme forecast. Result is subject for budget planning.

budget authorization Review budget development figures to ensure that company policies are applied.

C

CAD, Computer Aided Design Computer unterstütztes Entwickeln/Konstruieren.

CAM, Computer Aided Manufacturing Computer unterstützte/gesteuerte Fertigung.

CAP, Computer Aided Planning and Manufacturing Method Computer unterstützte Planungs- und Fertigungsmethode.

CAD, computer aided design Computer supported construction.

CAM, computer aided manufacturing Computer supported/performed manufacturing.

CAP, computer aided Planning and manufacturing method Computer supported planning and manufacturing system.

Carryover-Effect Übertragener Materialumfang der gegenwärtigen Produktion auf zukünftige Bauumfänge.

Cash - Flow Netto Geldmittel-Verfügbarkeit. Zugang aus einer Abrechnungsperiode.

Charakteristik Feinabstimmung einer Fertigungseinrichtung.

chartern Mieten oder pachten von Transportmitteln.

CIM - Computer Integrated Manufacturing Systems Computer integrierte Fertigungssysteme.

Codeverzeichnis Alpha-numerisch geordnete Namensabkürzungen der Produkte zwecks Verwendung in Computerprogrammen.

Container Genormter Behälter für den Transport und Aufbewahrung von Gütern.

Controller Mit der Auswertung von Betriebsdaten zur Kontrolle des Betriebsgeschehens beauftragte Person.

Cross - Shipping Kreuzender Materialversand zwischen Zweigstellen des Unternehmens.

Cross - Check Methode der Überprüfung durch Kreuzvergleich.

carry over effect Carry forward of current production material for future products.

cash - flow Net money availability. Income in a settling period.

characterization Adjustment of manufacturing equipment.

charter Rent or hire of transportation equipments.

CIM, computer integrated manufacturing systems Computer supported manufacturing methods.

schedule formula index Alpha-numerical order of product description abbreviation for processing in computer programme.

container Standardized packing unit for transport and storage of goods.

controller Person who evaluates manufacturing data to control progress of business.

cross - shipping Cross-wise flow of material between subsidiaries.

cross - check Verifying method by cross checking.

D

Datenauflistung Aufgliederung der Produktionsmaterial-Teilnummern, auch als Stammdaten bezeichnet.

Datenbank Computer gespeicherte Datensammlung.

Datenerstellung Organisation des Computer Inputs für die sachgerechte Bedienung der Anwenderprogramme.

Datenübertragung Übertragung von Daten über Fernmeldewege, vom Ort der Erfassung zur EDV oder vom Ort der Verarbeitung zur Datenausgabe.

Datenverarbeitung Die Art der Zuordnung und Verbindung von Informationen zu einer systemgerechten Weiterverarbeitung entsprechend Programmvorgaben.

Dauerverpackung Verpackungseinheit mit langer Verwendungszeit, in der Mehrheit Norm-Container.

Dauerversuch Teil der Materialprüfung. Bevor neue Teile in den laufenden Produktionsprozeß übernommen werden, erfolgt vielfach ein zeitlich begrenzter Versuch, die Materialbeständigkeit unter Produktionsbedingungen zu testen.

De-Integration Die Verlagerung von Fertigungsvorgängen in Fremdbezug.

demontieren Aggregate in ihre Einzelteile zerlegen, zum Zwecke der Stichprobenkontrolle nach

data file Sequence of production material in part number order.

data bank Computer filed data collection.

data file generation Arrange initial computer input as base for customer programme requirements.

data transmission Data transfer via telefon from place of generation, to the place of data processing or from data processing to the place of output station.

data processing The method of relation and links of data to system assisted progress according forecast.

duarable packing Packing unit with long life time, mostly a standard container.

duarability test Quality control check to material specification. Prior new parts will be released for introduction in production, a limited durability test will be performed, to test quality of new material under condition of production.

de-integration / outsourcing Transfer of production to suppliers.

dismantle Down-stripping of assemblies for the purpose of quality control after functional test or for

Versuchen oder zum Zwecke der Reparatur.

Diebstahl Die unrechtmäßige Entwendung von Material. Für diebstahlgefährdete Materialien sind besondere Maßnahmen erforderlich.
(Verschlußlager, Ausgabe über Bezugsschein)

Dienstanweisung Vorschrift über die Ausübung der Funktion. Genaue Beschreibung des Sachverhalts im Arbeitsablauf.
-▶Arbeitsanweisung

Direkter Lohn Mit der Produktherstellung verbundener Direkt-Aufwand.
(Positiver Aufwandbezug) Gegensatz: Indirekter Lohn.

Disponent Verantwortlicher Sachbearbeiter für die Gestaltung und Kontrolle des Materialbezugs.

Disposition Organisationseinheit verantwortlich für den termin- und mengengerechten Materialbezug.

Dispositionskarte Materialplanungskartei der manuellen Materialdisposition.

Dispositionskennzeichen Klassifizierung der Materialverwendungsordnung zur Wahrnehmung der Kontrollfunktionen.
Verbrauchswichtung. (Aktiv/Auslauf/ Verwertung/Verschrottung)

Durchführung Ausführung der Aktionen.

reasons of repair.

pilfrerage Stealing of material.
For material with risk of pilfrerage special action for protection are required. (Closed store, issuance of material based on material requisition slip.)

procedure Instruction to perform a function. Detailed description of functional steps. -▶Operating procedure

direct labour End-product related labour cost. (Positive work payment) Contrary: Indirect labour.

parts analyst Parts control analyst responsible for planning and scheduling of production material.

scheduling and parts control Departmental section responsible for material receipts in quantity and time as scheduled.

scheduling card/record Index card for manuell requirement calculation.

record status indicator Classification of material in order to perform related control actions. Priority weighting. (Active / Deleted / Disposal / Scrap)

realization Performance of action.

Durchlaufplan Aufzeichnung von chronologisch folgenden Aktionen. Datenflußplan / Programmablaufplan -▶Arbeitsablaufplan.

Durchlaufzeit Die Zeit, in der ein Auftrag den Betrieb durchläuft.

Durchschnitt Mittelwert

durchzählen

E

ECU - Europäische Rechnungseinheit Ab 01.01.1981 Grundlage der -▶EG Haushaltsplanung und dient als Verrechnungseinheit bei allen finanziellen Transaktionen. Wert einer ECU und Kursbestimmung: (s. Tabelle „Währung")

EDV - Elektronische Daten Verarbeitung -▶Datenverarbeitung

effektiv wirksam / wirkungsvoll / real

EG - Europäische Gemeinschaften Zusammenschluß von nunmehr zwölf europäischen Staaten mit dem Ziel, eine wirtschaftliche und technologische Integrität herbei zu führen, um dadurch zu einer politischen Einheit zu gelangen. Erklärtes Nahziel: „Die Realisierung des Europäischen - Binnenmarktes bis Ende 1992." Mitgliedstaaten: 1958 Bundesrepublik Deutschland, Frankreich, Italien, Belgien, Niederlande und Luxemburg als Gründerstaaten.
1973 Großbritannien, Dänemark und Irland.
1981 Griechenland.
1986 Portugal und Spanien.

sequece chart Cronological of action. Data flow chart/Programme sequence planning -▶flow chart

respond time Time span of order processing.

average Mean value

count-up

ECU, European Currency Unit commencing 01.01.1981 basis for -▶EG budget planning and account unit on financial transactions. ECU value and exchange rate: (s.index "Currency")

electronical data processing - EDV -▶data processing

effective actual / real

Common Market, EG Community of now twelve European countries with the objective to commonize their economically and technologically achievements, as a foundation to achieve political commonality. Next major objective: „Realization of free trade market by end of 1992." Membership: 1958 Fed. Rep. of Germany, France, Italy, Belgium, Netherlands, and Luxembourg as nations of foundation. 1973 Great Britain, Denmark and Eire. 1981 Greece 1986 Portuguese and Spain.

Eigenfertigungsteile In Eigenproduktion hergestellte Teile, zur Weiterverwendung im Fertigprodukt.

Einbauprobe / Funktionsbau Neuentwicklungen unter Produktionsbedingungen montieren, zur Sicherstellung, daß der Großserieneinsatz nicht zur Produktionsstörung führt.

Einfuhr / Import Bezug von im Ausland hergestellten Waren.

Einführungsdatum Datum der effektiven Einführung von Produktänderungen.

Eingabe Organisation des Datenflusses zur Weiterverarbeitung in der EDV. (Weitgehend über Terminal)

Eingang Die Anlieferung und Vereinnahmung von Materiallieferungen.

Eingangsbericht Status über eingegangene Lieferungen.

Eingangsdatum Bearbeitungsvermerk, den Wareneingang bestätigen.

Eingangsschein Warenbegleitschein, Spezifikation der Lieferung.

Einheit Größenordnung bei Lieferungen und Produkten.

Einkauf Organisationseinheit verantwortlich für den Bezug von Zulieferungen.

Einkäufer Funktion der Einkaufsverantwortung.

manufactured parts Home made parts to be used in end-product.

functional build Capability test of new designed items to ensure uninterupted production under normal production conditions.

importation Material deliveries from abroad.

introduction date Effective date of product modification.

input Perform data flow for further process by data processing. (Mostly via terminal)

receival Deliveries and booking of receivals.

receiving report Status report of receipts.

receival date Remarks, confirming receipt of deliveries.

delivery document Specification of delivery.

unit Fixed quantity for products and deliveries.

purchase Organizational activity responsible for external source.

buyer Functional responsibility for buying.

Einkaufskostenanalyse Organisationseinheit zur Überwachung und Festlegung der Einkaufspreisgestaltung.

Einkaufspreis Der vom Lieferanten für eine Ware in Rechnung gestellte Preis, vielfach um die Kosten der Anlieferung erweitert.

Einkaufsrechnung Kostenmäßiges Gesamt-Einkaufs-Volumen / Kontrollgröße in Bezug auf Budgetvorgaben / Richtwert für Einsparungen.

Einkaufsteil / EP Von Fremdfirmen bezogenes Material.
-▶Einkauf

Einkaufsverbindlichkeiten Anerkennung der aus dem Kaufvertrag resultierenden Verpflichtungen über die Abnahme von Bestellungen.

Einrichtung Betriebsausstattung - Maschinen Vorrichtungen usw.

Einrichtungsabnahme / Maschinen Die Fähigkeitsüberprüfung von Einrichtungen und Maschinen durch verantwortliche Ingenieure des Bestellers beim Hersteller.
(Grundsatz der Bestellung)

Einrichtungsplan / Fabrik Genaue Aufzeichnug der geplanten Installations-Vorhaben und räumlichen Abgrenzungen für die Herstellung von Produkten.

Einsatzgewicht Rohmaterialgewicht, das für die Herstellung des Produktes eingesetzt wird.

purchasing cost analysis Organizational activity to control and determ purchase price.

prime cost From supplier calculated price for goods, sometimes increased by transportation costs.

purchase invoice Grand total of purchase costs / Medium to compare with budget forecast / Guideline to establish objectives for cost-reductions.

EP external purchase Items/parts purchased from suppliers.
-▶ purchase

purchasing commitments Acceptance of responsibilities as part from purchase contract with regard of material deliveries.

facility Manufacturing equipments machines tools etc.

acceptance of equipments/ machines Capability check of facilities, mainly machines by buyers personnel at the suppliers shop.
(Key feature of contract)

layout / plant Detailed plan of installation, requirements and plant size for processing of products.

rough weight Rough material weight required for machining of finished products.

Einsatzmeldung Bericht über den erfolgten Einsatz einer Produktänderung mit Angaben des Einsatzdatums und Serienbaunummer.

Einsatzmenge Eine bestimmte Menge neu entwickelter Produkte für Versuchszwecke, in bezug auf den geplanten Serieneinsatz.

Einwegverpackung Verpackungsform mit größtenteils einmaliger Verwendung, führt zur Platzersparnis und vermeidet Leergutrücktransport.

Einzelpreis -▶Einkaufspreis

Elektronische Bedarfserrechnung Computer gesteuerte Bedarfskalkulation. -▶Bedarfserrechnung

Elektronische Bestandsführung Computer gesteuerte Bestandskontrolle auf Basis des Anfangsbestandes und Zu- und Abgänge.

Elektronische Warenidentifizierung Auflösung der mittels Strich-Codes verschlüsselten Artikeldaten durch eine elektronische Leseanlage, führt zur automatischen Bestandsveränderungsbuchung bei Warenein- und Ausgang und regelt die Rechnungsschreibung.

Empfehlung Preisempfehlung / Unterstützung / Rat.

Endkontrolle Funktionstest des Fertigproduktes, letzte Qualitätsprüfung vor der Auslieferung.

notification of effective date Report of effective introduction date of product change, indicates implementation date and job-number.

initial quantity Limited number of new designed production material for line trial in regard of planned mass production.

one-way package Method of packing mainly one time posibility of utilization, leads to space saving and avoids transport costs for empties.

pice price -▶prime cost

mechanical requirement calculation Computer performed requirement calculation. -▶requirement calculation

mechanical stock control Computer controlled stock calculation considering starting inventories receipts and shipments.

bar code reading Identification of bar coded article data by electronical readers, initiates automatically stock amendments by material movements and invoice writing.

recommendation Recommendation of quotation / Support / Suggestion.

final Inspection Functional test of end-product, last quality check prior shipping.

Endkostenstelle Hauptkostenstelle - Endstelle der Leistungsverrechnung - Basis für die Kalkulation.

Endlosformular Vordrucke, die wiederholtes Einspannen in Schreib- oder Buchungsmaschinen ersparen.

Endmontage Fabrikbereich, wo die Fertigstellung des Produktes erfolgt.

Endprodukt / Fertigprodukt Produkt nach letzter Berarbeitungs- oder Montagestufe, versandfertig.

Energie / Strom / Wasser / Oel

Energieverbrauchswerte Meßgröße der aufgewandten Energie. Steht in Relation zum Produktionsergebnis, zur Kontrolle der produktbezogenen Energieverbrauchskosten.

Engpaß Absolut begrenzte Kapazitäten.
Problemstationen bestimmen die Auslastung der weiteren Fertigungseinrichtungen.

Entladestelle Ortsbezeichnung der Warenannahme - Anlieferungspunkt.

Entwicklung Planmäßige Tätigkeit zur Verbesserung und Neuentwicklung von Produkten.

Entwicklungsbüro In eine Organisationseinheit zusammengefaßte Abteilung mit Versuchseinrichtungen, verantwortlich für die Neu-

main cost centre / buy off centre Basic cost centre summarization of total performance - Basis for planning matters.

continuous stationery Printed forms avoiding multiple paper fitting into type- or account machines.

final assembly line Plant area were final assembly for end-product is performed.

end-item / finished product Product after final process operation, ready for dispatch.

utilities / electricity / water / oil

utility consumtion data Measurement of consumption used in relation to performance for utility cost control.

bottleneck Absolut limited capacity. Problem stations determing utilization of further process equipments.

unloading area Receiving area.

development Planning function to improve and develop new products

engineering office Organizational activity with experimental research, responsible for new product design and rationalization re-

entwicklung von Produkten und Rationalisierung im Hinblick auf kostengünstige Fertigung.

Entwicklungskosten / technische Zusammenfassung der projektbezogenen Kosten für Entwicklung, Forschung und Versuch als Meßgröße gegenüber den Budgetvorgaben.

Entwurf / Konstruktion Entwicklung von neuen Produktionsvorhaben.

Entwurf / Projekt-Plan Zusammenfassung geplanter Vorhaben und entstehender Kosten.

Erfassungsliste Automatische Auflistung der täglichen Computeraktionen der einzelnen Verarbeitungsprogramme.

Erfolg Arbeitsleistung / Nutzeffekt / Wirkungsgrad.

Erfolglosigkeit Nichterreichung der Planvorgaben / Mehraufwand Erreichung des Planzieles, Leistungsverlust.

Erfordernisse / Auflagen Die Beachtung der staatlichen Auflagen bei der Entwicklung von Wirtschaftsgütern und Wahrnehmung von Dienstleistungen. -▶gesetzliche Vorschriften

Ersatz Im Rahmen der Verkaufs- und Garantiebedingungen, Leistung auf Warenersatz oder Reparatur durch den Produzenten.

Ersatzbeleg Dokument als Ersatz für nicht mehr vorhandene Originalurkunde.

garding economical process performance.

engineering costs Summary of project related expenses regarding development, research and initial test phase, to compare with budget forecast.

design / construction Development of new products.

project plan Summary of planned actions and expected expenses.

holding list / transaction register Computer generated record indicating status of daily processed data.

efficiency Effectiveness of performance / Profitability.

inefficiency Off-standard position / Ineffectiveness of performance / Additional workload to meet achievements.

legal aspects Consideration of national principles in conjunction with development of new products and performance of services. -▶legal requirements

replacement Commitment for warrenty claims on condition of sales and guarantee contract by producer.

substitute document Document as replacement for loss of original.

Ersatzteil Teil gleicher Entwicklung oder gleiche Funktion wahrnehmende Alternative, als Ersatz für funktiongestörte Produkte.

Ersatzteile und Zubehör Organisationsbezeichnung für die Ersatzteillagerhaltung.

Ersatzteilfertigung Besondere Einrichtung oder Kapazitätsbindung für die Herstellung von Ersatzteilen. Die Ersatzteilfertigung für vergangene Großserienfertigungen wird vielfach in Fremdbezug verlagert, zur besseren Nutzung der Eigenkapazität und Reduzierug der In-Haus-Komplexität.

Ersatzteillager Lagereinheit in der zur schnelleren Bedienung der Kunden nur Ersatzteile gelagert werden.

Ersatzteillager-Verwaltung / PSO Organisationseinheit für Verwaltung und Planung der mit der Ersatzteilversorgung im Zusammenhang stehenden Aufgaben.

Ersatzteilliste / Katalog Von der -▶Ersatzteillager-Verwaltung erstellte Teileliste über verfügbare Bestände, mit Angaben der Serienbauzeit, zwecks Steuerung der Austauschaktionen und der Bestellung von Ersatzteilen durch den Service.

ersetzen Erneuerung von abgenutzten Wirtschaftsgütern / Produkterneuerung oder Verbesserung / Austauschaktionen.

service part/spare part Part of same design or same function performing alternative as replacement for defect products.

Parts and Accessories Description of organizational activity for parts depot.

service part manufacturing Special equipments or reserved capacity for manufacturing of spare parts. For better utilization of in-house capacity and complexity reductions, service demand is sometimes resourced to outside suppliers.

spare / service parts depot Separate storage for spare parts to provide quick customer service.

PSO parts supply operation Organizational unit responsible for administration and planning matters related to parts supply.

spare parts catalogue Bill of available service material issued by -▶PSO, indicating life time of production series to support replacement action and ordering of spare parts by service.

replace Replacement of used up material / Product replacement or improvements / Exchange action.

Ersparnisse / Einsparungen Zielsetzungsfaktor bei der Budgetplanung durch Rationalisierungsmaßnahmen in der laufenden Produktion. „Produktionsoptimierung"

Erstattung Die wertmäßige Rückerstattung für eine bezahlte, aber nicht in Anspruch genommene Ware.

Erstfertigung Fertigungsbeginn einer Neuentwicklung.

Erstmuster Unter Serienbedingungen hergestellte Teile zum Zwecke der Qualitätsprüfung und Einbauprobe, bevor Serienfertigung erfolgt. -▶Einbauprobe/Funktionsbau

Erstmusterkontrolle Die Überprüfung der neu zur Verwendung kommenden Teile auf ihre spezifikationsgerechte Herstellung. Prüfergebnis bestimmt den Beginn der Serienfertigung.

Erstmustertermin Teil der Serienanlaufplanung, berücksichtigt den Prüfzeitraum vor Serienfertigung.

Ertrag Der vom Unternehmen in einer Zeiteinheit durch Leistung erwirtschafteter Gesamtzuwachs.

Erweiterung Die Ausdehnung / Vergrößerung

Etatkontrolle Budgetkontrolle / Kontrolle der während eines Geschäftsjahres in den einzelnen Kostenstellen anfallenden Kosten, im Vergleich zu den Vorgaben.

Exportversand Den Transfer von

Savings / economics Objective for budget planning by rationalization of current production process. „Optimizing production flow."

refund / reimbursement Refund of payment for delivered but not used products.

job number one / initial production Initial build of new design.

initial sample Under regular process condition manufactured parts for the purpose of quality check and functional build prior mass production. -▶functional build

initial sample inspection Quality check of new designed parts to ensure that technical specification is fully applied prior release of mass production.

initial sample date Part of timing plan, considering test phase of sample approval prior job one.

income earned Total company return on performance within a limited time of business.

expansion Extension / Widening

budget control Controls of cost center related expenses and comparing actuals against forecast during a business year.

export shipping Transfer of pro-

Waren oder Dienstleistungen ins Ausland.

Expressendung Warenbeförderung als Stückgut im Gepäckwagen von Personenzügen oder durch andere spezielle Zustellmethoden.

ducts or services to foreign countries.

express shipment / 1st.class mail Transportation of goods in luggage-van of express train or special services by alternatives.

F

Fabrik Mit Einrichtungen zur Herstellung von Produkten ausgestattete Wirkungsstätte.

Fabrik - Direktion Fabrik-Leitung, Planung, Aufsicht. Verantwortlich für die Gestaltung der optimalen Fertigung.

Fabrikation Die Produktherstellung der Fertigungsverlauf.

Fabrikationsplanung Planung und Entwicklung der für die Produkterzeugung erforderlichen Anlagen.

Fabrikationstechnik Überwacht und unterstützt die Fertigung durch optimale Gestaltung der Fertigungsprozesse.

Fabrikleiter Manager, verantwortlich für die spezifikationsgerechte Herstellung der Produkte und Erreichung der Progammplanvorgaben. Vorgesetzter der betrieblichen Organisation.

Fabrikmarke / Zeichen Herstellerzeichen kennzeichnet den Warenursprung, die Echtheit und Güte der Ware.

Facharbeiter Der in einem Aus-

plant / factory Working place equiped with facilities for product manufacturing.

manufacturing staff Management with supervision and planning responsibilities and responsible for optimized production flow.

production / manufacture Processing of products manufacturing progress.

manufacturing planning Planning and development of required process equipments for product-manufacturing.

manufacturing engineering Controls and assists manufacturing by optimizing process performance.

plant manager Manager, responsible for manufacturing of products according engineering specification and achieving of programme planning objectives. Leads plant organization.

trade-mark Symbol indicating source of product as well as authenticity and quality.

skilled worker/specialist Person

bildungsberuf die Abschlußprüfung abgelegt hat und in dem erlernten Beruf beschäftigt ist.

Fähre Transport von Personen und Waren durch Schiffe.

Falschverbrauch Verwendung von Material an nicht vorgesehener Stelle oder von der Spezifikation abweichender Mehr- oder Minderverbrauch.

Farblager Verschlußlager mit besonderen Sicherheitsauflagen für die Lagerung von Farben und leicht brennbaren Materialien.

Fehlanzeige Wenn als Prüfergebnis keine Abweichungen von den Vorgaben festgestellt wurden.

Fehler-Analyse Ursachenforschung, Ermittlung der Fehlerhäufigkeit, Erstellung eines nach Prioritäten geordneten Problemkataloges mit Abstellmaßnahmen und Verlauf.

fehlerhaft Unrichtig, ungenau, falsch, irrtümlich.

Fehlmeldung Bericht über nicht stattfindende Realisierung eines geplanten Vorhabens, aufgrund unerwarteter Schwierigkeiten.

Fehlmenge Bedarf, der die verfügbaren Mengen überschreitet. Mengenmäßige Fehlplanung gegenüber dem tatsächlichen Verbrauch.

Fertigteile / Kaufteile Vom Lieferanten bezogene fertig bearbeitete Teile. -▶Einkaufsteil -▶Endprodukt

who passed an examination in a special field and works in this capacity.

ferry boat Transportation of passenger and googs by ferry.

incorrect usage/misusage Deviation from normal usage or usage of incorrect quantity.

paint store Locked store with specific safety regulations for storage of paint and inflammable items.

nil return/negative report Positive audit result. Functional check confirms in line performance.

error inquiry Error analysis, summary of error reported. Establishing of priority orientated problem report with solution proposals and timing.

incorrect Faulty, mistake, error, imperfect.

failure report Report of not achieved planned objective, caused by unexpected difficulties.

missing quantity Requirement exceeds available quantity. Wrong usage specification relative to actual demand.

purchased finished parts Finished EP-sourced parts. -▶EP-External Purchase -▶end-item

Fertigungsabweichung Dimensionelle Abweichung von der Spezifikation durch ungenaue Herstellungsmethoden.

Fertigungsauslastung Volle Nutzung der installierten Kapazität.

Fertigungsauslauf Programmäßiger Fertigungsabschluß einer Produktserie.

Fertigungsausschuß Teile, die während des Herstellungsprozesses durch Material- oder Fertigungsfehler zum Ausschuß führen.

Fertigungsbedingungen Durch Einrichtungen und Anweisungen vorgegebene Fertigungsordnung zur optimalen Gestaltung des Betriebsablaufes.

Fertigungsdauer Zeiteinheit für die Erstellung des Produktes.

Fertigungsdurchlauf Herstellungsverlauf eines Produktes über mehrere Fertigungsstationen oder Operationen.

Fertigungsengpaß -▸Engpaß

Fertigungserweiterung Ausdehnung der Kapazität durch Neuinvestitionen zur Befriedigung der Nachfrage. -▸Erweiterung

Fertigungsfreigabe Freigabe der Serienfertigung nach erfolgter Erstmusterabnahme. -▸Erstmuster

Fertigungsfrequenz Die Fertigungsfrequenz umfaßt die Fertigungsruhezeit, für die Material vor-

out of specification Deviation by dimension from specification caused by incorrect process.

capacity utilization Fully utilization of installed capacity.

production phase out Scheduled balance-out of product series.

scrap/wastage/rejects Parts, becoming rejects during manufacturing process caused by material- or machine defaults.

in-process condition Optimal manufacturing process supplemented by appropriate supportings and working instructions.

manufacturing period Time span required for manufacturing of products.

manufacturing process Progress of production or sequence of machining.

capacity bottleneck -▸bottleneck

capacity expansion Increasing manufacturing capacity by additional investments to satisfy customer demand. -▸expansion

manufacturing release Release of bulk production subseqent sample approval. -▸initial sample

manufacturing frequency Manufacturing frequency includes the period for tool-or machine-chan-

gefertigt sein muß und findet Anwendung, wenn kontinuierliche Umbauten oder Umstellungen der Fertigungseinrichtungen auf andere Produkte entsprechend der Prozeßplanung erforderlich sind.
-▶ Materialreserve Die Fertigungsfrequenz wird definiert in Produktionstagen zur Gestaltung der Materialvorplanung.

Fertigungsgemeinkosten Fertigungsnebenkosten, die nur zum Teil dem Produkt zugeordnet werden. (Energie, Hilfsmaterial, Dienstleistungen usw)

Fertigungsgröße Bestimmung der optimalen Losgröße, wenn gleiche Maschinen oder Einrichtungen zur besseren Auslastung für die Herstellung von anderen Produkten umgebaut werden. Für die Dauer der Fertigungsruhe ist entsprechend dem Materialverbrauch während dieser Zeit, eine Vorplanung erforderlich. -▶Fertigungsfrequenz

Fertigungsinspektion Die Kontrolle der spezifikationsgerechten Fertigung in den einzelnen Stationen der Herstellung durch die Qualitätskontrolle oder automatisch operierenden Prüfanlagen.

Fertigungskapazität Fabrikausstattung mit Maschinen, Anlagen und Personal als Erfordernis, um eine bestimmte Produktionsmenge herzustellen.

Fertigungskontrolle Organisationseinheit der Fabrikleitung, ver-

ge-over, for which required production material has to be pre-scheduled and is applied in case when equipments will be rebuild for manufacturing of different products, in accordance to process planning.
-▶production material float. For the purpose of advance material schedule, manufacturing frequency is defined in work days.

manufacturing overhead Manufacturing expenses which are only partly debited to production. (utilities, non production material, service etc.)

manufacturing lot Determination of optimal production rate, when for better capacity utilization machines or equipments will be rebuild for manufacturing of different products. During production stoppage material usage has to prescheduled accordingly. -▶manufacturing frequency.

in-process inspection Product quality check within various station of process by Quality Control or automatically operating checking equipments.

manufacturing capacity Plant installation with machines, equipments and labour as required, to achieve projected output.

production control Organizational unit of plant management re-

antwortlich für die Kostenkontrolle, Fertigungslenkung, Programmplanung, Maschinenbelegung, Terminplanung, Bestandsführung und -kontrolle, Materialbereitstellung sowie die Produktauslieferung.

Fertigungskosten Die bei der Be- und Verarbeitung von Material zu fertigen Produkten anfallenden Kosten. -▶Betriebskosten

Fertigungskostenstellen Umfassen Teilbereiche der betrieblichen Leistungsabrechnung. Zusammenfassung von operationsbezogenen Fertigungskosten. -▶Endkostenstellen

Fertigungsleiter Verantwortliche Führungskraft für den geordneten Fertigungsablauf.

Fertigungslenkung Organisationseinheit der -▶Fertigungskontrolle mit Verantwortung der Fertigungssteuerung zur Gewährleistung eines kontinuierlichen Fertigungsverlaufes.

Fertigungsmeldung / Bericht Bericht über das Produktionsergebnis in der Fertigungskostenstelle zur Erfassung der erbrachten Leistung und zur Übersicht der Materialbestandssituation, nach Abschluß einer Fertigungsperiode. (Schichtende)

Fertigungsmöglichkeit Die Fähigkeit zur Herstellung eines Produktes entsprechend den planerischen Vorgaben.

Fertigungsmuster -▶Erstmuster

sponsible for cost control, manufacturing coordination, programme-planning, balance of machine utilization, timing, stock control, housekeeping, material-handling and end-item shipping.

manufacturing cost/expense Arising costs by processing of material to finished products. -▶operating costs

manufacturing cost centre Control points for manufacturing performance. Summary of perational related process costs. -▶main cost centre.

superintendent Leader, responsible for the coordination of manufacturing progress.

manufacturing coordination Organizational unit of-▶Production Control with functnial responsibility of production coordination to support continuity of production.

production report Production count reporting within manufacturing cost center for reason of performance control and stock on hand situation at the end of production. (Shift change)

manufacturing feasibility Capability for product fabrication according pre-designed process.

production sample -▶initial sample

Fertigungsplan Die Aufgliederung der geforderten Bedarfe entsprechend den Herstellungsgegebenheiten unter Berücksichtigung der installierten Kapazität.

Fertigungsplaner Bedarfsplaner für den Bereich Eigenfertigung. Übertragung der herzustellenden Kundenbedarfe in Fertigungspläne entsprechend den Prozeßgegebenheiten. Maschinenbelegung, zyklische Fertigung. (Vielfach computergestützte Planung)

Fertigungsprogrammsteuerung Fertigungsplan über die in einem bestimmten Zeitraum zu erzeugenden Produkte. Einsteuerung der unterschiedlichen Bauumfänge entsprechend Kundenauftrag, unter Berücksichtigung der Komplexitätsgröße und vorhandener Kapazität.

Fertigungsreserve Erforderliche Materialmenge, um einen kontinuierlichen Fertigungsdurchlauf zu gewährleisten. (Gebundene Materialmenge im Prozeß) Die Fertigungsreserve ist Bestandteil der -▶System-Menge.

Fertigungsschlüssel Indikator zur Bestimmung der -▶Fertigungsfrequenz und Steuerungsmerkmal für die Kalkulation der benötigten Materialmengen während der Fertigungsruhezeit.

Fertigungssteuerung -▶Fertigungslenkung

Fertigungstiefe Größenordnung

manufacturing plan Product manufacturing schedule according to process capability and capacity limitations.

scheduling analyst Person responsible for requirement planning of own manufacturing parts based on customer demands. Establishing of production schedules and planning of cyclic production to suit installed capacity. (In many cases computer assist requirement planning)

manufacturing programme coordination Production plan for the fabrication of products within a certain period. Performing order segmentation according customer demand, considering product complexity and available capacity.

material in process Required number on material to support continuous flow of process. (Pipeline fill) Material in process is part of -▶system float.

manufacturing frequency code Indicator fixing -▶manufacturing frequency and key feature for calculation of required material during machine change over times.

production coordination -▶manufacturing coordination

range of company produced

der in -▶Eigenfertigung hergestellten Anteile vom -▶Endprodukt/Fertigprodukt. Mitbestimmend für den Grad der -▶Flexibilität.

Fertigungsüberschuß Über die Programmvorgaben hinaus produzierten Waren, für die keine Kundennachfrage besteht. Belastung der Kapitalbindung und Bindung von losem Material im Produkt. Führt zu Materialengpässen, wenn im Produkt gebundene Einzelteile,auch gleiche Verwendung in anderen Produkten finden.

Fertigungsumstellung Umbau von Fertigungsmaschinen zur Herstellung von anderen Produkten, im Rahmen des Maschinennutzungsplanes.

Fertigungsunterbrechung Störung des Produktionsflusses durch fehlendes Material oder Maschinenausfall,als Hauptursache.

Fertigungsverlust Nichterreichung der Planziele durch Ablaufstörungen.

Fertigungszahl Anzahl der produzierten Güter in einer bestimmten Zeiteinheit. -▶Fertigungsmeldung

Fertigungszyklus Periodische Fertigung von Produkten durch Einrichtungen mit Mehrfachverwendung oder aus Gründen der Rationalisierung beim Arbeitsablauf.

Festabruf Einmalige feste Bestellgröße.

assets Amount of -▶manufactured parts required for -▶end-item/finished product. - Factor for extent of -▶flexibility.

excess material Products produced in excess to schedule for which no customer demand exists. Leads to excess of capital binding and binding of loose material in higher production level and generates material shortages if already assembled single parts are required for other products.

machine change over Re-lining of production machines to enable change over to other products as part of machine utilization plan.

process interruption Interruption of production flow due to material or machine break down as main reason.

manufacturing losses Not achieving objectives by inefficiency within processing.

production quantity Number of produced products within a certain manufacturing period. -▶production report

cyclic production Periodical product manufacturing by multiple manufacturing equipement or for reason of product simplification.

fixed order Limited order quantity.

Festpreis Frei von Schwankungen vereinbarter Preis für den Bezug von Waren. Betriebliche Abrechnungsvereinfachung für innerbetriebliche Leistung.

Feuerschutz Sicherungsvorkehrungen zur Erhaltung von Fabrikanlagen. Installation der zur schnelleren Bekämpfung von Feuer auferlegten Anlagen und räumliche Besonderheit für leicht brennbares Material.

Filiale Dem Konzern angeschlossene unselbständige Zweigstelle mit eigenverantwortlicher Produktionsverantwortung, aber zentraler Verwaltung.

Finanz Betriebliche Organisationseinheit, verantwortlich für die monetären Bewegungen - Gewinn und Verlustrechnug - Publizierung des Betriebsergebnisses Budgetplanung.

first in - first out a) Materialbewertungsmethode unter Annahme, daß der Materialbezug vom Betriebslager (first out) analog der Einlagerung erfolgt. (first in) Bewertung nach vorhandenen und verbrauchten Materialien.
b) Wichtige Grundfunktion im Lagerwesen. Vermeidung von Qualitätsverlust bei eingelagertem Material, durch Alterung, aber auch Sicherstellung, daß bei Änderungen der Bestand der vorherigen Ausführung vor Einsatz der geänderten Produkten aufgebraucht wird.

fixed price Fixed price condition for EP-supplied products, not influenced by floating. Simplification of internal company performance account.

fire protection Safety regulations to protect company buildings and equipments. Installation of fire protection facilities to enable quick reaction in case of fire. Availability of special store for inflamable items.

subsidiary Company connected not autonomous factory with unique manufacturing responsibility and central office performed administration.

finance Organizational department responsible for company chash flow, controlling all monetary movements and publishes book balance. Responsible for budget planning.

first in - first out A method of stock value calculation under the assumption that material receipt (first out) from company store is analog to incomings (first in). Calculation based on actual stock on hand and effective usages.
b) Principle of material handling function. Avoidance of deterioration in quality due to long term material storage (ageing problem) - but also appropriate material turnover, in case of product changes use old stock first.

Fixmenge / Materialreserve Materialmenge in fester Größenordnung. Die Fixmenge findet Anwendung, wenn die kontinuierliche Fertigung nur durch eine bestimmte Systemfüllmenge möglich ist. (Einrichtungsabhängig) -▶Materialreserve

Flexibilität Folgerichtige Organisation des Fertigungsablaufes durch Rationalisierung der Durchlauf- und Verkürzung der Umbauzeiten bei Einrichtungen und Werkzeugwechsel.
Das Höchstmaß an Ausstattung steht in Relation zur Produktkomplexität und der vom Markt verlangten Produktverfügbarkeit wie auch der Reaktionszeit bei Änderung der Produktnachfrage.

Forderungen Anspruch auf Leistung - Kundenforderung auf Rechnungsausgleich.

Formaländerung Änderung der technischen Unterlagen, Spezifikation oder Zeichnung, im Angleich an die Produktherstellung. Legitimation von Fertigungsabweichungen aufgrund Herstellungsschwierigkeiten, ohne daß die Funktion des Produktes beeinträchtigt wird.

FPV- Finanzplanungsvolumen Produktionsgrößenermittlung aufgrund Marketing-Ergebnissen zur Kalkulation der Gesamtinvestierung und Planung der Fertigungsanlagen.
Die Verkaufserwartungen werden als Planzahlen um den Prozentsatz der dem Markt entsprechen-

fix float Fixed quantity as system fill to support continuous production flow. (Equipment related) -▶production material float

flexibility Optimal production flow governed by process sequence and changeover time. Degree of installation is relative to product complexity and market requirement on product availability, considering reaction time of customer consumption.

receivables Claim of payment - Customer claim to balance invoice.

record change Revision of technical specification or drawing in accordance with processing. Legitimation of deviated production as consequence of manufacturing difficulties, without affecting functional performance.

FPV- financial planning volume Calculation of expected sales on Marketing assumptions to be used as initial planning figure for calculation of overall investment.
Planning figure will be up-graded according market orientated flexibility. (Effective planning assumtions:-▶CPV -▶DPV)

den Flexibilität aufgerundet.
(Effektive Einrichtungsplanung: -►CPV -►DPV)

Frachtbrief Vom Absender ausgestellte Warenbegleitpapiere für den Frachtführer über das zu befördernde Gut.

frachtfrei Die Lieferung von Bestellungen erfolgt ohne Transportkostenbelastung für den Käufer. Transportkosten gehen zu Lasten des Verkäufers.

Freigabe Freigabe einer Neuentwicklung oder technischen Änderung durch die Produktentwicklung zur Realisierung in der Produktion.

Freigabenummer Klassifizierung und Numerierung der Produktänderung.

Fremdleistung Beschaffung von Produkten und Dienstleistungen von anderen Unternehmen.

Frequenz -►Fertigungsfrequenz / -►Lieferfrequenz

Frist / Zeitraum Zeitraum zur Herstellung und Bereitstellung von Waren. -►Lieferzeit

Fuhrpark Die Gesamtheit der hausinternen Fahrzeuge.

Führungskräfte Wahrnehmung von Verantwortungen in leitender Position durch Zuweisungen aufgrund der unternehmerischen Organisationsstruktur.

Funktion Spezifiziertes Aufgabengebiet im Rahmen einer Gesamtorganisation. -►Arbeitsplatz

consignment note Fright bill issued by the consignee to instruct the forwarding agent to transport goods.

free freight Deliveries on orders are free of transportation costs for customer. Freight is fully paid by shipper.

release Release of new design or product modification by Product Development Group for implementation in production.

release number Classification and numbering of product change.

outside services Ordering of products and services from other companies.

frequency -►Manufacturing frequency/ -►Delivery frequency

lead time Time span for production and availability of material. -►term for delivery

transport and supply unit Whole range of company vehicles.

supervisory personnel Personnel who carry out responsibilities in leading positions as directed by companies organizational structure.

function Specified working place as part of overall organization. -►job position

funktionieren Im Sinne der Entwicklung, ablaufendes Geschehen.

Funktionsbeschreibung -▶Arbeitsplatzbeschreibung

Funktionsprüfung Überprüfung der Funktion bei Neuentwicklungen, vor Aufnahme der Serienfertigung. -▶Einbauprobe/Funktionsbau

Funktionsüberprüfung Überprüfung der Aufgabenwahrnehmung durch interne Kontrollinstanz.

G

Gabelstabler Fahrzeug mit gabelförmiger Hebevorrichtung, das zum Bewegen und Heben von Paletten dient.

Garantie / Gewährleistung -▶Ersatz

Gebrauchsanweisung -▶Bedienunganleitung

gebrauchsfähig Durch Überprüfung festgestellte Verwendungsfähigkeit von Produkten und Einrichtungen.

gebrauchsfertig Fertigerzeugnisse fähig für die vorgesehene Verwendung.

Gebühren Abgaben für die Inanspruchnahme einer öffentlichen Leistung.

gebührenfrei Öffentliche Leistungen die nicht der Gebührenerhebung unterliegen.

Gebührenordnung Verzeichnis

operate Performance in working order.

statement of function -▶job description

functional test Functional test for new designed products, prior release of mass production. -▶functional build

audit of function performance Revision of function performance by internal control.

fork track Truck equiped with forks to handle palettes.

warranty -▶replacement

operational instruction

usable / serviceable Confirmed usage of products and equipments by testing.

ready for use Finished products ready for planned utilization.

fees / taxes Duty for service performed by administrative authority.

free of charge Public services which do not require duty.

tariff Index indicating fees for pub-

über Abgaben für die Inanspruchnahme von öffentlichen Leistungen.

Gegenstand / Sache Objekt, Subjekt, Artikel

Gegenstück Gleiche Funktionswahrnehmung mit gleichen oder anderen Mitteln.

gegenwärtiger Stand Derzeitige Position einer Verrichtung.

Gehaltsabzüge Vom Arbeitgeber vorzunehmenden Abzüge vom Verdienst aufgrund der Abgabenordnung. (Steuer / Versicherungsbeiträge)

Gehaltsempfänger Angestellte die nach Zeitabschnitten bemessene Vergütung erhalten.

Gehaltserhöhung Erhöhung der bisher für eine bestimmte, auf Zeit bezogene Leistung gewährte Vergütung, durch tarifliche Änderungen oder als Anerkennung für besondere Leistung bei Ausübung der Funktion.

Geldfluß -►Cash-Flow

Geldfreigabe Freigabe der für die Realisierung eines Vorhabens über Projekt oder Budget beantragten Geldmenge.

Geldmittel Verfügbare Geldmenge für die Bedienung von kurzfristigen Verpflichtungen.

Geltungsbereich Räumliche Begrenzung zur Anwendung von Anordnungen.

lic services.

item Object, subject, article

counterpart Same function performance by equivalent or different equipments.

current status Current position of performance.

salary deductions Reductions from salary by employer based on liability order. (Tax/insurance payment)

salaried employee Salaried people earning wages for timly working periods.

salary increase Increase of current payment level by wage negotiation or as merit for excellent job performance. -► cash - flow

cash flow funds release

release funds Release of required amount of money for the realization of investment as requested by project application or budged planning.

funds on hand Available funds to finance short-term demand.

scope of validity District where applications are in force.

Gemeinkosten Kostenarten, die im einzelnen nicht erfaßbar sind und somit nicht immer dem Produkt direkt zugeordnet werden können. -▶Fertigungsgemeinkosten

overheads Indirect cost which are not in all cases end-product related. -▶manufacturing overheads

Gemeinsamer Markt -▶EG Europäische Gemeinschaften

Common Market -▶EG Common Market

Genehmigung Zustimmung eines beantragten oder geplanten Vorhabens durch die hierfür bevollmächtigte Institution.

approval Formal agreement of requested application by responsible authorities.

Geplanter Verbrauch vor geplanter Verfügbarkeit Vorproduzierte Materialbedarfsmenge zur Bedienung der Produktion während der Fertigungsruhezeit für dieses Material. Vielfach, wenn Einrichtungen zur Herstellung von anderen Produkten umgebaut sind. -▶Fertigungsfrequenz

planned usage prior planned availability Advance production of material required to support production during the phase of interruption for machining. Mainly used in case of machine-changeover. -▶manufacturing frequency

geringfügig wenig - unbedeutend - unwichtig Kleinigkeit

insignificant trifling - unimportant little - minor

Gesamtansicht Übersicht

general view

Gesamtbedarf Zusammenfassung der in der Produktion an unterschiedlichen Stellen zur Verwendung kommenden Materialmengen, gleicher Ausführung zu einer Bedarfs- oder Bestellgröße.

total requirement Generation of total production material demand by adding up all various usages of same design to an accummulated value.

Gesamtertrag Gesamtgewinn des Betriebsgeschehens. -▶Ertrag

total profit / return Overall profit of business. -▶income earned

Gesamtforderung Forderung aller Verbindlichkeiten. -▶Forderung

total charges Total claim of obligation. -▶receivables

Gesamtleistung Die Effektivität in

overall efficiency Company effec-

seiner Gesamtheit, bezogen auf Arbeitsleistung, Nutzeffekt, Wirkungsgrad und Wirksamkeit.

Gesamtübersicht Das Verständnis hinsichtlich dem Zusammenwirken in einer Organisationseinheit.

Gesamtwert Gesamtgröße einer Investition.

Gesamtzahl Erfassung mehrer Einzelwerte in einer Totalen.

Geschäftbericht Bericht über den Geschäftsverlauf einer Aktien-Gesellschaft.

Geschäftsgrundsatz Von der Geschäftsleitung erlassene Anordnung, die die Verhaltensweise der Beteiligten zu einem bestimmten Sachverhalt regelt.

Geschäftsjahr Größtenteils gleich dem Kalenderjahr, wo jedes Unternehmen nach Ablauf von 12 Monaten das Geschäftsergebnis erstellen muß.

Geschäftskenntnis Die Erfahrung im Ablauf der einzelnen Funktionen zur Erreichung der Betriebserwartungen.

Geschäftsordnung Richtlinien nach denen die Arbeit abgewickelt wird, soweit nicht schon durch Gesetzgeber bestimmt.

Geschäftsreisender Im Auftrage einer Firma reisende Person.

Geschäftssprache Spezialisierte- fachbezogene Sprache zur

tiveness in overall performance, execution, achievement and output.

general survey Comprehensive view of cooperation within an organizational unit.

aggregate value Total investment.

total number Adding-up of various single values to a cumulative figure.

company report Business trend report of a stock company outlining year-end position.

policy letter From company management published principles determing the behaviour of affected persons with respect to certain objects.

business / trading year Generally equal to calender year where every company is requested to establish their company results, after 12 months of business.

business experience Knowledge of function to be performed to achieve company objectives.

standing orders Guidelines to coordinate progress of work, as far as not already laid down by goverment.

commercial traveler Person travelling on behalf of a company.

commercial language Unique job related language to cover business

Abwicklung der Geschäftsvorgänge.

Geschäftsverbindung Die Beziehungen zu außerbetrieblichen Institutionen und Geschäftspartner zur Koordination des Betriebsgeschehens.

Geschäftsverkehr Transaktionen von Waren und Dienstleistungen mit Geschäftspartner.

geschätzt Angenommener Zeitpunkt zur Realisierung eines Vorhabens.

Gesellschaft Zusammenschluß von Personen zum gemeinsamen Betrieb von Handel.

Gesenkedisposition Die Planung und Bestellung von Press- Stanz- und Schmiedewerkzeuge im Rahmen der Neuplanung oder des Werkzeugabnutzungsplanes.

Gesenkelager In sich abgegrenztes mit Bedienungshilfen ausgestattetes Lager für Gesenke.

gesetzliche Vorschriften Vom Gesetzgeber erlassene Bestimmungen, die bei der Entwicklung von neuen Produkten zu berücksichtigen sind. (Sicherheitsauflagen)

gesetzlicher Feiertag Besonderer Tag im Kalenderjahr, der zum Gedenken an ein geschichtliches Ereignis von der Staatsführung als arbeitsfreier, aber vom Arbeitgeber zu bezahlender Tag bestimmt wurde.

Gewerbeaufsichtamt Die be-

matter.

business connexion Relationship to outside economic institutions and associated partners to coordinate business progress.

commercial intercourse Transaction of products and services with associated partners.

estimate Expected timing for realization of projected action.

company Combination of business partner to perform corporate trade.

die scheduling Planning and ordering of die tools in line with initial production or die replacement plan.

die store Seperate store with special handling equipment for dies.

legal requirements From goverment published legislation which are mandatory for development of new products. (Savety regulations)

legal holiday Special day based on historical event, free of work but fully paid as directed by law. In some countries known as bank holiday.

trade control office Control of

hördliche Überwachung der Einhaltung der arbeitsrechtlichen- und Arbeitsschutzbestimmungen.

Gewerbeordnung Rechtsordnung über Zulassung, Umfang und Ausübung eines Gewerbes. Bestimmt die Beschäftigung und enthält Schutzbestimmungen zur Beschäftigung.

Gewerkschaften Nach Berufszweigen oder Industriegruppen gegliederte Vereinigungen von Arbeitnehmern zur Verbesserung der sozialen und wirtschaftlichen Lebensbedingungen. Vertretung der Arbeitnehmer gegenüber Arbeitgeber und Behörden.

Gewinn Differenz zwischen Erträgen und Kosten in einer Periode.

Gewinn nach Steuer Verbleibender Ertrag nach Abzug der Steuer.

Gewinn vor Steuer Ertrag vor Abzug der Steuer.

Gewinnprognose Gewinnprojektion auf Basis der zu erwartenden Umsatzerlöse.

grenzüberschreitender Verkehr Der Warenverkehr über Landesgrenzen zur Erfüllung der Kundennachfrage oder Bedienung von Zweigstellen unter Beachtung der Zollbestimmungen.

Großraumbehälter Genormter Großraumcontainer für den Transport von Gütern mittels Zugmaschine zur besseren Nutzung und Rationalisierung der Transportka-

proceeding in accordance with working rule and safety regulations.

trade regulations Regulations for licencing operation, range and kind of business, containing safety regulations to protect employment.

trade unions Organized communities of labour to improve social and economical style of life. Elected representative of workers to negotiate with employer and official representatives.

profit Difference between income and losses within a period of business.

profit after tax Remaining earnings after deduction of tax.

profit before tax Pre-tax earnings.

profit forecast Profit projection based on sales planning.

border- crossing traffic Material shipment to foreign countries to satisfy customer demand or support foreign branch under consideration of customs regulations.

high cube container Standardized metal packing unit for transportation of goods by special truck for better utilization and rationalization of trans port capacity as well as

pazitäten und Reduzierung der Transportkosten.

Großversuch Die Verwendung einer größeren Anzahl von neuen Produkten zur Gewinnung der Erfahrungswerte vor Großserieneinsatz. -▶Dauerversuch

Grundlohn Tariflich festgelegtes Entgelt für die Arbeitsleistung, gegliedert nach Leistungsgruppen.

Grundrißplan Anlageplan für Neuplanung und Installierung von Vorhaben.

Gruppe Abgegrenzte Anzahl von Personen deren Zusammenarbeit auf ein gemeinsames Ziel gerichtet ist.

Gruppenleiter Führungskraft mit Verantwortung zur Erreichung der Gruppenplanziele.

Gruppenstab In der Stabsorganisation angesiedlte Einheit zur Wahrnehmung von übergeordneten Aufgaben.

Gültigkeitsdauer Periode in der nach einer Abweichungsgenehmigung verfahren werden darf.

Gültigkeitsverlängerung Ausdehnung der ursprünglichen Begrenzung einer Abweichungsgenehmigung.

Gutachten Beurteilung eines Ergebnisses durch einen Sachverständigen.

Güter Waren, Produkte, Teile

Güterbeförderung Transport von

cost reduction.

large quantity trial Large-scale test of new designed products to obtain experience prior release of mass production. -▶durability test

base rate / base wage Wage determined by tariff for work performance, structured according to function responsibility.

layout Shop-floor and installation plan for new investments.

section / group Restricted number of people who are working together on common objectives.

supervisor Team leader responsible for achievments of group objectives.

group staff Organizational unit with subordinate responsibility reporting to group management.

validity Period for which a deviation request is valid for proceeding.

extension of validity Extension of originally approved validity period of a deviation request.

appraisal Rating of achievement by an advisor.

goods Articles, products, parts

forwarding of goods Transporta-

Produkten vom Hersteller zum Verbraucher.

Gutschrift Anspruch auf eine Leistung aufgrund bezahlter aber nicht funktioniernder Bestellung.

H

Haftung Wiedergutmachung für persönliches Fehlverhalten oder fehlerhafte Warenlieferung.

Halbfabrikate Fabrikate, deren Fertigstellung an anderen Verarbeitungsorten erfolgt.
(Rationalisierung, auch steuerliche Gründe)

Halle / Fabrik -▶Fabrik

Handbuch Richtlinien und Beschreibungen hinsichtlich der Funktion und der Funktionswahrnehmung.

Handel Austausch von Waren zwischen den einzelnen Wirtschaftspartnern.

Handelsangelegenheit Die Vereinbarung zwischen Hersteller und Abnehmer von Waren über Geschäftsbedingungen.   -▶INCOTERMS

Handelsgesellschaft -▶Gesellschaft

Handelsgesetz Regelt die Rechte bei der Abwicklung von Handelsgeschäften.

handelsübliches Material Dem Allgemeinzweck dienendes Standardmaterial für universale Verwendung.

tion of products from supplier to consumer.

crediting Claim for support for paid but not operating goods/articles.

liability Compensation for personal faults or deficient delivery.

semi finished production goods Semi finished material which will be finished at different manufacturing places. (Rationalization, sometimes for reason of tax savings.)

Plant / Building

manual Instructions and descriptions for proceeding and performance of function.

trade Exchange of commodities between section of economy.

trade matter Arrangement between producer and consumer of goods based on terms of trade.
-▶INCOTERMS

trading company -▶company

commercial law Regulation to perform commercial transaction.

general supplies Standard material available to suit multi-purpose utilization.

Händler Verkaufsorganisation für die Produkte der Serienhersteller und verantwortlich für die Kundenbetreuung.

Handlung Abwicklung, Verrichtung, Durchführung, Aktion, Handel.

Handlungsregister In einem Register nach Art und Umfang zusammengefaßten täglichen Bewegungen von Wert- und Bestandsveränderungen in einem Unternehmen, zum Zwecke der Kontrolle.

Harmonisierung Die Abstimmung der betrieblichen Leistungsfaktoren zur Gestaltung eines reibungslosen Fertigungsverlaufes.

Häufigkeit Festlegung der Frequenz für durchzuführnde wiederkehrende Aktionen.
-▶Bestandsaufnahmehäufigkeit -▶Fertigungsfrequenz -▶Lieferfrequenz

Hauptlager Zentrale Lagereinheit zur Aufnahme von besonderen Materialien wie Betriebsstoffe, Werkzeuge, Rohstoffe.

Hauptmerkmal Besonderheit, die eine Sache oder Sachverhalt kennzeichnet oder hervorhebt.

Haushaltsplan -▶Budget -▶Wirtschaftsplan

Hausmitteilung/DC Innerbetriebliche Mitteilung zur Information angrenzender Bereiche.

Heizmaterial Brennstoff, Hausbrand, Öl, Kohle, Holz, Elektrizität, Gas.

dealer Sales organization for mass produced products and responisible for customer service.

transaction Proceeding, performance, realization, action, business.

transaction register Index of daily movements within the company, affecting value and stock position, for the purpose of business control.

harmonization The balance of overall economic potential to achieve high level of efficiency.

frequency Establishing of frequency for performing repetitive action. -▶cycle count frequency - ▶manufacturing frequency -▶delivery frequency

main store Central storage to store special material e.g. oil, tools, raw material.

main feature Special facts of a case indicating the speciality of subject.

budget -▶economic planning

DC- departmental communication Interoffice mail as information for associate departments.

fuel Burn material, house heating oil, coal, wood, electricity, gas.

Heizwert Heizkraft, Wärmewert.

Herstellungskosten Fertigungskosten unter angemessener Berücksichtigung der Betriebs- und Verwaltungskosten. -▶Fertigungskosten -▶Betriebskosten

Hilfsarbeiter Mit einfacher Arbeit Beschäftigter Arbeiter ohne besondere Qualifikation zur Verrichtung dieser Arbeit.

Hilfsmaterial Im Unterschied zum Produktionsmaterial, Betriebsmittel wie Öle, Fette, Putzmittel. Material, was dem Produkt nicht direkt zugeordnet werden kann.

Hilfsmaterialanforderung
Vom zuständigen Organisationsbereich genehmigter Antrag zur Entnahme von Hilfsmaterial aus dem Zentrallager.

Hilfswerkzeug Werkzeuge mit deren Hilfe eine vereinfachte Durchführung von mechanischer Verarbeitung, hauptsächlich im Reparaturdienst, ermöglicht wird. Die Entwicklung erfolgt unter Beachtung der vorgesehenen Standzeit mit relativem Kostenaufwand.

Hochbaulager Grundfläche sparendes, mittels Stahlkonstruktion in der Höhe ausgedehntes Lager, wo durch völlige Automatisierung die Einlagerung und Ausgabe von Material erfolgt. (computergesteuert)

Hochbauregal Lagereinrichtung

calorific value Heating power, thermal efficiency.

expense of production Manufacturing costs under appropriate consideration of operating costs, overheads and administrational costs. -▶manufacturing cost/expense -▶operating costs

unskilled worker With simple work employed employee without specific qualification to perform this work.

non production material Material not used directly for the manufacturing of a product such as oil, grease, cleaning material.

non production material requisition From responsible organizational department approved stock requisition for requesting of non production items from general store.

auxiliary tool Tools which supporting mechanical process, mainly for repairs. Auxiliary tools are developed under considering a minimum of investment.

high-bay warehouse On limited floor space up-rising steal construction used as material store, where material is handled completely automatically. (computer controlled)

high-bay shelf Warehouse equip-

zur Aufnahme von verpackten Materialien. Auch besondere Lagereinrichtung in Hochbaulager.

Höchstarbeitszeit Höchstzulässige vom Arbeitgeber angeordnete Mehrarbeit. (Durch Gesetz geregelt)

Höchstgrenze Im Rahmen der Produktion, die Nutzung der vollen Kapazität.

Höchstleistung Die Erreichung der maximalen Effektivität.

Höchstpreis Der höchstmögliche Preis, der für eine Ware zu erzielen ist.

Humanisierung der Arbeit Organisatorische Maßnahmen, die darauf gerichtet sind, die Arbeitsbelastung zu verringern, wie auch Veränderungen an Einrichtungen, die dazu führen, die körperlichen Anstrengungen zu reduzieren.

equipment to store packed material. Special requisit for high bay warehouse.

maximum working time Maximum hours of work allowed by employer. (Controlled by law)

limit With regard to production, to reach peak level of capacity.

best performance / maximum output Achieving maximum efficiency.

maximum price Highest achieveable price.

humanization of work Organizational measures to reduced stress situation including change of equipments to minimize heavy workload.

I

i.O. Teile Begriff der Qualitätskontrolle für im Rahmen der Toleranzen hergestellten und durch die Qualitätskontrolle geprüften Teile. (i.o.= in Ordnung)

Import -▶Einfuhr

Importware -▶Einfuhr

inaktives Material Aus dem aktiven Materialbestand entnommene Materialmenge, die für produktive Verwendung nicht zur Verfügung steht.

o.k. parts Terms of quality control for parts produced in line with tolerance limit and approved by quality control (o.k.= okay)

import -▶importation

articles of import -▶importation

inactive material Number of material extracted from stock on hand and blocked for productive utilization.

Inanspruchnahme öffentlicher Mittel Die Nutzung der im Rahmen von öffentlichen Investitionsprogrammen gegebenen staatlichen Förderungsmaßnahmen zur Verbesserung der Beschäftigung. (Zinsgünstige Kredite oder steuersparende Investierungen)

Inbetriebnahme Die Eröffnung einer neuen Fertigungsanlage.

INCOTERMS - International Commercial Terms Internationale Regeln für die Auslegung der handelsüblichen Vertragsformeln.

Zusammengestellt und veröffentlicht durch die -►Internationale Handelskammer /ICC mit dem Zweck: Internationale Verträge unter Bezugnahme auf eine INCOTERMS-Klausel abzuschließen,- um hierdurch die Möglichkeit von Mißverständnissen auszuschließen.

In der Publikation Nr.350, Ausgabe März 1980, sind von der -►Internationalen Handelskammer 14 Grundregeln als Bezugspunkte zusammengefaßt:

1. Ab Werk

2. FOR/FOT Frei (Franko) Waggon

3. FAS Frei Längsseite Seeschiff (benannter Verschiffungshafen)

4. FOB Frei on Bord benannter Verschiffungshafen)

5. C&F Kosten und Fracht (benannter Bestimmungshafen)

6. CIF Kosten, Versicherung,

utilization of public money resources Utilization of goverment-public supporting offer to improve employment. (Credit with low interest or tax-reduced investments)

starting / opening Start of new manufacturing operation.

INCOTERMS- international commercial terms International rules for the interpretation of trade terms. Established and published by -►ICC, for the purpose of reference to one of the INCOTERMS-Rules by foreign trade contracts, to eliminate any posibility of misunderstanding. In the -►ICC-publication No.350, 1980 edition, are 14 rules included, as reference items:

1. Ex works

2. FOR/FOT Free on rail / Free on truck

3. FAS Free alongside ship (named port of shipment)

4. FOB Free on board (named port of shipment)

5. C&F Cost and freight (named port of destination)

6. CIF Cost, insurance, freight

Fracht (benannter Bestimmungshafen)	(named port of destination)
7. Ab Schiff (benannter Bestimmungshafen)	7. Ex ship (named port of destination)
8. Ab Kai (verzollt - unverzollt benannter Bestimmungshafen)	8. Ex quay (duty paid - duty on buyer's account named port of destination)
9. Geliefert Grenze (benannter Lieferort an der Grenze)	9. Delivered at frontier (named place of delivery at frontier)
10. Geliefert verzollt (benannter Bestimmungsort im Einfuhrland)	10. Delivered duty paid (named place of destination in the country of importation)
11. FOB Flughafen (benannter Abgangsflughafen)	11. FOB airport (named airport of departure)
12. Frei Frachtführer (benannter Ort)	12. Free carrier (named point)
13. Frachtfrei (benannter Bestimmungsort)	13. Freight carriage paid to (named point of destination)
14. Frachtfrei versichert (benannter Bestimmungsort)	14. Freight carriage paid to and insurance (named point of destination (s. index: Incoterms)
(s.Literatur - Qellennachweis: Incoterms)	

Index Inhaltsverzeichnis, Register

indirekter Lohn Beschäftigung, die nicht im direkten Zusammenhang mit der Produkterstellung steht.
(Nebentätigkeiten, Dienstleistungen) Gegenteil: -▸direkter Lohn

individuelle Disposition Kalkulierung des zukünftigen Materialverbrauches auf Basis von historischen Verbrauchswerten. Die individuelle Disposition findet Anwendung, wenn durch Stücklistenauflösung, die zukünftigen Be-

index Table of contents, register.

indirect labour Labour employment, business etc. not directly related to manufacturing of a product. Opposite: -▸direct labour

as required scheduling Calculation of future material requirement derived from historical data. Individual requirement calculation is applied, when usage cannot be determinated by bill of mateterial breakdown. (In case where mate-

darfsmengen nicht bestimmbar sind. (Unregelmäßiger Verbrauch durch Toleranzüberschneidung in der Fertigung.) Vielfach wird der Materialbedarf durch eine Mindestbevorratung abgedeckt.

Industrieausstellung Öffentliche Veranstaltung zur Presentation der eigenen Erzeugnisse zum Zwecke der Werbung und Absatzförderung.

Industriestreik Auf bestimmte Industriebereiche bezogene organisierte Arbeitsniederlegung als Kampfmittel zum Zwecke der Durchsetzung von Tarifänderungen. -▶Arbeitskampf

Inhalt Rauminhalt, Fassungsvermögen, Inhalt eines Briefes.

Inhaltsverzeichnis Stichwortartige Zusammenfassung der Inhaltsangaben einer Darbietung.-▶Index

inländische Transportzeit als Teil der -▶Transitzeit zum Zwecke der besonderen Planung und Transportkostenrechnung, wenn vor Grenzüberschreitung Konsolidierung erfolgt. (Seeweg)

Inlandversand Nur für inländische Verwendung bestimmte Warenlieferung.

Innenrevision Interne Kontrolle der Ordnungsmäßigkeit im Geschäftsverlauf, durch hausinterne Revision.

innerbetrieblich Interne Behandlung von Angelegenheiten.

innerbetriebliche Zuordnung In-

rial usage is relative to manufacturing tolerance.) In many cases material requirement is covered by minimum stock-keeping.

industrial exhibition Public exposition for presentation of own products for the purpose of publicity and sales promotion.

industrial strike Industrial-wide labour dispute to achieve tariff revisions. -▶industrial dispute

content Amount, matter, volume, capacity, contents of a letter.

table of contents Summary of a presentation. -▶index

inbound time Part of -▶transittime for the purpose of planning and calculation of transportation costs, when prior border-crossing traffic, material consolidation is performed. (sea route)

inland shipping Only for domestic consumption specified goods deliveries.

internal audit Internal control of business performed by in-house audit office.

intra-plant Intercompany treatment of matters.

internal allocation In-house as-

terne Zuweisung, Zuteilung, Verteilung oder Bestimmung von Bezugsmerkmalen auf Sachverhalte.

innerbetrieblicher Versand Zwischen den eigenen Fertigungsbereichen stattfindender Materialversand.

inoffiziell Äußerungen, Meinungen und Beurteilungen von und über Sachverhalte in nicht amtlicher, öffentlicher oder betrieblicher Funktion.

Inspektion Organisation der Qualitätskontrolle zur Überwachung der spezifikationsgerechten Fertigung. -▶Fertigungsinspektion

Instandhaltung / vorbeugend Die Überwachung des Anlagevermögens, insbsondere der Fertigungseinrichtungen hinsichtlich ihrer Funktionskontinuität.- Die regelmäßige Wartung und Erneuerung von Verschleißteilen an Maschinen im Rahmen des Reparaturplanes durch die Reparaturdienste.

Installation Ausstattung einer Fabrik mit Betriebseinrichtungen.

Instanz Für die Entscheidung zuständige Stelle in der Organisationsstruktur.

Instanzenweg Die Ordnung des Informationsflusses nach der Organisationsstruktur.

Instruktion Anordnung, Anweisung, Vorschrift, Verhaltensmaßregel.

Integration Die Übernahme von

signment, distribution or determination of reference items based on facts.

intra-plant shipment In-house material deliveries between areas of manufacturing.

unofficial Not offical expressed statements, opinions and comments to subjects.

inspection Organization of quality control to check quality level of manufacturing progress. -▶in-process inspection

preventive maintenance Control of installed manufacturing investments particulary of process equipments, to support continious production capability.- The frequently performed maintenance and replacement of machine parts according to a repair plan.
(Functional responsibility of maintenance department)

installation Equiping a plant with machines.

instance Responsible organizational unit for decision-making.

normal channel Order of instruction flow in line with organizational structure.

instruction Direction, order, policy behaviour.

integration In-house sourcing of

Kaufumfängen in Eigenfertigung zur Verbesserung der Wirtschaftlichkeit.

Interimsmaßnahme Vorläufige Maßnahme zur Lösung eines Sachverhaltes, auch Zwischenlösung als Sofortreaktion zur Abstellung eines Problems.

Internationale Handelskammer / ICC Die internationale Handelskammer ist die Weltorganisation der Wirtschaft; sie fördert die Interessen der Wirtschaft auf internationaler Ebene. Die Kammer, mit Sitz in Paris, ist durch Landesgruppen in über 50 Ländern vertreten. -▶INCOTERMS

Inventur Körperliche Bestandsaufnahme des Vermögens und der Schulden eines Unternehmens zu einem gegebenen Zeitpunkt - Bilanzstichtag. Für aktives Produktionsmaterial vielfach durch permanente Bestandsfortschreibung ersetzt. Bestandsaufnahmen erfolgen dann während des Geschäftsjahres nach einem Prioritäts-Plan.

Inventurstichtag Vorgesehener Zeitpunkt der körperlichen Bestandsaufnahme als Grundlage der Bilanzerstellung.

Investition Kapitalanlage für die kapazitätsmäßige Ausstattung einer Fertigungsanlage.

Investitionsantrag Beantragung der im Investitionsplan vorgesehenen Geldmittel zur Anschaffung und Modernisierung von Betriebs-

buy parts as own manufacturing content to improve economics.

provisional measure Temporary action to solve a problem, also interims solution to overcome faulty condition.

ICC- International Chamber of Commerce The International Chamber of Commerce is the world business organization. It acts to promote the greater freedom of world trade at international levels. The chamber is based at Paris and represented by national communities in over 50 countries.-▶INCOTERMS

inventory / stock-taking Physical stock-taking of total company inventories and debits at a given point in time- balance-sheet date. For active production material sometimes replaced by permanent stock accounting. Stock-taking is than performed according to a cycle count frequency plan during year of business.

annual inventory day Fixed calendar day for stock-taking, required to establish balance sheet.

investment Capital investment for capacity installation of a manufacturing plant.

appropriation request Application of investment for installation and modernization of manufacturing equipments according invest-

einrichtungen. Der Geldbedarf ist Teilbetrag des Finanzplanes.

Investitionsausgaben Ausgaben der über Projekt oder Budget genehmigten Geldmittel für Investitionszwecke.

Investitionsbudget Einbringung der geplanten Investitionskosten in den Finanzplan.

Irrtum Fehler, Versehen

Ist - Kosten Alle während einer bestimmten Abrechnungsperiode angefallenen tasächlichen Kosten.

ment plan. Funds requirement is part of the budget plan.

capital phasing / expenditure Spending of funds for investments as approved by project or budget.

capital investment budget Budgeting of proposed capital investment demand.

error mistake, fault

actual costs All costs incurred during a certain period of business.

J

Jahresabschluß Entsprechend dem Gesetz zu erstellende Bilanz mit Gewinn- und Verlustrechnung.
-▶Geschäftsbericht

Jahresabschlußprüfung Pflichtprüfung des Jahresergebnisses durch unabhängige Sachverständige.

Jahresbericht In der Bilanz zusammengefaßtes Ergebnis der wirtschaftlichen Tätigkeit zum Schluß des Geschäftsjahres.
-▶Geschäftsbericht

Jahresdurchschnitt Umlage des Jahresergebnisses auf Jahreszeitleistung.

Jahresergebnis -▶Jahresabschluß

Jahresproduktion Gesamtzahl der im Geschäftsjahr produzierten Waren.

Jahresvertrag Von Geschäfts-

annual account Establishing of annual balancesheet as directed by law outlining profit and loss.
-▶company report

year-end audit Legally required balancesheet-audit performed by outside auditors.

annual report Summarization of economics by year-end for balance sheet reporting.
-▶company report

year average Allocation of annual results based on annual achievements.

annual return -▶annual account

annual production output Annual output of products produced.

contract for one year Agreed

partnern getroffenen, auf ein Jahr befristeten Bedingungen zur Abwicklung von Geschäftsvorgängen.

Jahreswechselroutine Beendigung der fortschreibenden akkumulativen Bewegungen zum Jahresende und Bildung von Anfangsbestandswerten für die neue Planungsperiode.

Jahreszahlen Erreichte Jahreszahlen von Akkumulativen zu irgend einem Zeitpunkt während des Jahres.

jährlich

Joint Venture Engl. Bezeichnung für Kooperationsvorhaben von Gemeinschaftsunternehmen, zur besseren Nutzung der unterschiedlichen Ressourcen bei den verschiedenen Partnern.

Just in Time /JIT Umfassender Begriff für die optimale Gestaltung der Geschäftstätigkeit: Mit einem Minimum an Investition,bei hoher Qualitätsforderung,ein Maximum als Produktionsergebnis zu erreichen.
JIT-Prinzipien, bezogen auf die optimale betriebswirtschaftliche Gestaltung einer Fertigung, sind in der strengen Beachtung der folgenden Kriterien gegeben:

-▶Kapitalbildung -▶Komplexität (minimum Angebot)

-▶lagerlose Fertigung -▶Lagerumschlag -▶Lieferanteninformationssystem

contract between business partner to do business within one year.

year-end routine Ending of cumulative movements at year end and establishing starting inventory figure for the new period of scheduling.

year-to-date figure Cumulative value at any time during the year.

annual yearly

joint venture Cooperation agreement of business partner for more economical utilization of individual resources.

JIT, just in time Definition for optimal performance in order to achieve with minimum of investment a high quality standard and maximum output. JIT-principles are related to an optimal economical process-achievement and needs an exact attention of the following items:

-▶capital binding -▶complexity (minimum offer) -▶out of stock production -▶inventory turnover -▶supplier communication system -▶delivery frequency -▶logistic/ material management -▶produc-

-▶Lieferfrequenz -▶Logistik/Material Management

-▶Materialreserve -▶Materialwirtschaft -▶optimale Produktionsgestaltung

-▶Prinzipien zur Bestimmung der Materialreserve -▶Verfahrensplanung

-▶Vertrag

tion material float -▶materials supply -▶OPT, optimized production timing -▶principles of float allocation -▶planning of operation method -▶contract

K

Kapazität -▶Fertigungskapazität

Kapazitätausdehnung -▶Fertigungserweiterung

Kapazitätsengpaß -▶Engpaß

Kapazitätsgrenze Nutzbare Einrichtungen bis zu einer bestimmten Stückzahl.

Kapazitätsnutzung -▶Fertigungsauslastung

Kapazitätsplanungsvolumen / CPV Genaue Abgrenzung der Planzahlen für die Planung der Einrichtung und Bestellung von Maschinen, Werkzeugen und Hilfsgüter.
Planzahlen sind kleiner als -▶FPV, beinhalten aber Flexibilitätsanteile, um Marktschwankungen abzufangen. -▶DPV

Kapital Bestand an Produktionsausrüstung, Geldmittel für die Investierung, aber auch der in der Bilanz ausgewiesene Wert des Gesamtvermögens.

Kapitalanlage Investition der

capacity -▶manufacturing capacity

capacity extension -▶capacity expansion

capacity bottleneck -▶bottleneck

capacity limitation Utilization of equipments up to a limited quantity.

work to capacity -▶capacity utilization

CPV-capacity planning volume Planning figure used for commitments of equipments, machines, tools and general supplies.
CPV figure is less than -▶FPV but reflecting flexibility to support market fluctuations. -▶DPV

capital Total range of installation, funds for investments as well as total assets as outlined in the balancesheet.

capital investment Investment of

Produktionsausrüstung. -▶Investition

Kapitalbindung Die Bindung von Kapital durch Bestellungen - Materialbevorratung, Vorrat an Werkzeugen - Reparatur und Ersatzteilen. Die Kapitalbindung ist Kernpunkt der -▶Prinzipien zur Bestimmung der Materialreserve.- Die Kapitalbindung durch Material muß der absolut kleinsten Menge entsprechen. -▶Just in Time /JIT

Kapitaldienst Die Zahlungen von Zinsen, Tilgungen und Rückzahlungen von Krediten und Anleihen, wie auch die Bedienung der laufenden Verpflichtungen.

Kapitalinvestierungsbudget/ CIB -▶Investitionsbudget

Karton Aus Pappe, hauptsächlich als Einwegverpackung hergestellte Verpackungseinheit.

Kasten Kiste, Behälter, Schaukasten.

Katalog Systematische, geschlossene Übersicht über die Produkte der eigenen Herstellung, als Broschüre oder Liste zum Zwecke der Verkaufswerbung.

kaufen Beschaffen von Material und Dienstleistungen von Anbietern durch den Einkauf.

Kaufpreis -▶Einkaufspreis

Kaufteil -▶Einkaufsteil

Kaufvertrag Gegenseitige Abmachungen über den Bezug von Wa-

production equipments. -▶investment

capital binding Binding of capital by commitments of production material and excessive stock holdings on material, tools repair- and spare parts. Capital binding is key point of -▶principles of production float allocation. Capital binding by material has to reflect absolut minimum level -▶JIT Just in Time

annual capital charge Payment of interest, annuities and payment of credits and loans as well as payments of other services of current commitments.

CIB-capital investment budget -▶capital investment budget

cardboard box Paper box made from carton mostly used as one way packing.

box case, coffer, showcase

catalogue Systematical listing of products, publishing as brochure or list for the purpose of sales advertising.

purchase /buy Procure material and services from outside supplier by purchase department.

purchase price -▶prime cost

purchase part -▶EP-external purchase

purchase contract Business agreement for delivery of goods

ren und der damit verbundenen Anerkennung der Lieferbedingungen. -►Einkaufsverbindlichkeiten -►INCOTERMS

Kenn-Nummerung Nummerung von Begriffen, Artikeln, Einzelteilen und Fertigprodukten, um sie mittels EDV erfaßbar und kontollierbar zu machen.

Kennwort Verschlüsselung von Namen zur Gewährleistung des persönlichen Zugriffes zu systemgebundenen Vorgängen.

Kennzeichnung Die Kennzeichnung von Produkten, durch Anbringung von Teilnummer oder Herstellerzeichen.

Kennziffer Numerierung von Vorgängen zum Zwecke der einfacheren Registratur und Ablage.

Kettenförder-Anlage Zur optimalen Raumnutzung entwickeltes und im Überkopfbereich operierendes Transportsystem, wo mittels einer Zugkette und besonderen Vorrichtungen der Materialfluß organisiert ist.

Kilometerzähler Anzeigegerät in Fahrzeugen zur Darstellung der effektiven Fahrgeschwindigkeit und Aufzeichnung der Fahrleistung.

klären einer Sache Die Klärung von Abweichungen.

Klassifizierung Rangordnungsbestimmung für Produktionsmaterial entsprechend dem täglichen Verbrauchswert. -►Kostenklassen

and acceptance of delivery conditions -►purchase commitments -►INCOTERMS

code number Numbering of subjects, articles, production parts and finished products to enable processing and control of electronical data.

pass word Coding of names to allow only personal access to system related subjects.

identification Marking of products by labelling of partnumber or trademark.

reference number Numbering of transaction to enable simple registration and filing.

overhead conveyer For optimal space utilization developed and in overhead position operating transport system, whereby chain drive and special equipments material transport is performed.

milometer Instrument in vehicles to indicate effective speed situation and distance covered.

clear-up a matter Clarification of discrepancy.

classification Ranking of production material according daily usage value. -►cost classification

Knappheit Das zur Verfügung stehende Warenangebot ist kleiner als die Nachfrage.
Bei der Materialbereitstellung vielfach dann, wenn infolge von technischen Änderungen der Verbrauch von bestimmten Artikeln ansteigt, ohne rechtzeitige Erhöhung der Herstellungskapazität.

shortage Availability of goods offered is less than market demand. Shortage condition in production material availability exist by incremental usage without timely required capacity expansion.

Kombination Zusammenwirken von Faktoren, Maschinen und Werkzeugen zur optimalen Gestaltung des Fertigungsablaufes.

combination Combined action of machines and tools for optimizing process condition.

Komplexität Die Gesamtheit der unterschiedlichen Erzeugnissen und die zur Herstellung einer Produktvielfalt erforderlichen Einrichtungen.

complexity Total range on different products and number of manufacturing equipments required for complex of product range.

Konferenz Zusammenkunft von beteiligten Personen zur Erarbeitung von Lösungsmaßnahmen anstehender Probleme.

conference Meeting of affected people to find resulution to overcome existing problems.

Konjunktur Zyklischer Ablauf des Wirtschaftsgeschehens.

market condition Cyclical trend of business condition.

Konjunkturverlauf Die gegenwärtige Situation des Wirtschaftsverlaufes.

economic trend Current position of economics.

Konkurrent Mitbewerber oder Mitanbieter.

competitor A business rival.

Konkurs Die nach der gegenwärtigen Kenntnislage auf Dauer festgestellte Zahlungsunfähigkeit eines Unternehmens. Die anstehenden Zahlungsverpflichtungen sind größer als die verfügbaren Geldmittel unter Berücksichtigung der Kreditgewährung.

bankruptcy Based on current assumption the inhability to pay companies obligation. Indebtedness exceeding availability of funds, even considering of available credits.

Konsignation 1) Die Ablieferung von Produkten in ein Konsignationslager, wobei die Bezahlung des Herstellers erst durch den Verkauf aus dem Konsignationslager erfolgt. Konsignationsbestand ist Eigentum des Herstellers.
2) Die weitere Veredelung von Produkten bei anderen Unternehmen und anschließende Rückführung zum Ursprung erfolgt ohne Berechnung des Eigenanteils.
Die so gelagerten Transaktionen werden durch Ein- und Ausgang über ein Konsignationskonto kontrolliert.

konsolidieren Zwischenlagern von Einzellieferungen zur Organisation von Sammeltransporten zum Empfänger.

Konsolidierungsort Sammelpunkt für regionale Materiallieferungen, von wo der Weitertransport zum Empfänger durch Zusammenstellung von Sammeltransport, unter optimaler Nutzung von Transportraum erfolgt. (Hafen - Spediteur Lagerort)

Konstrukteur Ingenieur mit planmäßiger Tätigkeit in der Produktentwicklung zur Verbesserung und Neuentwicklung von Produkten.

Konstruktion -▶Entwurf / Konstruktion

Konsum Die Verwendung oder der Verbrauch von Waren.

Konsument Der Bezieher und Verbraucher von Konsumwaren.

consignment a) Taking goods in consignment stock whereby payment of invoice is performed on sale out of consignment store.
Consignment material remains the property of the owner.
2) In case of material refinement only the improvement is invoiced if material is returned to the original supplier.
All transactions on consignment goods will be controlled by a special consignment account.

consolidate Intermediate storage for individual shipments to arrange gross deliveries for recipient.

consolidation point Collecting for point local material deliveries, from where material to recipients is forwarded considering optimal utilization of transport space. (Harbour - Carrier - Shipping destination)

designer Engineer with functional responsibility for product design improvement and develop work for new design.

construction -▶design

consumption Utilization or usage of goods.

user / **consumer** Customer and user of consumer goods.

Konten Rechnungen zur wertmäßigen Erfassung von Geschäftsvorgängen mit Soll- und Habenseiten. Zur Ordnung des betrieblichen Rechnungswesens sind die Konten in einen Kontenplan aufgegliedert, der internationale Anwendung findet.

Kontierung Die Feststellung eines Geschäftsvorganges durch ordnungsgemäße Buchung in der jeweiligen Kontenordnung.

Kontingent Wert- oder mengenmäßige Quoten zur Begrenzung eines Warenangebotes. Zollfreie Ein- und Ausfuhr von bestimmten Mengeneinheiten an Waren.

Kontingentierung Wert- oder mengenmäßig begrenzte Ein- und Ausfuhr von Produkten zum Schutz der eigenen Wirtschaftlichkeit.

Kontinuität Annahme, daß die gegenwärtigen Bedingungen zur Erreichung von Ergebnissen auch für die Zukunft fortbestehen und somit gleichbleibende Verhältnisse gewährleistet werden.

Kontenauszug Für den Bankkunden als Information über den letzten Saldostand erstellten Rechnungsauszug mit Angaben der Umsatzbewegungen.

Kontokorrent Laufende Rechnungen bei Geschäftsverbindungen, wo Leistung und Gegenleistung in Rechnung gestellt sind und in bestimmten Zeitabständen ausgeglichen werden.

accounts Accounts to outline value of business transaction showing debit and credit positions. To ensure correctness of accounting, accounts are classified by international standards.

allocation of accounting Appropriate allocation of business transaction to an account in line with given standards.

contingent Value or quantity related quotation as restriction to buy and sell. Duty-free regulation for ex- and import of goods.

fixing quota Value or quantity limitation on im- and export of products for the protection of inland economics.

continuity Assumption that current rules for achieving results, will be forwarded in the future to generate same outcome.

statement of account Service to bank customers about the last account balance and account movements.

current account Business accounts where debits and credits are considered and from time to time balanced.

Kontrollabschnitt Kupon, Kontrollblatt, Gepäckzettel, -schein.

Kontrolleur Mit Prüfung und Kontrollaufgaben beauftragte Person.

kontrollieren Die Güteprüfung der Erzeugnisse.

Kontrollpunkt Besondere Station im Fertigungsablauf oder im Warenein- und Ausgang, wo Materialkontrollen entsprechend den Spezififikationsvorgaben durchgeführt werden.

konvertierbar Die Weiterverarbeitung von Daten in lokalen Systemen beim internationalen Austausch von Daten.

Konvertierbarkeit Eine Währung zum Paritätskurs in ein anderes Zahlungsmittel zu tauschen.

Konzeption Konzept oder Idee zur Lösung einer Aufgabe.

Konzern Zusammenfassung der einzelnen Fertigungsbereiche in eine zentrale Organisation zur rationeller Planung und Koordination der Betriebsabläufe.

Konzession Die behördliche Genehmigung zur Ausübung eines Gewerbes durch Erteilung der Lizenz.

Kooperation Zusammenarbeit zwischen Organisationseinheiten zur Optimierung des Betriebsgeschehens.

Koordination Die Aufeianderabstimmung von ineinander greifen-

control tag Coupon, luggage tag

checker Clerk with functional responsibility of controlling.

checking Inspection of product quality.

check point Special area in manufacturing or receiving and shipping where check operation are carry out according to specification.

convertible The posibility of data processing in local systems, when international data exchange is performed.

convertibility Conversion of currency in other standards considering exchange rate.

concept First draft or idea to overcome a problem.

group of companies Amalgamation of various manufacturing plants in one central organization to achieve optimal efficiency by planning and coordination of progress.

allowance licence A privilege granted by a goverment to perform a specific business.

cooperation Teamwork between organizational units to improve companies output.

coordination Adjustment of connected functions to a harmonious

den Funktionen zu einer geschlossenen Einheit.

Kopfzahl Anzahl der Beschäftigten.

Kopie Zweitschrift, Durchschlag, Fotokopie

kopieren Vervielfältigen von Schriftsätzen oder Zeichnungen, aber auch die Anfertigung von Nachbildungen.

Korb Tragbarer Behälter, hauptsächlich in der Landwirtschaft genutzt.

Korrektur Berichtigung oder Richtigstellung einer abweichenden Darstellung. -▶Berichtigung

Korrekturmaßnahmen Im einzelnen spezifizierte Aktionen zur Durchführung von Berichtigungen bei Abweichungen.

Korrespondenz Brief- Schriftwechsel eines Unternehmens.

Kosten Aufwand an Geld, Zeit und Arbeit, um ein gewünschtes Resultat zu erzielen.

Kostenanalyse Die kostenmäßige Bewertung bei Programmvorhaben, die Investitionen erfordern.

Kostenbewertung Die kostenmäßige Bewertung einer Leistung.

Kostenermittlung Dem Genehmigungsverfahren eines Vorhabens vorgelagerte kostenmäßige Untersuchung der projektbezogenen Gesamtinvestition.

Kostenersparnis -▶Ersparnisse /Einsparungen

economic integrated unit.

head count Number of employees.

copy duplication, carbon copy photo copy

duplicate / imitate Copying of documents or drawings, but also reproductive work.

basket Hand portable case, mainly used in agricultural.

correction Change from wrong to right. -▶adjustment

corrective action Detailed action plan to initiate correction.

correspondence Exchange of letters, memos etc. of a company.

costs Amount of money, time and labour to achieve a required result.

cost analysis Estimation of costs for planned investments.

cost evaluation Evaluate a work in material terms.

cost finding Investigation of project related costs prior initiating of project approval.

cost savings -▶savings/economics

Kostenklassen Einteilung des Produktionsmaterials in Kostenklassen entsprechend dem teilbezogenen Tagesverbrauchswert. (Mengeneinheit mal Preis mal produktbezogener Menge mal geplanter Tagesverbrauch) Die Größenordnung der Kostenklassen sind %-Anteile vom Gesamtmaterial-Tagesverbrauchswert.
z.B. Dreiteilung des Materialtageswertes:

A = 80 % vom Tageswert

B = 15 %

C = 5 %

Enstprechend der wertbezogenen Größenordnung erfolgt die Klassifizierung des Materials in A / B oder C und unterliegt somit den mit der Kostenklasse verbundenen Kontrollmerkmalen, die Bestandteil der -▶Prinzipien zur Bestimmung der Materialreserve sind.

Kostenkontrolle Innerbetrieblicher Kostenvergleich über verschiedene Perioden. Gegenüberstellung von Istkosten mit den Plankosten.
Überwachung der Wirtschaftlichkeit.

Kostenrechnung Die Ermittlung der im Betrieb entstehenden Kosten für die Erstellung einer Leistung.

Kostenstelle -▶Fertigungskostenstelle

Kostenstellenplan Nach betrieblichen Fabrikationszweigen aufgeteilte Kostenstellenkonten.

cost classification Classification of production material in cost class according to part related daily usage value (Multiplication of unit of measure by price by usage by daily rate) Level of cost class is percentage of total daily usage value.
e.g. Categorization of daily usage value in three section:
A = 80 % of daily usage value
B = 15 %
C = 5 %

Determination of cost classification in A/B/C is based on daily usage value of production material.
Production material control is performed on its cost class as specified in the -▶principles of float allocation.

cost control Internal cost comparison over various periods of production.
Comparison of estimates and effective costs.
Efficiency control.

account of charges Calculation of arising company costs for performance of work.

cost centre -▶manufacturing cost centre

cost centre plan Expense accounts in line with departmental process condition.

Kostenumlage Die Verteilung der Kosten auf die Produkte.

Kostenvergleich Vergleich der Wirtschaftlichkeit mit anderen Unternehmen gleicher Branche. -▶Kostenkontrolle

Kraftanlage Energieerzeugende Anlage Elektrizitätswerk, Wasserwerk, Atomkraftwerk.

Krafteinheit Meßeinheit für den Verbrauch an Energie.

kraftlos Ineffektiv, ohne Kraft.

Kraftquelle -▶Kraftanlage

Kraftstoff Benzin, Dieselöl, Gas

kraftvoll effektiv

Kriterium Ordnungsbezugspunkte zur Beurteilung von Zusammenhängen.

Kritik Die Beurteilung der sachgerechten Ausführung.

Küchengüter Warensortiment für den Verpflegungsdienst.

Kumulative -▶Akkumulative

Kunde Konsument,Verbraucher oder Abnehmer von Produkten.

Kundendienst Freiwillige Dienste eines Herstellers oder Händlers zur Betreuung der Kunden.

Kündigung Die Auflösung des Arbeitsverhältnisses zu einem bestimmten Zeitpunkt.

Kündigungsfrist Zeitraum der

cost allocation Distribution of costs to products.

cost comparison Comparison of cost with other companies of same branche and comperable application. -▶cost control

power station Energy producing facilities - electric utility, water supply, nuclear station.

unit of work Unit of measure for energy consumption.

powerless Inefficient, without power.

source of power/energy -▶power station

fuel/petrol gasoline, diesel-oil, gas

powerfull efficient, effective

criterion Point of orientation to view connections.

critique Review of appropriate performance.

cantine supplies Goods for cantine service.

accumulative -▶cumulative

customer Consumer, user or purchaser of products.

customer service Service provided free of charge by producer or dealer to customer.

termination Notice of termination of employment to a given at a point in time.

period of notice Term of notice is

Kündigungsfrist richtet sich nach dem Arbeitsvertrag und Dauer der Beschäftigung. (gesetzlich geregelt)

Kurs An der Börse festgestellter Wechselkurs zum Tausch von Währungen.

Kursbericht Offizieller Börsenbericht mit Angaben der täglich neu festgestellten Wechselkursen.

Kursbuch Amtliches Verzeichnis der Fahrpläne für regelmäßigen Verkehr von Bahn-, Bus-, Schiffahrts- und Fluglinien.

Kursfestsetzung Feststellumg der an der Börse amtlich notierten Werte.

Kurswert Der sich aufgrund Börsenkurs ergebende Wert eines Wertpapieres.

Kurzarbeit Die Reduzierung der Normalarbeitszeit zur Anpassung der Produktion an die Nachfrage.

Kurzbericht Auflistung von Produktionsmaterial, wo der Mindestbestand unterschritten ist.

Kurzform Abkürzungen für feste Begriffe. (Länderkennzeichen)

kurzfristig Reaktion innerhalb eines kurzen Zeitraumes.

Kürzungs-Auflage Vorgaben zur Reduzierung von Kosten in bestimmten Planbereichen in zukünftigen Abrechnungsperioden.

subject of working contract and relative to the duration of employment. (controlled by law)

exchange rate Rate of exchange to convert currency fixed by stock market.

market report Official list of quotation publishing daily fixed exchange rates.

time table Official time schedule for regular traffic of railway, bus-, sea- and airline.

rate fixing Determination of exchange value by stock market.

market value Quoted value for securities.

short-time work Reduced normal working time to balance production with customer demand.

shortage report Index of production material indicating critical stock on hand position.

abbreviation Abbreviated form for fixed conceptions. (country code)

short-dated Short-timed reaction.

task Cost reduction within certain areas as objective for future planning periods.

L

Laboratorium Überprüfungsraum für chemische und physikalische Materialprüfung.

Lackiererei Fabrikanlage mit besonderen Einrichtungen zur Lackierung von Produkten.

Ladebrief -▶Frachtbrief

Ladeeinheit Die Größe einer Transporteinheit.

Ladeliste Verzeichnis der Ladung -▶Frachtbrief

laden -▶Beladung

Laderampe Plattform zur ebenerdigen Be- und Entladung von Transportmittel.

Ladestation Versandstelle, Versandplatz

Ladung Maximal faßbare Materialmenge, die ein Fahrzeug aufnehmen kann.

Lageplan Gebäude-, Flächen-und Einrichtungsplan einer Fertigungsstätte.

Lager Ort der Vorratshaltung mit entsprechenden Einrichtungen zur Aufnahme, Ausgabe und Kontrolle von Material.

Lagerbestand Der Bestand an Roh-, Hilfs- und Betriebsstoffen, halbfertigen und fertigen Erzeugnissen, aber auch in Kommission gegebenen Waren.

Lagergebühren Entgelt für die

laboratory Control room for chemical and physical material testing.

paint shop Plant area equiped with facilities to paint products.

bill of loading -▶consignment note

unit-load Standard of tranportation unit.

freight list Package list, loading list -▶consignment note

freight -▶load

loading dock Platform to ground floor level for load and unload of material.

loading station Shipping point, loading place.

load / freight Maximum loading capacity of transportation.

layout Building-, space- and installation plan of a manufacturing plant.

store/warehouse/depot Place of inventory holding with special equipments for receiving, delivery and control facilities for storages.

stocks inventory Stock on hand of rough material, general supplies, utilities, semi- and finnished products as well as consignment material.

charge for storage Charges for

Lagerung von Gütern im Lagergeschäft.

Lagerkosten Kosten, die im Zusammenhang mit der Materiallagerung entstehen für Gebäude, Einrichtungen, Energie, Schutzmaßnahmen für Bestände und Verwaltungkosten, aber auch Kosten der Kapitalbindung durch Material und die daraus resultierende Verzinsung. Lagerkosten sind wesentlicher Faktor bei der Ermittlung der optimalen Bevorratung.

lagerlose Fertigung Die Bereitstellung von Material durch die Lieferanten im Rahmen des Verbrauchsplanes durch terminlich genau fixierte Anlieferungen zum Verbrauchsort, wobei der tägliche Materialverbrauchswert für die Bestimmung der Anlieferhäufigkeit von Bedeutung ist. -▶Just in Time JIT

Lagerplatz Abgegrenzter Raum oder Fläche zum Lagern von Material. -▶Lager

Lagerreserve -▶Materialreserve/ -▶Operationsreserve

Lagerumschlag Betriebswirtschaftliche Kennzahl. Die Umschlaghäufigkeit des Materialbestandes ergibt sich aus dem Verhältnis der jährlichen Anforderungen und des durchschnittlichen Bestandes. Die Höhe der Umschlaghäufigkeit ist Merkmal für eine optimale Lagerhaltung.

Lagerverwalter Verantwortlich für den organisatorischen Geschäfts-

storage goods in warehouse business.

cost of storage Costs in conjuction with material storage related to building, equipments, energy, safety protection for inventories and administration cost, but also cost for capital binding by material and interest resulting from material holding. Costs of material storage are key feature for the calculation of optimal stock planning.

out of stock production Delivery of material by supplier in line with customer programme requirements by timly controlled deliveries to the place of utilization, whereby daily usage value is significant to determine delivery frequency. -▶JIT Just in Time

storage location Special room or area to store material. -▶store/ warehouse/depot

inventory reserve -▶production material float/-▶operationreserve

inventory turnover Economical key point. Inventory turnover ratio resulted from annual demand and average stock on hand. The number of turnover indicates optimalization of stock keeping.

store - keeper Warehouse man responsible to organize and control

ablauf und Kontrollmaßnahmen bei der Lagerhaltung.

Länge Ausdehnung, Entfernung

langfristig Die sachbezogene Reaktion zu einem späteren Zeitpunkt.

lastenfrei Frei von Verpflichtungen an Gebühren, Abgaben oder Zusatzkosten.

Lastkraftwagen Motorfahrzeug für den Transport von Gütern.

Lastschrift Belastung der Soll-Seite eines Bankkontos, aber auch Rechnungseinzugsverfahren durch den Gläubiger zu Lasten des Schuldners.

laufender Monat

Laufkarte Etikett an der Warenlieferung mit Bezeichnung und Mengenangabe des Artikels, manchmal auch mit Preisangaben.

Laufzeit / Lebensdauer Die Dauer der Funktionsfähigkeit eines Gebrauchsgegenstandes.

Leasing Die Vermietung von Industrieanlagen, Gebäuden und Gebrauchsgüter durch die Hersteller oder Vermieterorganisationen.

Leergut Bei Warenanlieferung anfallende Verpackungen oder Container, die zwecks Wiederverwendung einer besonderen Kontrolle unterliegen. -▶Verpackungsart

Leergutlagerreserve Den Nominalbedarf übersteigende Anzahl an Standardverpackungen als Flexibilität bei plötzlich auftreten-

methods of business in a warehouse.

length extent, distance

long - term Delayed reaction.

free of taxes/charges Free of duties, charges or additional costs.

truck / lorry Vehicle for transportation of goods.

debit Entry on the debit side of an account, but also direct debiting system by creditor to charge account of debitor.

current month

pallet tag Delivery label indicating part description, quantity and sometimes price of quotations.

time span / life time Duration of a functional period of article in every day use.

leasing Letting of equipments, buildings and consumable by producer or out-hiring organizations.

empties Package or containers from material deliveries, under special control for multiple use -▶type of packing.

empties stock reserve Net demand exceeding number on standard packing for flexibility to cover extra demand by supply

dem Mehrbedarf durch Materialbevorratung. Die Größenordnung der Leergutlagerreserve richtet sich nach der Komplexität und Volumen der zur Anlieferung kommenden Produkte.

Leergutprüfer Verantwortlich für die Leergutbestandskontrolle und den planmäßigen Rückversand.

Lehrling Zum Zwecke der Berufsausbildung in einem Lehrverhältnis stehende Auszubildende.

Lehrvertrag Berufausbildungsvertrag zwischen dem Ausbilder und dem Auszubildenden oder seines gesetzlichen Vertreters, über die wesentlichen Punkte der Berufsausbildung.
(Berufsbild, Dauer der Ausbildung und Arbeitsordnung.)

Lehrwerkstatt Mit besonderen Einrichtungen für die Berufsausbildung ausgestattete Werkstatt.

Leiharbeitskraft -▶Agenturkraft/-Aushilfskraft

Leihverpackung Verpackungseinheit mit Mehrfachverwendung, die Eigentum des Zustellers ist und daher als Leergut an den Lieferer zurückzusenden ist.
(Standard-Container)

Leistung -▶Gesamtleistung

Leistungsbericht Täglicher Bericht mit Ergebnissen in den betrieblichen Leistungsstellen.

Leistungseinstufung Die Beur-

protection.
Number of add. packing units is relative to complexity and volume of receivings.

empties checker Responsible person for empty-stock control and planned return shipments.

apprentice Person who undertakes a special training for the purpose of professional education at an employer.

indenture of apprenticeship Education contract between educator and apprentice or his legal representative, outlining key elements of education. (Profession of education, period of apprenticeship and working order.)

training department Workshop equiped with special facilities for the purpose of vocational education.

agency clerk -▶agency labour

returnable packing Packing unit with lifetime utilization which are property of supplier and thereof returnable as empty to the source of supply. (Standard container)

performance -▶overall efficiency

performance report Daily report outlining achievements in company cost centre structure.

merit rating Personal perfor-

teilung der persönlichen Leistung in Ausübung der Funktion nach Leistungskriterien durch den Vorgesetzten.

Leistungsfähigkeit Die Nutzung der betrieblichen Kapazität- auch Effektivität oder Wirkungsgrad.

Leistungslohn Arbeitsentgelt für vollbrachte Leistung.

Leistungsverlust Umstände, die dazu führen, daß die vorgegebene Leistungserwartung in den Kostenstellen nicht erbracht werden kann.

Leistungszulage Geldliche Zuwendung aufgrund besonderem Geschäftsergebnis.

Leiter Für eine Organisationseinheit Verantwortung tragende Führungskraft.

Leute - Anzahl -►Kopfzahl

Lieferant Hersteller von Zustellprodukten - Einkaufsmaterial und Dienstleistungen.

Lieferanten-Informations-system Die elektronische Übermittlung der Bedarfs- und Bestandsangaben über zu beziehendes Material an den Lieferanten. Regelt die Organisation der zeitgerechten Materialversorgung. -►Just in Time JIT

Lieferanten-Situationsbericht Statistische Erfassung und Auswertung der Geschäftstätigkeit mit Lieferanten über Zuverlässigkeit und Qualitätsstandard.

mance rating in achieving functional objectives according weighted performance criteria, by department manager.

commercial efficiency Utilization level of installed plant capacity, but also level of effectivity or efficiency term.

incentive wage Wage payment for efficiency of output.

inefficiency/ off standard Circumstances which are reason for not achieving forecasted efficiency demand in manufacturing cost centre.

merit / salary increase Valuable consideration as bonus for outstanding business achievement.

manager Responsible person in leading position to manage an organization.

number of people -►headcount

supplier / vendor Producer of supplies purchase material and services.

supplier communication system Electronical data communication system, submitting production material requirement and stock status position to supplier. Initiates timely required material supply. - ►JIT Just in Time

supplier performance report Statistical data collection and analysis of business transaction to proof supplier reliability and quality standard.

Lieferantenanpassung Nivellierung der Lieferquoten zur Erfüllung der Lieferbedingungen, wenn mehrere Lieferanten mit festen Anteilen an der Lieferung von gleichen Produkten beteiligt sind.

Lieferantenfehler Die Zustellung von nicht spezifikationsgerechtem Material.

Lieferantenkartei Verzeichnis der mit einem Unternehmen in Geschäftsverbindung stehenden Lieferanten.

Lieferantenkontonummer Nummer unter der das Konto des Lieferanten bei einer Bank geführt wird.

Lieferantenschlüssel Vercodungsmerkmal für den Lieferanten zur Erfassung der Geschäftvorgänge mittels EDV.

lieferbar Verfügbarer Artikel, bereitstehend zur Lieferung.

Lieferbedingungen Zwischen Käufer und Verkäufer getroffenen Vereinbarungen über Art, Zeitpunkt, Qualitätsstandard, Verpackung und Versand beim Bezug von Waren. -►Kaufvertrag -►INCOTERMS

Lieferdifferenzen Mengenmäßige Abweichung von der avisierten Liefergröße oder Fehlbezeichnung des Artikels, bei Materialzustellungen.

Liefereingang -►Eingang

Lieferfrequenz Häufigkeit der Anlieferungen. Wichtiger Faktor zur Kontrolle der Kapitalbindung durch

supplier adjustment Balance of quotations between suppliers to fulfil purchase contract, where more then one supplier is involved with fix order deliveries for same component.

supplier error Out of tolerance material delivery.

supplier card file Card-index of suppliers in business relationship with producer.

supplier account number Number of suppliers bank account.

supplier identification code Coding symbol for supplier to enable electronical data processing of business transaction.

available for delivery Goods ready for delivery.

delivery conditions Contract agreed between user and producer regarding delivery, timing, quality and transport of supplies. -►purchase order -►INCOTERMS

delivery discrepancies Quantities deviating from advised level of delivery or misinterpretation of supplied articles.

receiving / receipt -►receival

delivery frequency Turn of deliveries. Key element to control capital binding by stock on material.

Material. Bei großen Verbrauchsmengen oder sehr teuren Zulieferungen soll die Anlieferung so erfolgen, daß mit dem absolut kleinsten Bestand eine geordnete Produktion möglich ist. -▶Just in Time JIT

Liefermenge Größe der Lieferung.

Lieferprozentsatz Prozentuale Aufteilung des Liefervolumens gleicher Produkte auf mehrere Hersteller.

Lieferreserve Vorgezogene Materiallieferung zur Überbrückung von zu erwartenden Lieferstörungen bei Hersteller oder Zustellorganisationen.

Lieferschein -▶Frachtbrief

Lieferscheinberichtigung Berichtigung zum Lieferschein, wenn effektive Anlieferungen mit den avisierten Daten nicht übereinstimmen.

Liefertermin -▶Lieferzeit

Liefervertrag -▶Kaufvertrag

Lieferzeit Vertraglich vereinbarte Zeit für die Lieferung von Waren.

Lieferzusage Die verbindliche Erklärung des Lieferanten gegenüber dem Auftraggeber über die termingerechte Zustellung der Bestellungen.

Linie /Produktionsstraße Pro-

High material usages or expensive deliveries require maximum turnover, so that absolut minimum stock supports continious production. -▶JIT Just in Time

quantity delivered Bulk of delivery.

delivery percentage Quotation of delivery percentage for deliveries of same commodities by various supplier.

supply protection Advance material schedule to overcome anticipated supply problems by producer or traffic organization.

bill of delivery -▶consignment note

discrepancy note Correction to bill of delivery, when actual receipts are deviating from statement of delivery.

time of delivery -▶term for deliveries

delivery contract -▶purchase order

delivery time Time span for delivery of goods as outlined by purchase order.

delivery promise Firm commitment by the supplier to the buyer for delivery on time.

production line Production or as-

duktions- oder Montagestätte, wo das Produkt im Rahmen von Taktzeiten von Operation zu Operation geführt wird - Fließbandfertigung.

Linienbestückung Die Versorgung der Montagelinie mit Material.

Linienverteiler Mit der Verteilung von Material zu den einzelnen Montagestationen beauftragter Arbeiter.

Liste Aufzeichnung, Katalog, Aufstellung, Verzeichnis, Tabelle, Spezifikation, Terminliste, Register.

Lizenz Gewerbeerlaubnis - Genehmigung der Geschäftstätigkeit. -►Konzession

Lochkarte Datenträger und Datenspeicher aus Karton, findet bei der heutigen EDV nur noch begrenzte Anwendung.

Logistik/Material Management Die Konzeption, den Material- und Produktionsfluß einer Betriebswirtschaft als kooperierendes System vom Einkauf der Einzelartikel und dem Ursprung des Rohmaterials über mehrere Stationen der Fertigung bis zum Endprodukt und der Produktverteilung bis zum Endverbraucher zu koordinieren.
In seiner Effizienz voll wirksam, wenn Mindestmengen an Material zum rechten Zeitpunkt am richtigen Ort bereitstehen und die Produktpalette wie auch die installierte Kapazität den Marktverhältnissen entsprechen, so daß für die Abnahme der Endprodukte eine gesembly operation, where product moves from operation to operation within time limitation - assembly line.

line feeding Provide assembly line with material.

line feeder Employee with functional responsibility of providing material to assembly stations.

bill List, catalogue, tables, specification, index, register, schedule.

licence Permission to transact business. -►concession

punch card Data transmitter and data storage made from carton, currently nearly out of use for electronical data processing.

logistic/material management Concept of material and production flow seen as a cooperating system for EP deliveries from the source of of raw material through various stages of process to finished condition and the subsequent distribution of the final product to the customer. Most effective if minimum quantities of material are available at the right place and time and the level of complexity and capacity installation supports marketing demand. -►JIT Just in Time

nügende Nachfrage besteht.
-▶Just in Time JIT

Lohn Entgelt für Arbeitsleistung.
-▶Grundlohn

Lohnempfänger Arbeiter, der für seine Tätigkeit Lohn erhält.

Lohnerhöhung -▶Gehaltserhöhung

Lohnkosten Summe der Bruttolöhne, die ein Unternehmen in einem Zeitabschnitt als Arbeitsentgelt aufwendet.

Lohnnebenkosten Zusätzliche zum Arbeitsentgelt anfallende Kosten für den Arbeitgeber aufgrund gesetzlicher und tariflicher Bestimmungen. (Anteile zur Sozialversicherung, Lohnfortzahlung bei Krankheit, Urlaub und Feiertage.) Aber auch aufgrund von freiwilligen Leistungen. (Aus- und Weiterbildung, Altersversorgung, Werksverpflegung, Sonderzuwendungen und andere.)

lokalisieren Positionsbestimmung

Löschkennzeichen Indikator bei der EDV zur Löschung von Daten. Anwendung unterliegt besonderen Aufsichtsbedingungen.

Losgrößen - Produktion -▶Fertigungsgröße

Luftfracht Güter, die mit dem Flugzeug befördert werden.

wage Payment for labour performed. -▶base rate / base wage

hourly employee Person who works for wages.

wage increase -▶salary increase

labour cost Total amount of gross wages which a company has to spent as labour cost in a certain period of time.

incidental wage cost Costs in addition to normal payment based on legal and tariff requirements. (Social security benefits, payment in case of illness, holidays.) But also gratia payment. (Fringe benefits, education cost, provision for pension liabilities, cantine services, extra payments and others.)

determine the position Localization of subject.

cancellation indicator Indicator in data processing system to cancel data. Application mostly restricted by security procedures.

batch production ▶limited quantity

air - freight Forwarding of goods by an air carrier.

M

machen Herstellung / Fabrikation der Erzeugnisse.

Magazin -▶Lager

mangelhaft Die unsachgemäße Ausführung eines Auftrages.

Manufakture Fabrikmäßige Herstellung oder Bearbeitung von Produkten.

Marke Produkt-, Hersteller-, Ursprungs-, Qualitätskennzeichen, Schutzmarke, Klasse oder Sorte. -▶Kennzeichnung

Markenartikel Besondere Güter, die sich durch ihre Herstellung und Hersteller in der Art, Qualität und Preis auf dem Markt durchgesetzt haben.

Markenschutz Durch Patentrechte geschützte Herstellung von besonderen Produkten.

Markt Ort, Handelsplatz, Absatzraum für Produkte, wo durch Angebot und Nachfrage die Preisgestaltung bestimmt wird.

Marktanteil Erfolgskennzahl des Unternehmens über das marktgerechte Warenangebot.

Marktbericht Berichterstattung, hauptsächlich durch Presse und Institute, über die Marktsituation und Aufnahmefähigkeit für Produkte.

marktfähig Das zielgerechte

make / manufacture / produce Production or fabrication of products.

magazine -▶store / warehouse / depot

defective Imperfect execution of an order.

manufacturing Factory-made or produced products.

label/brand/identification mark Trademark, source code, quality sign, supplier identification mark or brand. -▶identification

branded article Special goods, trade-marked commodities which have an unique market-number by special process conditions and producer, quality performance and price conditions.

protection of trademarks Protection for manufacturing of branded goods by patent rights.

market Place, trading center, sales area for products, where supply and demand are basis for price formation.

market share Key point, indicates business success of company saleable products.

market letters Reports outlining market position on sales potential,- published by news or market analysis.

marketable/saleable Availability

Warenangebot zur Befriedigung der Nachfrage.

Marktordnung Behördliche Ordnungsprinzipien oder Bestimmungen, die Herstellung und Verkauf von Gütern regulieren.
(Schutzmaßnahmen bei der Verwendung von bestimmten Grundstoffen, Festlegung der Verkaufzeiten, Transportbestimmungen, usw.)

Maß Dimension, Extent, Größe, Ausmaß, Volumen, usw.

Maschinenausfallzeit Bei Mehrzweckmaschinen, wenn Umbau für die Herstellung von anderen Produkten erforderlich ist. Auch Reparaturzeiten im Rahmen des Wartungsplanes oder plötzlicher Ausfall durch Störung der Systeme. Soweit die Ausfallzeit erfaßbar ist, ist eine vorgezogene Materialdisposition zu berücksichtigen.

Maschinenauslastung Die volle Nutzung der Maschinenkapazität in der zur Verfügung stehenden Arbeitszeit.

Maschinenbelegungsplan Optimale Aufteilung der zu fertigenden Bedarfsmengen auf die verfügbare Bearbeitungskapazität unter Berücksichtigung der Umbauzeiten, wenn mehrere Produkte über gleiche Einrichtungen laufen.
-▶Fertigungsplan

Maßeinheit Standardgröße einer Meßeinheit zur Abwicklung der Geschäftstätigkeit.   -▶Bezugsmengeneinheit

of products in conformity with market demand.

market regulation Legal principles or rules for manufacturing and sales of products. (Safety regulations in conjunction of certain material usage, opening hours transportation rules and others.)

measurement Dimension, extent, size, scale, quantity, volume, etc.

machine down-time Changeover time, to rebuild multi-purpose machines for machining of different products as well as repair times according maintenance plan and machine break-down.
As far as idle time can be calculated, pre-scheduling of material is required.

machine utilization Complete utilization of machine capacity during normal course of working time.

machine sequencing Appropriate reqirement allocation to utilize available machine capacity considering change-over time, if same machine is used for different products. -▶manufacturing plan

work unit Standard size of measure for business transaction of goods. -▶unit of measure

Massengüter Industrieprodukte, die in großen Mengen hergestellt und verbraucht werden.

Massenverbrauch Großverbrauch - Bedarfsartikel.

massenweise Große Mengen oder Serien.

Materialart Grundstoffe aus denen Produkte hergestellt werden.

Materialbestand -▶Lagerbestand

Materialbestandswert Wert der Materialvorräte.

Materialbewegung Materialumschlaghäufigkeit -▶Lagerumschlag

Materialdisponent -▶Disponent

Materialdisposition -▶Disposition -▶Bedarfserrechnung

Materialentnahmeschein Beleg zur Erfassung des Materialabgangs aus dem Lager. Dient als Buchungsbeleg für Materialabgang.
-▶Bezugsschein

Materialfluß Die Kontinuität der Materialbereitstellung vom Ort der Herstellung bis zum Verbrauch.

Materialfreigabe Freigabe zur Bestellung von Ausgangsmaterial zur Herstellung von Einzelteilen,im Rahmen der Lieferbedingungen für Rohmaterial.

Materiallager -▶Lager

Materiallieferung -▶Eingang

bulk articles Mass produced and consumed goods.

bulk consumption Large-scale consumer goods.

large quantities Bulk material.

type of material Substance for manufacturing of products.

stock on hand -▶stocks inventory

material stock value Stock on hand value.

material movement Material turnover -▶inventory turnover

disposal clerk -▶parts analyst

material scheduling -▶scheduling and parts control -▶requirement calculation

material requisition Record to document material issues from storage. Booking slip for stock deduction.
-▶requisition

material flow Continuity of material supply from place of source to place of usage.

material authorization Release for ordering of raw material for production of components, considering order condition for raw material.

store / depot -▶store / warehouse / depot

material delivery -▶receival

Materialplanung und Kontrolle Organisationseinheit der Materialwirtschaft, verantwortlich für die Erstellung der Planungsunterlagen zur Beschaffung und Kontrolle von Produktionsmaterial, die Programmplanung und die Koordination zur Einführung von Produktänderungen.

Materialreserve Vorgezogene erforderliche Materialmenge zur Gewährleistung einer kontinuierlichen Fertigung. Die Materialmenge muß der absolut kleinsten Kapitalbindung durch Materialvorrat entsprechen. Die Größe der Materialreserve gliedert sich streng nach den Fertigungserfordernissen, wobei der Fertigungsprozeß entsprechend dem Wert der Produkte in einem hohen Maße flexibel sein muß, um somit ein Minimum an Kapitalbindung zu erreichen. Die Materialreserve umfaßt acht Hauptkriterien, denen im einzelnen Materialvortrag zugeordnet werden kann.

1.-▶Transitzeiten

2.-▶Operationsreserve

3.-▶Zusätzliche Operationsreserve

4.-▶System-Menge -▶Fertigungsreserve -▶Montagesystem

5.-▶Fixmenge

6.-▶Versandreserve

7.-▶Fertigungsfrequenz

8.-▶Lieferfrequenz

material planning & control Organizational unit of materials supply, responsible for generation of parts planning records for scheduling and controlling of production material, for programme planning and coordination and implementation of product changes.

production material float Prescheduled material requirement to support production process.- Number of material has to reflect absolut minimum quantity to minimize capital binding by production material float holding.

Allocation of production material float is relative to manufacturing process, whereby high flexibility for manufacturing of expensive products is essential, to achieve minimum capital binding by production float allocation.

Production material float consist of eight criterias to which individual float can be allocated.

1.- ▶Transit times

2. -▶Operational reserve

3. -▶Add. operational reserve

4. -▶System float -▶Material in process -▶Assembly line float

5. -▶Fix float

6. -▶Shipping bank

7. -▶Manufacturing frequency

8. -▶Delivery frequency

Der planerischer Wert soll mehr in Produktionstagen als in fixen Mengen dargestellt sein. Fertigungs- und Lieferfrequenz werden mit Hilfe von Tabellen ermittelt. Transitzeitwert wird bei der Akkumulation der Materialreserve nicht brücksichtigt, da wert- und bestandsmäßig noch nicht vereinnahmt.

Materialreserve-Wert
Materialwert der -▶Materialreserve.

Materialschaden Mangelhafter Warenzustand.

Materialwirtschaft Die Koordination der Materialversorgung in einem Unternehmen, die dazu dient, Material nach Menge und Qualität rechtzeitig unter günstigen Bedingungen am richtigen Ort bereitzustellen, daß eine effiziente Erstellung der Leistung oder des Produktes gewährleistet ist.
Organisationststruktur: -▶Einkauf - ▶Materialplanung und Kontrolle -▶Zoll und Verkehrsdienste

Maximalbelastung Höchstgrenze der Leistungsfähigkeit eines Betriebes oder Einrichtung entsprechend der technischen Installation.

Maximalbestand Höchstzulässiger - wirtschaftlich vertretbarer - Materialbestand.

Maximalleistung Höchste Produktionsrate. -▶Fertigungsauslastung

Mehrarbeit Über die Normalarbeitszeit hinausgehende Beschäf-

Float should basically be expressed in production days rather than in fix quantities.
Manufacturing- and delivery frequency is calculated by table of frequency.

Material in transit is excluded from total float, as not yet received and booked inventories.

production material float value
Material value of -▶production material float.

material damage Defective condition of material.

materials supply The coordination of supplying material with the objective to arrange material availability in appropriate quantity and quality by the required time under economical conditions, to the place of usage, so that efficient performance will be supported.
Organizational structure: -▶purchase -▶material planning & control -▶customs and traffic

maximal load Peak capacity of efficiency from a plant or equipment, according level of technical installation.

maximum stock Maxiumum - economical justified - number on material holdings.

maximum output Work to capacity. -▶capacity utilization

overtime work Extra work, exceeding standard working time, re-

181

tigung gegen besonderes Entgelt.

Mehrfachsatz Formularsatz

Mehrfachversand -▶Cross - Shipping

Mehrkosten Nicht geplante Kosten, die über das normale Maß hinausgehen und unvermeidbar sind. (Zeit- und Lohnüberschreitungen, Materialnachforderungen, fehlgelaufene Entwicklungsarbeiten, Veränderung der Fertigungseinrichtungen, Materialbevorratung zur Überbrückung von zu erwartenden Lieferstörungen, Absatzschwierigkeiten)

Meister Handwerker mit bestandener Meisterprüfung, beaufsichtigt Teilbereiche der Fertigung.

Meldestelle Registratur zur Erfassung von Geschäftsvorgängen.

Mengeneinheit -▶Bezugsmengeneinheit -▶Maßeinheit

Methodenverbessrung Prozeßverbesserung - Verfahrensänderungen zur Optimierung der Fertigung.

methodisch Methodisch arbeiten.

Mindestbestand Kleinste Menge an Materialbestand, ausreichend zur Stützung einer kontinuierlichen Fertigung. Die Größenordnung ist im wesentlichen durch Lieferzeiten für Material bestimmt.

Mindestfertigungsmenge Kleinste, wirtschaftlich noch vertretbare

quires extra payment.

multi-page document Form set

multiple shipping -▶cross-shipping

excess costs Not expected, but unavoidable costs, exceeding level of limitation. (Time losses, extra wage payment, add.material requirement, imperfect engineering, modification of process equipments, stock-pile programme, sales losses.)

foreman Workman educated as foreman with trade examination, controls manufacturing process.

reporting point Registration office for recording of business transaction.

unit of quantity -▶unit of measure -▶work unit

method of improvement Process improvements change in manufacturing techniques for optimal production.

methodical Work with method.

minimum stock Lowes level of inventories sufficient to support continious production. Stock holding is restricted by delivery times for material.

minimum production-run Minimum, economical justified number

Menge an Produkten, die hergestellt werden muß, wenn Einrichtungen für die Produkterzeugung umgebaut werden, oder Mindestmengen erst eine Fertigung ermöglichen.

Mindestliefermenge Kleinste wirtschaftliche Liefermenge. Begrenzung durch -▶Mindestfertigungsmenge, Verpackung oder Transportraumnutzung.

Minus-Buchbestand Fehlerhafte Zuordnung von Einzelteilen oder Materialien zum Endprodukt, für die keine praktische Verwendung mehr gegeben ist.durch -▶Produktionsmeldung über das Endprodukt erhalten diese Positionen Verbrauchsmeldung und generieren aufgrund Null - Bestand eine Minus-Kondition. Beim Endprodukt entsteht hierdurch eine unberechtigte Preisbewertung. Minus-Buchbestands-Positionen müssen zur Richtigstellung der Finanzberichte unverzüglich geklärt werden.

Modellanlauf -▶Anlauf/Produktion

Modifcation Abänderung/Umstellung -▶Änderung

monatliche Akkumulative Erreichte Zahl einer monatlichen Aufrechnug von Geschäftsvorgängen. (Produzierte Teile, Liefereingänge usw.)

Monatsrate Die Begleichung einer Schuldsumme durch festgesetzte Monatsraten.

Montage Zusammenbau von Tei-

of products, to be produced in case of rebuild of equipments/machines for product manufacturing, or where minimum-run is required to support production.

minimum delivery quantity Minimum commercial delivery. Limitation by -▶minimum production-run, packing unit or utilization of transportation capacity.

minus stock balance Incorrect link of detail parts or material to end-item, for which no further requirement excists.
Resulting from-▶production count of end-item and zero stock position for wrongly linked single parts, generates production count minus condition and leads to incorrect pricing level of end-item.
Minus stock balances require immediate corrective action, to clear financial record.

model launch -▶start initial production.

modification Improvement -▶change

month-to-date figure Cum-achievement at any time of the month on business transaction. (Produced products, received deliveries etc.)

monthly installments Payment of debts by stated monthly installments.

assembly Assembling of single

len und Fertigungsstufen zum Enderzeugnis.

Montagelinie -▶Linie/Produktionsstraße

Montagesystem / Materialbindung Zeit, in der das Material bis zum Ablauf des Produktes in der Montageline gebunden ist. -▶Materialreserve -▶System-Menge

Montagewerk Betriebsstätte, wo fertig bezogene Produkte zu einem Endprodukt zusammengebaut werden.

Mußänderung Klassifizierung für eine wichtige Produktänderung, die zum frühestmöglichen Zeitpunkt durchgeführt werden soll.

Muster -▶Erstmuster

Musterbefund Bericht mit den Ergebnissen der Bemusterung von Produktionsteilen.

parts and sub-assemblies to an end-item.

assembly line -▶production line

assembly line float Period of time from assembly up to buy off of finished product, for which production material is on hold. -▶production material float -▶System float

assembly plant Factory, where finished received products are assembled to an end-product.

mandatory change Classification of product change, requiring urgent action to realize earliest possible implementation.

sample -▶initial sample

sample report Report outlining inspection result of sample check for production parts.

N

Nacharbeit Extra Aufwand, um im eigentlichen Sinne durch Herstellungsprozeß fertig gestellte Produkte auf den Stand der geforderten Vorgaben zu bringen.

Nacharbeitskosten Kosten, die entstehen durch die Beseitigung von Fehlern an Produkten nach der eigentlichen Fertigstellung.

Nachbestellung Über die Ursprungsplanung hinausgehender Bedarf zur Abdeckung der Nachfrage.

rework Extra work to achieve required level of specification on products, which under normal circumstances are produced as finished parts during manufacturing process.

rework expense Costs resulting from rework of products, subsequent end of finished process.

re-order Additional order exceeding initial planning, to support market demand.

Nachbezahlung Nachträgliche Entgeltung einer vollbrachten Leistung.

Nachfrage Der auf dem Markt vorhandene Bedarf an Gütern und Dienstleistungen.

Nachholtag Besondere Arbeitsleistung zum Ausgleich für arbeitsfreier Arbeitstag.

Nachlieferung Zusätzliche Lieferung von Gütern zur Abdeckung der Bedarfsnachfrage.

Nachnahme Zustellung von Warensendungen durch die Post gegen Bezahlung der Ware.

Nachricht Die Weiterleitung einer Information an den zuständigen Bereich.

Nachtschicht Verrichtung der Arbeitszeit während der Nacht. (22oo-6oo) Vorwiegend, wenn der Arbeitsrhythmus eines Unternehmens in Schichtbetrieb aufgeteilt ist, aber auch zur Durchführung von Reparatur- und Aufbereitungsarbeiten an Anlagen.

Nachtschichtzulage Zulage zum Arbeitsentgelt bei Nachtarbeit.

Nachweis Dokumentation für die Richtigkeit einer Aktion.

nachzählen Nachprüfung eines zahlenmäßig festgestellten Ergebnisses.

Nebenwirkung Nichtbeabsichtigte Begleiterscheinungen bei Neuentwicklungen, die besonderer Beachtung bedürfen.

subsequent payment Additional payment for work performed.

demand / request Market requirement on goods and services.

make-up day Extra working time to recover normal working day losses.

additional delivery Subsequent supply of goods to overcome customer demand

collection on-delivery Delivery of goods by mail and collecting amount on delivery.

message Dispatch of information to affected area.

night shift Working time during night.
(22oo-6oo hrs.) In majority, when working time consist of shift-pattern, but also to perform repair and maintenance on equipments.

night shift premium Bonus for nightwork as extra payment to normal wage.

supporting record Documentation to proof evidence of action.

recount Verifying of stated results.

secondary effect Consequences not intended deriving from development work, which require special attention.

Nennbelastung Die Nutzung von Maschinen bis zur Nennleistung. -▶ausgelegte Kapazität

Nettoeinkünfte Das nach Abzug aller Abgaben verbleibende Kapital.

Nettogewicht Das Gewicht, das sich nach Abzug der Verpackung vom Gesamtgewicht ergibt.

Nettogewinn Differenz aus Erlösen und Gesamtkosten eines Unternehmens in einer Abrechnungsperiode. -▶Gewinn

Nettopreis Festpreis ohne Gewährung von Nachlässen.

Neuanschaffung Ersetzen von Anlagen und Werkzeugen nach Erreichung der Standzeiten.

Neueinstellungen Die Einstellung von Personal zur Erreichung der betrieblichen Ziele.

Neugestaltung Die technische Neuentwicklung der Produkte.

Neugruppierung Neubewertung der Produktionsteile, entsprechend den für die neue Fertigungsperiode gültigen Kriterien. -▶Kostenklassen

Neuordnung Änderung der bestehenden Ordnung.

nicht auffindbares Material Nach Belegen vorhandenes, aber physisch nicht verfügbares Material.

Nicht-Produktionsmaterial
-▶Betriebshilfsmittel)
-▶handelsübliches Material
-▶Hilfsmaterial

nominal load Utilization of machines to quoted capacity. -▶rated capacity

net earnings Amount of money after deduction of all duties.

net weight Weight, after deduction of packing from total weight.

net profit Difference between total income and total expenses in a period of business. -▶profit

net price Fix price without any discount.

retool Replacement of equipments and tools, after lifetime.

new hirings Recruitment of personnel to suit companies objectives.

innovations New technical development of products.

re-classification Re-grouping of production parts based on criterias applying to new period of business. -▶cost classification

re-arrangement Re-organization of current order.

missing material According record available, but physical not on hand material.

non production supplies -▶non production items -▶general supplies -▶non production material

Niederlassung Ort, an dem ein Unternehmen geführt wird. Erfüllungsort für alle geschäftlichen Aktivitäten.

Nivellierungsprozeß Die leistungsmäßige Auslastung der Produktionseinrichtungen durch gleichmäßige Fertigungsprogramme.

Norm Festlegung von anerkannten Begriffen, Standards, Vorschriften, Arbeitsnorm, Abmessungen, Richtmaße.

Normalarbeitszeit Durch Arbeitsrecht geregelte Zeit der täglichen-wöchentlichen Beschäftigung.

Notmaßnahmen Sofortmaßnahmen zur Wiederherstellung der Geschäftsmäßigkeit bei plötzlich auftretenden Störungen im Geschäftsablauf.

nutzbar produktiv, profitabel, lukrativ, sinnvoll

Nutzen Die Befriedigung von Bedürfnissen durch die Nutzung von Gütern oder Dienstleistungen.

business location Place where a company is registred and business transaction are performed.

leveling process Efficient utilization of manufacturing process by equal production programme.

standard Established standards, norms, regulations, work rates, specifications, guidelines.

normal operating hours By labour law scheduled daily- weekly working time.

emergency actions Immediate corrective action to re-establish business, after unexpected interruption of production.

useful productive, profitable, lucrative, meaningful

utilization Satisfaction to supply the needs, by using products or services.

O

Obergrenze Rahmen der Leistungsfähigkeit.

Obermeister Verantwortlich für mehrere Meisterbereiche der Fertigung.

Objekt Sache, Gegenstand, Angelegenheit.

Obliegenheit Die Wahrnehmung

border line Limit of efficiency.

general foreman Person controlling various foreman areas in manufacturing.

object Article, property, matter.

obligation Carry out of assigned

einer zugewiesenen Verantwortlichkeit.

offener Posten Offenstehender Rechnungsbetrag.

Öffentlichkeitsarbeit Öffentliche Meinungspflege, Werbemaßnahmen zur Steigerung des Umsatzes.

offerieren Bekanntmachen, anzeigen und anbieten von Produkten.

offiziell Amtlich festgestellt.

ökonomisch wirtschaftlich, profitabel, effizient.

Operationsreserve Materialmenge, die zur Überbrückung von Lieferstörungen zur Verfügung steht. Die Größenordnung richtet sich nach Wert und -►Lieferfrequenz des jeweiligen Materials. Die Operationsrerve findet keine Anwendung, wenn die Anlieferung nach den -►Just-in-Time JIT Prinzipien geordnet ist. -►Materialreserve

optimale Losgröße -►Fertigungsgröße -►wirtschaftliche Fertigungsgröße

optimale Produktionsgestaltung Die volle Nutzung der installierten Kapazität mit einem Minimum an Materialreserve und Personal bei einem hohen Flexibilisierungsgrad, wenn gleiche Einrichtungen für die Herstellung von unterschiedlichen Produkten dienen. -►Just-in-Time JIT

ordungsgemäß Die entsprechend Vorgaben korrekte Durchführung einer Anordnung.

responsibility.

unpaid item Uncovered amount.

public relation work Publicity of product information, to increase sales.

offer Publication notification and offers for sale of products.

official Confirmed by an authority.

economical Effective, profitable, efficient.

operational reserve Quantity of material as protection for supply interruption. Quantity is related to value and -►delivery frequency of material. Operational reserve is not applied, if deliveries are coordinated in line with -►JIT, Just in Time principles -►production material float

optimized production rate -►manufacturing lot -►economical production rate

OPT optimized production timing Fully utilization of installed capacity with a minimum of production float and manpower as well as high degree of flexibility when equipments are used for different products. -►JIT, Just in Time

properly Correct performed order according regulation.

Ordnungsstrafe Strafanordnung- Bußgeld.

Organisationsgrundsätze Richtlinien für die Erstellung einer Organisationsstruktur.

Organisationsplan Planerische Darstellung einer betrieblichen Organisation mit Gliederung der Verantwortung.

organisieren Die Einrichtung des geordneten Arbeitsablaufes.

Ortsbehörde Die Ortsverwaltung.

Ortsbesichtigung Die Überprüfung der örtlichen Verhältnisse.

Ortsbezeichnung Die genaue Bezeichnung der Örtlichkeit, wo besondere Aufgaben zu erfüllen sind.

Ortsverkehr Innerörtlicher Verkehr.

Ortszuschlag Zulage zum Arbeitsentgelt zum Ausgleich für Erschwernisse am Arbeitsort.

Output Mengenmäßiger Ertrag - Produktionsausstoß - Ergebnis von Eingaben.

Overhead Fixe Kosten, aber auch -▶Fertigungsgemein- oder -▶Gemeinkosten.

administrative fine Disciplinary punishment, fine.

prinziples of organization Guidelines for establishment of organizational structure.

organization chart Organization plan showing positions of responibility.

organize Arrangement for orderly work-flow.

local authority local goverment.

local inspection View of local areas.

indication of place Description of area, where special action will be performed.

local traffic Local transport.

local allowance Additional payment to normal wage rate as compensation for aggravating circumstances on working place.

output Rate of production - result of input.

fix cost Fix cost content, but also -▶manufacturing overheads or -▶overheads.

P

Pacht Vertragliche Überlassung und Nutzung von Gebrauchsgütern gegen Entgelt. -▶leasing

Pachtbedingungen Bedingun-

tenancy Lease and use goods against payment.-▶leasing

terms of tenancy Conditions to

gen, unter denen die Nutzung von Gebrauchsgütern erfolgt.

Packzettel Auftrag zur Zusammenstellung und Verpackung einer Bestellung.

Paginierstempel Stempel mit fortlaufender Numerierungseinrichtung zur Vollzähligkeitskontrolle von Geschäftsvorgängen.

Paket Verpackte Kleingüter, die sich auch für die Beförderung mit der Post eignen.

Palette Beförderungspalette zur Aufnahme und Transport von Material.

PC Personal Computer Unabhängig operierender Klein Computer, der am Arbeitsplatz aufgestellt werden kann und für alle üblichen EDV- Aufgaben geeignet und frei programmierbar ist.

periodische Fertigung -▶Fertigungszyklus

Personalbedarf Festlegung des Arbeitskräftepotentials, das ein Unternehmen zur Erfüllung seiner Aufgaben benötigt.

Personalkosten -▶Lohnkosten

Personallohnliste Gehalts-Lohnverzeichnis der Beschäftigten eines Unternehmens.

Personalstärke Gesamtzahl der Beschäftigten eines Unternehmens.

Personalverwaltung / IR Organisationseinheit eines Unterneh-

lease goods / products.

packing slip Order to pick and pack material.

pagination stamp Stamp with continious numbering facility for completenes control of business transaction.

parcel Small packing of goods acceptable for mail transport.

palette Flat board to carry and transport material.

PC personnel computer Independent programmeable operating compact computer, capable of electronical processing.

periodical manufacturing -▶cyclic production

manpower requirements Planned manpower requirement to meet companies objectives.

personnel expenses -▶labour cost

payroll Wage- salary index of employed staff of a company.

head count Total range of employed personnel of a company.

IR, industrial relation Organizational activity of a company to per-

mens zur Wahrnehmung aller administrativen- personalbezogenen Maßnahmen.

Personalvorschätzung Ermittlung des Personalbedarfes aufgrund von festen Bezugsgrößen. (Produktionszahlen)

Planbestand Vorhandener Materialbestand entspricht den planerischen Vorgaben. -▶Materialreserve

planmäßig Aktionsverlauf wie geplant.

Planung Festlegung der betrieblich notwendigen Aktionen zur optimalen Ablaufgestaltung eines Vorhabens.

Planzahl Vorgabe der zu erreichenden Produktionsmenge während einer Planungsperiode.

Platz/Stelle/Ort Bereich

Platzmangel Nicht ausreichender Raum zur Durchführung der vorgesehenen Aktionen.

Plombe Verschlußsiegel im amtlichen Verkehr zur Verhinderung vom unbefugten Öffnen von Behältern, Fahrzeugen, amtlichen Meßgeräten und Eindringen in amtlich verschlossene Räume.

plombieren Amtliche- durch Zoll vorgenommene Verschließung von Warensendungen im grenzüberschreitendem Verkehr.

Positionsbeschreibung
-▶Arbeitsplatzbeschreibung

Posten Eine Warenmenge.

form all personnel administrative actions.

head count forecast Calculation of manpower requirement based on fixed conditions. (Production quantities)

target inventory Stock on hand in line with material authorization -▶Production material float

according to plan Progress as scheduled.

planning Determination of operational requirements to optimized process condition for new projects.

target figure Planned output figure expected to be achieved during a planning period.

location / place Area

short of space Insufficient space to perform action as forecasted.

seal Seal used by authorities to prevent opening of boxes, vehicles,- measurement equipments and rooms, by unauthorized persons.

lead Sealed bond of material deliveries in border crossing traffic.

position description -▶job description

lot Quantity of goods.

Postzeichen Organisationskennzeichen einer Abteilung.

Preis Der Geldwert für eine Ware oder Leistung. -▶Einkaufspreis

Preisabweichung Differenzen zwischen Ist- und Planwerten.

Preisangabe Preisangabe im Zusammenhang mit Angebotsabgabe zur Lieferung von Waren oder Dienstleistungen.

Pressmenge Optimale Fertigungsmenge, wenn zur Herstellung von Teilen, Pressen oder Preßstraßen umgebaut werden. -▶optimale Losgröße

Pressteile Teile, deren Herstellung durch Pressen aus Rohmaterial erfolgt.

Presswerk Fabrikausstattung mit Pressen zur Herstellung von Pressteilen.

Presswerkzeuge Besondere Werkzeuge zur Aufnahme in Pressen mit hoher Festigkeit zur Gewährleistung einer angemessenen Standzeit.

Prinzipien zur Bestimmung der Materialreserve Grundsätze zur Bestimmung der quantitativen und zeitlichen Größenordnung der einzelnen Kriterien der -▶Materialreserve. Der jeweilige Toleranzbereich steht relativ zur -▶Mengeneinheit bezogenen -▶Kostenklasse und ist somit wertorientiert. Die Prinzipien zur Bestimmung der Materialreserve sind die Fakten zur Gewährleistung einer optimalen

mailing symbol Departmental organizational code.

price Value of money for goods or services.-▶prime cost

price variance Difference between actual und target figure.

quotation of price Statement of price in connection with quotation for supply of goods or services.

press load Optimal production rate for press-parts, when press facilities are used for multi purpose production. -▶optimized production rate

stampings/press parts Manufacturing of parts by stamping from rough material.

press shop Plant equiped with stamping machines for the production of stampings.

dies/press tools Special tools to be used in press-machines with high resistance to meet projected life time.

principles of float allocation Policy letter outlining standards to establish float level relative to the various criterias of -▶production material float.Quantity of float is related to parts -▶cost classification and thereof value orientated.
Principles of float allocation are basic rules of economics to meet optimized capital binding by material-holding -▶production material float value

Kapitalbindung durch Materialvorrat. -▶Materialreserve-Wert

Probe Warenlieferung zur Feststellung der Gebrauchsfähigkeit von größeren Bestellmengen. -▶Erstmuster

Produktenwicklung -▶Entwicklung

produktionsabhängig Betriebsfaktoren, die in Relation zum Fertigungsplan stehen.

Produktionsänderungsanzeige -▶Änderungsanzeige

Produktionsänderungstermin Einsatztermin für eine Änderung in der laufenden Fertigung.

Produktionsauslauf Geplante Fertigungseinstellung einer Serienproduktion. -▶Fertigungsauslauf

Produktionsausschuß Bei der Herstellung angefallene fehlerhafte Teile durch Fertigungs- oder Materialfehler. -▶Fertigungsausschuß

Produktionsbeginn Start der Serienfertigung. -▶Anlauf Produktion

Produktionsbericht -▶Fertigungsmeldung

Produktionserhöhung -▶Fertigungserweiterung

Produktionsfähigkeit Die Überprüfung der Fertigungsanlagen auf ihre Funktionsfähigkeit.

Produktionsgefahr Störung im organisierten Fertigungsablauf auf-

pattern Delivery of test parts to proof utilization of bulk supply. -▶initial sample

product design development -▶development

production related Manufacturing elements which are in relationship with production plan.

product change notice - ▶change notice

break point Timing to implement a product change during running production.

phase out of production Termination of mass-produced products. -▶production run out

rejects Production parts which becoming defective during course of process or by material defaults. -▶scrap/wastage/rejects

start of production Start of volume production. -▶start of initial production

production account -▶production report

increase in output -▶capacity expansion

productive capacity Efficiency check of production equipments.

production risk Interuption of production due to lack of material

grund Materialmangel oder anderer Ursachen.

Produktionskontrolle -▶Fertigungskontrolle

Produktionskosten -▶Betriebskosten -▶Fertigungskosten -▶Herstellungskosten

Produktionsleistung Die Menge der produzierten Güter in einem bestimmten Zeitraum.

Produktionslenkung Steuerung des Produktionsverlaufes. -▶Fertigungslenkung

Produktionsmaterial Zusammenfassender Begriff für Material, das zur Erstellung von Produkten dient.

Produktionsmeldung -▶Fertigungsmeldung/Bericht -▶Produktionsbericht

Produktionsprogramm Plan über die Produktherstellung in einem bestimmten Zeitabschnitt. -▶Abrufprogramm

Produktionssteigerungsrate Die Steigerung der Produktionsraten bis zur Erreichung der installierten Kapazität.

Produktionsteil Teil, was dem Endprodukt zugeordnet ist. -▶Eigenfertigungsteile

Produktionsüberschuß Über dem Produktionsprogramm liegende Fertigungsmenge, für die keine Nachfrage besteht. -▶Fertigungsüberschuß

or other reasons.

production control -▶production control

production expense -▶operating costs -▶manufacturing costs / expenses -▶expenses of production

manufacturing efficiency Number of products produced during a certain period.

production allocation programme Planning and control of production schedules. -▶manufacturing coordination

production material Collective description for material required for product manufacturing.

production rate report -▶production report -▶production account

production schedule Production plan for manufacturing of products within a certain period. -▶master schedule formula

production rate of climb Increasing of production rates up to the level of maximum output.

production part Part linked to end-item. -▶manufactured parts

excess to schedule Surplus production for which no demand exist. -▶excess material

Produktionsunterbrechung - ▶Produktionsgefahr

Produktionsverzögerung Die zeitliche Verschiebung einer vorgesehenen Produktionsaufnahme.

Prognose Vorhersage zukünftiger Situationen in bezug auf die geschäftliche Entwicklung.

Projekt Investmentvorhaben- Zusammenfassung aller Kosten, die zur Realisierung einer Neuentwicklung entstehen. -▶Investition -▶Investitionsantrag -▶Investitionsausgaben

Projektvorschlag Studie über die Realisierung eines Vorhabens zum Zweck der Kostenerfassung.

Protokollabfassung Schriftliche Wiedergabe von Verhandlungsergebnissen.

Protokolländerung Änderung der Verhandlungsniederschrift aufgrund Fehldarstellung in der Urschrift.

Prototyp/Musterbau -▶Einbauprobe -▶Funktionsüberprüfung

Prüfeinrichtung Lehren, Vorrichtungen, Laboranlagen zum Prüfen von Produktionsgütern.

Prüfer Hausinterner Revisor zur Überwachung der Rechtmäßigkeit bei den verschiedenen Geschäftsvorgängen.

Prüfergebnis Befund der Qualitätsprüfung von Produkten.

Prüfungshäufigkeit Die im Prü-

production interruption -▶ production risk

production delay Postponement of scheduled initial production build.

forecasting Prognosis of future situations as related to business expansion.

project Investment plan- Total range of expenditure, required for the realization of new development.
-▶investment -▶appropriation request -▶capital phasing/expenditure

project proposal Feasibility study for the realization of investment and calculation of expenditure.

minute writing Summary of subjects discussed during a conference.

alteration of the minutes Correction of conference minutes to eliminate misinterpretation in initial record.

prototype/pilot build -▶functional build -▶functional test

test facility Gauges, testing and laboratory equipments to inspect production goods.

auditor internal audit to check legality of business transaction.

check result Findings of quality check from products.

checking frequency Number of

fungsplan ausgewiesene Anzahl der durchzuführenden Prüfungen in einem bestimmten Zeitabschnitt. Die Anzahl der Prüfungen ist abhängig von gesetzlichen- oder internen Richtlinien, bezogen auf Sachgebiete und Sachwerte.

Prüfveranlassung Antrag mittels Form zur Überprüfung von Vorgaben durch den Anwender beim Verursacher.

Puffermenge Materialmenge zur Stützung der Produktion. -▶Materialreserve

Punkt der absoluten Kostendeckung Ausgleich einer Investition durch die bezogene Leistung. Plus - Minus - Null Position. Erreichung der Gewinnschwelle.

checks to be performed during a certain period and as outlined in a test programme. Frequence of tests determined by legal- or internal requirements and related to business transaction and inventory value.

query notice Request formulated by user in writing to review correctness of record integrity.

buffer stock Stock on material to support production. -▶production material float

break even point Recovery of investment by equalization of received efficiency. plus - minus - nil position.
Achieving of profit line.

Q

Qualifikation Befähigungsnachweis - fachliche Kompetenz.

Qualität Die Beschaffenheit oder Güte einer Ware.

Qualitätsabnahmeschein Prüfbericht über die Beschaffenheit der Ware und der spezifikationsgerechten Herstellung. -▶Erstmuster -▶Musterbefund

Qualitätsabweichung Nichterreichung der vorgegebenen Güte. -▶Abweichungsgenehmigungsantrag

Qualitätskontrolle Überwachung der Fertigung hinsichtlich Errei-

qualification Professional qualification competence.

quality Condition or quality of goods.

certificate of inspection Inspection report of material condition in relation to specification. -▶initial sample -▶sample report

deviation in quality Not achieving required level of specified quality. -▶deviation request

quality control Process control of productmanufacturing to ensure

chung der verlangten Qualität.
-▶Inspektion

Qualitätsnorm Richtlinien, die bei der Produktherstellung den Grad der Qualität bestimmen.

Quantität Große Menge - Anzahl Kleine Menge.

Quartal Kalenderperiode Deutschland / US 1./1. - 1./4. -1./7. - 1./10. England 25./3. - 24./6. - 19./9. -25./12.

Quelle/Ursprung Hersteller, - ▶Lieferant, Bezugsstelle von Produkten.

quittieren Bestätigung einer Warenlieferung.

Quittung Bestätigung, Beleg.

Quote Anteil, Rate, Verhältnis.

R

Rabatt Preisnachlaß.

Rahmen Bereich des üblichen Geschäftsverkehrs.

Rang Güteklasse - Qualitätsgrad einer Ware.

Rangordnung -▶Klassifizierung

Rate Festgelegte Mengen, auch Teilzahlung. -▶Tagesraten

Rationalisierung Durchführung von Maßnahmen zur Steigerung des wirtschaftlichen Erfolges, Steigerung der Produktion bei Anhebung der Erzeugnisqualität und

required level of quality.
-▶inspection

standards of quality Guidelines outlining level of quality for product manufacturing.

quantity Great lot - bulk small lots.

quarter Calendar period Germany / US 1./1. - 1./4. - 1./7. - 1./10. England 25./3. - 24./6. - 19./9. - 25./12.

source of supply Origin, -▶supplier/vendor, producer of products.

acknowledge of receipt Akknowledge receipt of goods.

receipt Acknowledgement, voucher.

share / contingent Quota, proportional, allocation, contribution.

R

discount Price deduction.

scope In the course of normal way of business.

grade Condition - quality rating of a product.

ranking order -▶classification

installment Fixed installments, also payment in installments.
-▶daily rate

rationalization Initiation of actions to increase economical efficiency. Increasing of production and improvement of product quality as well as optimizing of

Optimierung der -▶Herstellungskosten.

rationell Wirtschaftlich, sparsam, effizient.

Raum / Platz Fläche, Zone, Distrikt, Gebiet, Laderaum.

Raumeinheit Die Größe - Kapazität einer räumlichen Abgrenzung.

Raummangel Begrenzt zur Verfügung stehender Raum.

Raumverschwendung Unsachgemäße Raumnutzung.

Raumplanung -▶Lageplan

Reaktionszeit -▶Durchlaufzeit

Rechenzentrum Raum, in dem EDV-Anlagen installiert sind.

Rechnung Vom Lieferanten zu erstellende Spezifizierung über fälliges Entgelt, für gelieferte Waren oder Dienstleistungen, mit Zahlungsbedingungen.

Rechnungseinheit Rechentechnisches Hilfsmittel zur einfacheren Gestaltung des Zahlungsverkehrs bei internationalen Transaktionen. (In der -▶EG -▶ECU)

Rechnungsjahr -▶Geschäftsjahr

Rechnungsnummer Kennummer einer Rechnung für die Registrierung.

Rechnungsprüfung Die Prüfung des Rechnungswesens einer Unternehmung. (Bilanzprüfung, Wirtschaftsprüfung, Sonderprüfung, Revision)

process cost

rational Economical, saving, efficient

room / space Area, district, capacity.

unit of space Volume - Capacity of an area.

lack of space Restricted space available.

waste of space Careless storage.

area planning -▶layout

reaction time -▶respond time

data processing center Area where electronical data processing equipments are installed.

invoice Suppliers statement of account for payment due to delivered goods or performed services.

unit of account Technical unit of money to simplify payment routine of international transactions. (Within -▶EG -▶ECU)

financial year -▶business / treading year

invoice nummber Identification number of an invoice used for registration.

auditing Checking of companies accounting. (Ballancesheet audit, public accounting, special audit, verification review)

Rechnungsstelle Ort der Rechnungserstellung auf Basis der Lieferaufträge.

Recht Verordnungen und Normen als Ordnungsprinzip einer Gemeinschaft.

Rechtfertigung Die Begründung der getroffenen Maßnahmen zur Lösung einer Aufgabe - Problem.

Rechtsanspruch Anspruch auf -►Garantie -►Ersatz im Rahmen der Verkaufsbedingungen.

Regal Gestell aus Holz oder Stahl zur Lagerung von verpacktem Material. -►Hochbauregal

Regelfall Die gleichbleibende Wiederholung von Aktionen.

regeln Eine Angelegenheit in Ordnung bringen.

Register Verzeichnis, Index, Katalog

Reihenfolge Ordnungsprinzip in alphabetischer - chronologischer oder in der richtigen Reihenfolge.

Reinertrag Reingewinn des Geschäftsjahres. Summe der Erträge abzüglich Summe der Aufwendungen. -►Ertrag -►Gewinn -►Nettogewinn

Reinverlust Negatives Ergebnis eines Geschäftsjahres. Summe der Aufwendungen abzüglich Summe der Erträge. -►Ertrag

Reisespesenabrechnung Die Abrechnung der während einer Geschäftsreise entstandenen Ko-

accounting office Place where invoicing of accounts according to customer order are established.

law Rights and obligations as principle of order in a community.

justification Reasons to explain actions in order to solve problems.

claim Lawefull claim for -►warranty and -►replacement based on sales conditions.

shelf Storage rack made from wood or steal for storage of packed material. -►high bay shelf

normal case Constant - unchanged repetition of action.

regulate To settle a problem.

register Record, index, catalogue

sequence Order (alpha betical data) in which things occur.

clean profit Profit less expense. Surplus of a business year. -►income earned -►profit -►net profit

net loss Negative result of a business year. Total expenses minus -►clean profit.

billing of travel expenses Charging of travel expenses to the company account. In many cases sim-

sten - Vielfach durch -▶Tagessatz vereinfacht.

Reklame Die Werbung zur Absatzsteigerung der Produkte.

reklamieren Beanstandung einer Ware auf nicht sachgerechter Herstellung oder Funktion.

Reparaturkosten Kosten für die Instandhaltung der Fertigungsanlagen zur Aufrechterhaltung des Betriebsablaufes.

Reparaturwerkstatt Besonders ausgestattete Werkstatt zur Durchführung von Reparaturen an Produkten und Behebung von Reklamationen bei -▶Garantie / Gewährleistung.

Restbestand Materialmenge, für die im eigentlichen Sinne keine Verwendung mehr gegeben ist.
-▶ausgelaufenes Material

Restmaterialwert Aus der Verschrottung von -▶Restbestand an Material erzielter Gewinn.

Restposten -▶Restbestand

Restsumme Noch ausstehender Restbetrag.

Revision Prüfung von Geschäftsvorgängen und Veranlassung von Änderungen oder Ergänzungen.
-▶Rechnungsprüfung

RGW - Rat für gegenseitige Wirtschaftshilfe / COMECON Seit 1949 in der sozialistischen Marktordnung zusammengeschlossenen Staaten zur wirt-

plified by -▶travel allowance.

publicity Advertisement to increase sales of products.

complain Objection against goods regarding quality or performance.

expenditure on repairs Maintenance costs for manufacturing equipments to ensure continious production flow.

repair workshop Special workshop equiped with facilities to repair goods and eliminate -▶warranty claims.

remainder of stocks Remaining stock for which no further usage exist as original intended.
-▶obsolete material

scrap value Net gain resulting from scrapping of -▶obsolete material.

remaining stock -▶remainder of stocks

balance Outstanding value / sum.

revision Reviewing of business transactions and recommendation for amendments or modifications.
-▶auditing

COMECON -Council for Mutual Economic Assistance / RGW Community of socialist countries, founded in 1949, for economical specialisation and cooperation for

schaftlichen Spezialisierung und Kooperation bei der Produktion mit dem Ziel, eine wirtschaftliche Integration herbeizuführen.
Mitglieder: 1949: Albanien bis 12/62, Bulgarien, Polen, Rumänien, Sowjetunion, Ungarn, Tschechoslowakei, 1950: Deutsche Demokratische Republik bis 3. Okt. 90, 1962: Mongolische Volksrepublik, 1972: Kuba, 1978: Vietnam
Sitz: Moskau Seit 1988 in offizieller Beziehung zur -►EG Seit Ende 1989 durch Liberalisierung der politischen Verhältnisse in Osteuropa, mit Strukturveränderungen der planwirtschatlichen Grundordnung konfrontiert.

Richtlinien Anordnungen, Anleitungen. -►Arbeitsanweisung -►Bedienungsanleitung -►Geschäftsordnung -►Geschäftsgrundsatz -►Organisationsgrundsätze -►Instruktionen

Richtwert für die Fertigung Festlegung der Fertigungszeiten/ Taktzeiten.

Rohling Durch Schmieden, Pressen oder Gießen hergestellte Werkstücke.

Rohmaterial Ausgangsmaterial wie Stahl, Blech, Flüssigmetalle usw. zur Herstellung von Produktionsteilen. -►Produktionsmaterial

Rückgängigmachung Die Aufhebung einer getroffenen Entscheidung. Annullierung von Geschäftsvorgängen.

product manufacturing with the objective to achieve comprehensive economical integration.
Member: 1949: Albania until 12/62, Bulgaria, Poland, Rumania, UDSSR, Hungary, Czechoslovakia, 1950: German Democratic Republic until 3. oct. 90, 1962: Mongolian Republic.

1972: Cuba, 1978: Vietnam

Residence: Moscow Since 1988 offical relation with -►EG

As consequence of liberalization in political terms within the East-European Countries at end of 1989, are being modifications of central economy planning structure under discussion.

directives Rules, guidelines. -►operating procedure -►operating instruction -►standing order -►policy letter -►principles of organization -►instructions

production standards Establishment of standard time data/ process tact-time.

rough part Part produced by forging, stamping or castings.

raw material Basic material as steal, sheet metal, fluid metal etc. for manufacturing of production parts. -►production material

cancellation Withdrawal of decission. Cancellation of a business deal.

Rückgewinnung Die Aktivierung von -▶Fertigungsausschuß - ▶Verwerfungen durch -▶Nacharbeit.

Rückrufaktion Aufforderung des Herstellers an den Kunden, bestimmte Produkte einer Fertigungsserie zur Behebung von Herstellungsfehlern den Reparaturdiensten vorzustellen.

Rückstand Verzug bei der Abwicklung von Aufträgen.

rückständig Nicht dem letzten Stand entsprechend - altmodisch.

Rückversand Rücklieferung einer Warensendung an die Bezugsstelle.

salvage/recovery Activation of -▶scrap -▶rejects by -▶rework.

recall campaign Request by a producer to customers to return products for repair or exchange of defective parts.

arrears Behind on orders - Behind on schedules.

old-fashioned Not up-to-date, behind the times.

return shipment Return delivery of products to source of supply.

S

Sachverhalt Genaue Darstellung eines Vorganges.

Sammelladung Zusammenfassung von mehreren Artikeln zu einem Sammeltransport.

Sammelstützpunkt -▶Konsolidierungsort

Schaden Durch einen besonderen Umstand entstandene -▶Beschädigung eines Gutes.

Schadenersatz Ausgleich von entstandenem Schaden aufgrund vertraglich festgelegter Verpflichtung bei Vertragsverletzung, vielfach Schadenersatz wegen Nichterfüllung.

Schalterdienst Die Besetzung

facts of the case Detailed statement of an issue.

mixed cargo Consolidated delivery of various articles by collective transport.

collecting point -▶consolidation point

loss -▶Damage of goods caused by exceptional circumstances.

compensation for damage Payment for damages according to a contract, mostly compensation for nonfulfilment.

counter service Attending hours

der Warenannahme zu bestimmten Öffnungszeiten.

Schichteinteilung Übernahme des Arbeitsplatzes nacheinander durch verschiedene Mitarbeiter für eine Zeiteinheit, die die Normalarbeitszeit eines einzelnen Arbeitnehmers übersteigt. Zur Ausnutzung der installierten Kapazität und Bedienung der Marktnachfrage ist die tägliche Arbeitszeit vielfach in drei Schichten eingeteilt.

Schichtwechsel Nach Ablauf der Schicht Arbeitszeit, Fortsetzung der Tätigkeit durch die Folgeschicht. -►Schichteinteilung

Schichtzuschlag Erschwerniszulage zum normalen Lohn bei Schichtarbeit, in besonderer Weise bei Nachtschicht.

Schienenverkehr Die Transportabwicklung über die Schiene -Eisenbahn.

Schiffahrt Die Güterbeförderung über Wasserstraßen und See.

Schmiede Mit Schmiedeeinrichtungen, zum Teil Schmiedeautomaten, ausgestattete Fabrik zur Herstellung von konturbezogenen Werkstücken.

Schmiederohling Durch Schmieden über besondere Einrichtungen hergestellte Werkstücke. -►Schmiede

Schrott Bei der Herstellung von Produkten anfallende Materialreste und -►Fertigungsausschuß sowie vorhandene -►Restposten at the receiving office.

shift pattern Sequential takeover of work by different workers for a period exceeding normal working time of an employee. For reasons of capacity utilization and supporting of customer demand, daily working time sometimes is split-up in three shift operations.

shift change Subsequential turn off shift, continuation of function performance by shift change over. -►shift pattern

shift premium Extra payment to normal wage as shift allowance, in particular for night shift.

rail transport Transportations via rail.

navigation / shipping Transport of goods on waterways and ocean.

forge Plant equiped with forging facilities to produce form related forgings.

forging Forgings formed by special equipments. -►forge

scrap Restmaterial from production process and -►scrap/waste/rejects as well as -►remainder stocks, for which no further usage

an Fertigprodukten, für die keine produktive Verwendung mehr besteht.

Schrottmeldung Nach Ablauf der täglichen Fertigungsperiode erstellter Bericht mit Angaben der nicht zeichnungsgerecht hergestellten Produkten.

Schrottprozentsatz Bei der -▶Materialdisposition zu berücksichtigender Mehrbedarf, der basierend auf Vergangenheitswerten als -▶Schrott angefallen ist.

Schrottwert -▶Restmaterialwert

Schutt Abfall, nicht verwertbare Reste wie Asche, Rückstände aus Reinigung usw., die entsorgt werden müssen.

Schutzbestimmung Anordnungen, Maßnahmen, Vorsorge zum Schutz von Mensch und Material.

Schutzmarke Zur Unterscheidung von Waren anderer Hersteller angebrachte Merkmale. -▶Fabrikmarke / Zeichen -▶Warenzeichen

Schutzzoll Zum Schutz der inländischen Erzeugnisse, Erhebung von Einfuhrgebühr auf ausländische Produkte. Ab 1993 entfallen alle Einfuhrzölle für den -▶EG Binnenmarkt.

Schwerpunkt Ereignis, Mittelpunkt, Kernpunkt.

Schwund Unkontrollierter Abgang von Material

exist.

scrap report Report with details of out-of-tolerance products at the end of daily production.

scrap percentage Additional material to be considered by normal production -▶requirement calculation, based on historical -▶scrap data.

salvage value -▶scrap value

rubbish Waste, not salvageable refusal like ash, arrears from cleaning etc., which have to be disposed.

safety regulation Regulations and actions to be taken as provisions for the protection of personnel and material

brand Indication on products to differenciate between products of various producers. -▶trade marke -▶trade name

protective tariff Protection of domestic products by trade barriers for goods of foreign competitors. Commencing 1993 there will be no further tariff-protection for trade business within -▶EG countries.

keypoint Event, focal point, subject.

deficit Uncontrolled loss of material.

Seetransport -▶Schiffahrt

Seeverpackung Besonders konstruierte und aus seefestem Material hergestellte Verpackung für den Seetransport.

Selbstanfertigung Anteil der Eigenherstellung von Teilen die dem Endprodukt zugeordnet sind.
-▶Fertigungstiefe   -▶Eigenfertigungsteile

Serienfertigung Fertigungsverfahren im Mehrproduktbetrieb, wo nach- oder nebeneinander gleichartige Produkte hergestellt werden.

Sicherheitseinrichtungen Einrichtungen an Maschinen und Arbeitsplatz zum Schutze der Beschäftigten.

Sicherheitsfaktor Durch besondere Aktionen erreichter Grad der Sicherheit.

Skonto Prozentualer Nachlaß von der Rechnungssumme entsprechend den Zahlungsbedingungen.

Sollarbeitsstunden Die vertraglich festgelegte Normalarbeitszeit.

Sollbestand Vorhandener Materialbestand ist in Übereinstimmung mit den Planvorgaben.

Sonderbestellung Extrabestellung einer eigens herzustellenden Ware.

Sonderteile Zusätzliche Ausstattung, die den Standardumfang eines Produktes übersteigt.

carriage by sea -▶navigation/shipping

seaproof packing Special developed and from seawortly material manufactured packing for sea-transportation.

own make Content of own manufacturing parts to be linked to end-item -▶range of company produced assets -▶manufactured parts

serial production Production method, where either parallel or side by side similar products are produced.

safety facilities Facilities to ensure that machines and working areas are safe for employees.

safety factor By special action achieved level of safety protection.

discount allowance Percentage of discount allowance according to payment regulation.

nominal manhours Normal working time as stated in working contract.

target inventory Stock on hand in line with authorized schedule.

special order Once-off order for extra product-manufacturing.

options/accessories Additional product features, exceeding normal standard offer of product.

Sonderverpackung Besonders angefertigte Verpackung, insbesondere, wenn Standardverpackungen für Serienprodukte nicht zur Verfügung stehen.

sortieren Nach bestimmten Kategorien ordnen. -▶Klassifizierung

Sortiment Anzahl der unterschiedlichen Produkte.

Sparprodukt Veränderung des Produktionsumfanges durch Reduzierung der Produktausstattung zur Verminderung des Verkaufspreises.

Sparprogramm -▶Ersparnisse / Einsparungen

Spediteur Transportunternehmer. Übernimmt die Güterversendung im Auftrag des Versenders.

Speditionsabteilung Verwaltungsstelle in einer Spedition zur Koordination des Transportgeschehens.

Speicher Magazin, Depot -▶Lager

Sperrgut Großvolumige Warensendungen oder Güter, die nicht stapelbar sind.

Sperrlager Besonderes Lager für geliefertes, aber noch nicht zur Verwendung freigegebenes Material. Für zukünftige Produktion bestimmte Neuteile.

Spesen Aufwand durch Geschäftsreisen, der vom Unternehmen erstattet wird. -▶Reisespesenabrechnung

special wrapping Extra manufactured packing to bridge shortage of standard packing.

sort Selection of material -▶classification.

collection Range of different products.

economy product Modification of product by omitting product extras to reduce selling price.

cost reduction programme -▶savings/economics

carrier Forwarding agent carrying goods on behalf of shipper.

forwarding department Dispatching office to coordinate transportation.

storehouse Magazine, storage -▶store/warehouse/depot

measurement cargo / goods Voluminous material, bulky goods not for stapling.

storage area for unapproved parts Special storage for material delivered, but not yet released for production.
New designed production parts for future production.

expenses Travel expenses to be refunded by company. -▶billing of travel expenses

Spezialist In einem Fachgebiet besonders ausgebildete Person. -▶Facharbeiter

Spezifikation Detaillierte Beschreibung - Materialbeschaffenheit - Dimension - Herstellungsart -Kontrolldaten usw.

Spitzenleistung Höchstleistung. Erreichung der -▶Kapazitätsgrenze.

Spitzenlohn Höchstlohn.

staatliche Zuschüsse Subvention durch den Staat für die Schaffung neuer Arbeitsplätze, zum Teil in Entwicklungsgebieten.

Stammdaten-File Register der in einem Unternehmen zur Verwendung gelangenden Teile und Materialien mit detaillierten Angaben über Verbrauch, Laufzeit, Mengen, Bezug, Preis, Liefer- oder Fertigungsbedingungen und weiteren Kontrolldaten.

Stammkarte Registration der Einzelteildaten, Auszug aus dem -▶Stammdaten-File.

Standardteile Vereinheitlichung von Teilen durch Normung und einheitliche Typung im besonderen bei häufig zur Anwendung kommendem Kleinmaterial - Schrauben, Stiften, Scheiben, -▶Hilfsmaterial. -▶Norm

Standort einer Industrie Niederlassung eines Unternehmens.

Standzeiten für Werkzeuge Anzahl der mit einem Werkzeug her-

specialist Person with special skills. -▶skilled worker/specialist

specification Detailed statement -material condition - measurements process condition - control data etc.

maximum wages Maximum, top wages.

outstanding performance Top efficiency, -▶maximum output.

govermental grands Subvention by goverment for creating of new jobs, mostly in development areas.

parts master file Register containing companies parts usage records with detailed specification of usage, life time, quantities, source, price, delivery- or manufacturing conditions and further control data.

master card Basic data record showing parts specification, extract from -▶parts master file.

standard parts Standardization of parts by establishment of standards and standardization of types, mainly for multipurpose usage material - screws, pins, washers, ▶non production material -▶standard

location of an industry Residence of a company.

tool-life time Number of production parts produced by a tool set or

zustellenden Teile oder Betriebsdauer, die ein Werkzeug halten muß. (Normwerte für die Werkzeugentwicklung)

Stangenmaterial Rohmaterial in Stangenform.

Stapelplätze Läger oder Hafenstädte, an denen Welthandelsgüter gestapelt werden.

statistische Angaben Die Sammlung und Zusammenstellung aller geschäftlichen Ergebnissen zur Beurteilung der Geschäftstätigkeit.

statistische Qualitätskontrolle Qualitätskontrollverfahren bei Großserienprodukten.
Durch Entnahme von Einzelprodukten wird in regelmäßigen Abständen die -▶Qualität der Ware überprüft.

Steigerung Fortschritt, Verbesserung

Stellfläche Platz für Materiallagerung.

Stellung Position in der Organisation. -▶Arbeitsplatz/Funktion - ▶Funktion

Stellungnahme Antwort, Beurteilung, Entscheidung, Erklärung, Meinung, Kommentar, Gesichtspunkt.

Steuer Öffentliche Abgaben, die durch staatliche Organe in ihrer Höhe festgelegt und erhoben werden. Abgaben der Bürger zur Abdekkung der staatlichen Verpflichtungen.

required duration of tool operating time. (Standards for tool development)

bar material Raw material in form of bars.

staple locations Storage areas (seaports) where world trade goods can be stored.

statistical data Collection and listing of all business transaction, to rate business efficiency.

statistical quality control Method of quality control to check the performance for mass produced products.
Level of quality is checked by random sampling in regular sequence.

progression Step forward, improvement

shelf space Place for material storage.

position Job titel of organization. -▶job position -▶function

statement Answer, endorsement,- decission declaration, opinion, comment approach.

tax Public rates which are established and collected by authorities. Forced contribution by citizen to support Govermental obligation.

Stichprobe Teilmengenentnahme aus Großserien zum Zwecke der Güteprüfung. -▶statistische Qualitätskontrolle

Stichtag Fester Termin, Kalendertag, zu dem bestimmte Aktionen stattfinden. -▶Inventurstichtag, Steuerzahlung, Lohnzahlung.

Stillegung Betriebsschließung wegen Urlaub oder Auflösung.

Stillstand Betriebsunterbrechung, Störung der Fertigung.

Störung -▶Stillstand

Streik -▶Industriestreik -▶Arbeitskampf/Streik

Stück Einheit, Segment

Stückliste Von der Konstruktion erstellte Material-Teileliste, enthält Angaben über Werkstoff, Bezeichnung und Güte eines Erzeugnisses. -▶Spezifikation -▶Stammdaten-File

Stückzahl Anzahl, Mengenangabe, Fertigungseinheiten.

Stundenlohn Entgelt für die Arbeitsleistung einer Stunde.

Summe Gesamtzahl, Ergebnis, Totale

System-Menge System-Menge ist Teil der -▶Materialreserve und besteht aus: -▶Fertigungsreserve -▶Montagesystem

Systemfüllung Erstbestückung der Fertigung mit Material.

spot check Irregulary sampling taken from bulk deliveries to check product quality. -▶statistical quality control.

key date Fixed timing, calender day, where certain action have to be performed. -▶annual inventory day, tax payment, wage payment.

shutdown Plant shut down due to vacation or closure.

standstill Interruption of business, process breakdown.

disturbance -▶standstill

strike/dispute -▶industrial strike -▶industrial dispute/strike

piece Unit, segment

bill of material List of material containing parts -▶specification established by product development. -▶parts master file

piece number Number of pieces, volume, number of units.

wage per hour Hourly wage rate for one hour work.

amount Total amount, result, value

system float System float is part of -▶production material float and consist of: -▶material in process -▶assembly line float

system fill Initial material fill of production line.

T

Tabelle Plan -▶Inhaltsverzeichnis -▶Index -▶Liste

Tagesordnung Auflistung der zur Abhandlung anstehenden Geschäftsvorgänge mit Verantwortlichkeit der Berichterstattung.

Tagesplanungsvolumen /DPV Auf Basis von Markterwartungen und Marktergebnissen entwickelte zukünftige- tägliche Produktionsvolumen. Planwert für Werkzeugentwicklung, Kapazitätsinstallation für -▶Kaufteile, Planung von Verpackung und Transportraum. -▶Kapazitätsplanungsvolumen / CPV -▶FPV- Finanzplanungsvolumen -▶Budgetentwicklungsvolumen / BDV

Tagesrate Die Aufgliederung des -▶Produktionsprogramms auf Arbeitstage.

Tagessatz Festgelegter Abrechnungsbetrag für tägliche Reisekosten anstelle von Belegabrechnung, der unter Berücksichtigung der unterschiedlichen Kostenstruktur in den verschiedenen Ländern von der Finanzbehörde festgestellt wurde.

Tagesverbrauchswert Der Tagesverbrauchswert ergibt sich aus der Kalkulation, -▶Mengeneinheit mal Preis mal produktbezogener Verbrauch mal geplanter Tagesverbrauch. Dient zur Ermittlung der -▶Kostenklasse.

Tagung Konferenz, Kongreß

table schedule -▶table of content -▶index -▶bill

agenda Summary of business items to be discussed including responsibilities of reporting.

DPV- daily planning volume Developing of future daily production rates based on marketing assumptions and market positions.
Key figure for tool development, capacity installation for -▶EP sourced parts, planning of packing and transportation space.
-▶CPV, capacity planning volume
-▶FPV, financial planning volume
-▶BDV, budget development volume

daily rate Structuring of -▶production schedule into working days.

daily travel allowance Fixed travel amount to settle of daily travel expenses instead of voucher account as stated by finance authorities considering different cost structure between countries.

daily usage value Daily usage value calculated by -▶unit of measure by price by usage by daily rate. Result is base for calculation of -▶cost classification.

conference Meeting, congress, session

Taktzeiten -▶Richtwert für die Fertigung

Tarifabkommen Vertragliche Vereinbarung zwischen den Tarifparteien über Veränderung der Arbeitsbedingungen oder Lohnabkommen für einen bestimmten Zeitraum.

Tarifgebiet Gebietsbereich, für den Tariffestsetzungen erfolgen. Aufgliederung eines nationalen Fachbereiches in regionale Verbände zur Berücksichtigung von regional unterschiedlichen Aspekten bei Tarifabkommen.

Tätigkeitsbereich Aufgabenbereich -▶Funktion.

technische Änderung -▶Änderung

technische Einrichtung Technische Produktionsanlage -▶Fabrik

technische Unterlagen Entwicklungsunterlagen zur Produktgestaltung, -▶Spezifikationen, -▶Zeichnungen, -▶Normen.

technische Verbesserung Verbesserung der Produkte und Einrichtungen, durch -▶Neugestaltung, -▶Entwicklung.

Teilbezeichnung Teilbeschreibung, Teilnamen.

Teilefertigung Die Einzelteilfertigung. -▶Fabrikation

Teileklassifizierung -▶Kostenklassen

process tact time -▶production standards

wage settlement Regulations laid down in a contract between collective representatives for modification of working condition or wage rate setting for a certain period.

tariff area Territorial areas for which tariff settlements are to be taken. Splitting up of national trade organization into regional associations considering regional needs by wage settlements.

field of business activity Sphere of action -▶function.

technical change -▶change

engineering facilities Technical production facilities. -▶plant/factory

technical data Engineering develop work of product design, -▶specifications, -▶drawings, -▶standards.

technical improvement Technical product and facility improvement by -▶inovations, -▶development.

part description Part name

manufacturing of components Manufacturing of single parts. -▶fabrication/manufacture

parts classification -▶cost classification

Teileliste -▶Stückliste

Teilnummer Merkmal zur Identifizierung und Kontrolle der Produktionsteile,

Termin Bestimmter Zeitpunkt, Datum, -▶Einsatztermin, -▶Auslauftermin.

termingemäß Termingerecht, in der vorgesehenen Zeit, wie geplant, fertig nach Plan.

Terminplan Chronologische Auflistung der in einem bestimmten Zeitabschnitt durchzuführenden Aktionen mit Angaben der Fertigstellung.

Terminüberwachung Kontrolle der fristgerechten Erledigung der im -▶Terminplan vorgesehenen Aktionen.

Terminverfolgungsplan Plan zur Überwachung der zeitlich vorgesehenen Aktionen.

Terminzahlung Die Bezahlung einer Leistung zum vereinbarten Termin.

Toleranz Vorschrift, zum Teil genormt, über erlaubte Abweichungen von den Vorgaben bei Gewichten, Maßen, Festigkeiten, Bestandsabweichungen. -▶Norm

Toleranzüberschreitung Fertigergebnis liegt außerhalb der erlaubten -▶Toleranz, -▶Spezifikation -▶Fertigungsabweichung

Transit Im Durchlauf befindliche Materiallieferungen.

Transitzeiten Die Transitzeiten

parts list -▶bill of material

part number Number to identify and control parts.

stated time Appointed timing, date, -▶implementation date, -▶expire term

on the agreed time On schedule, in due time, as planned, finished on schedule.

time schedule Listing of planned action in sequence of effectivenes, to be performed during a certain period with details of expected execution.

follow-up of orders Controlling of actions to be performed as forecasted and stated in -▶time schedule.

follow-up chart Schedule to follow-up timly planned action.

payment in due time Payment for work performed in the agreed time.

tolerance Fixed limits regulated by standards, such as weights, measurement, resistance, inventory losses.
-▶standard

out of tolerance Deviating from limits of -▶tolerance, -▶specification -▶out of specification

transit Material in transit.

transit times Transit times com-

umfassen die Menge an Material in -▶Tagesraten für die Dauer des geplanten Transports vom Hersteller bis zum Empfänger. In Fällen von Überseebezug gliedert sich die Transitzeit in -▶inländische Transportzeit und allgemeine -▶Versandzeit. In der betriebswirtschaftlichen -▶Materialdisposition finden die Transitzeiten Berücksichtigung, wenn die -▶Bestellung auf ex Lieferant lautet. -▶Materialreserve

Transport Versendung der Güter.

Transportabteilung -▶Speditionsabteilung

Transportanweisungen Richtlinien, die den Versand von Gütern regeln.

Tranportkosten Kosten, die durch die Beförderung der Ausgangsprodukte und Abtranport der Erzeugnisse entstehen sowie Kosten des eigenen -▶Fuhrparks.

Transportschaden Während der Beförderung entstandener Schaden an Transportgut.

Typ Modell, Klasse

prising quantity of material in -▶daily rates for the duaration of planned transport from source of supply to the point of receiving in case of oversea deliveries, transit time is split-up in -▶inbound time and normal -▶transport time. In -▶material scheduling are transit times applied, when -▶purchase order stated, ex supplier. -▶production material float.

transport Shipping of products.

traffic department -▶forwarding department

shipping instructions Instructions to forward material.

transport charges Costs arising by transport of incoming material and shipping of own products, as well as costs resulting from own -▶transport and supply unit.

transport damage Damage of in transit material.

type Model/class

U

Überbestände -▶Fertigungsüberschuß -▶Produktionsüberschuß

Überbrückung Maßnahmen zur temporären Lösung von Problemen.

Übereinkommen Erzielung eines von Beteiligten erreichten gemein-

excess stocks -▶excess material -▶excess to schedule

bridge-over Interim measures to overcome problems.

agreement Enter into an agreement on a subject between parties

samen Ergebnisses zu einem Sachverhalt.

Überfällig Verzug nach -▶Terminplan.

Überholung Die technische Kontrolle und Nacharbeit von Einrichtungen oder Aggregaten, -▶Austauschmaterial / Teile.

Überkapazität Installierte Fertigungsmöglichkeit übersteigt die Bedarfsnachfrage.

Überlastung der Fertigung Bedarfsnachfrage ist größer als installierte Kapazität.

Überprüfung Kontrolle der sachgemäßen Ausführung einer Aktion. -▶Inspektion -▶Qualitätskontrolle

Überproduktion Die vorhandene Nachfrage übersteigende Produktion. -▶Fertigungsüberschuß -▶Produktionsüberschuß

Überschreitung des Budgets Die Finanzierung der im Budget vorgesehenen Vorhaben übersteigen die Vorgaben.

Überstunden -▶Mehrarbeit

Überstundenzuschlag Nach Tarif- oder Arbeitsvertrag festgelegtes zusätzliches Entgelt zum -▶Grundlohn als Ausgleich für -▶Mehrarbeit.

Überwachung - innerbetrieblich Die Kontrolle der einzelnen Geschäftsvorgänge. -▶Innenrevision

Umänderung Konvertieren, ändern, modifizieren.

concerned.

overdue Past-due according -▶time schedule.

overhoul Technical inspection and repair of facilities or assemblies, -▶reconditioning-material/ parts.

excess capacity Installed manufacturing rate exceeds market demand.

overload production Operate work is above installed capacity.

examination Controlling the correctness of action performed. -▶inspection -▶quality control

overproduction Market demand exceeding production output. -▶excess material -▶excess to schedule

exceeding the budget Financing of investments are in excess of budget authorization.

extra work -▶overtime work

overtime premium Amount paid in excess to -▶base rate / base wage as compensation for -▶overtime work, according to tariff or working contract.

in-house control Checking of company business transactions. -▶internal audit

alteration Conversion, change, modification, restyle.

Umbau Die -▶Umänderung von Produkten mit geringer oder keiner Nachfrage in marktgerechte Güter.

umbuchen Übertragung eines Buchungsvorganges auf ein anderes Buchungskonto.

Umklassifizieren Neubestimmung der -▶Kostenklassen aufgrund Preis- oder Bedarfsänderung.

Umrechnungskurs Amtlich festgestellter Wechselkurs, zu dem Währungen konvertiert werden.

Umsatz Die Summe aller Verkaufserlöse, die in einer bestimmten Zeit erzielt wurden.

Umschlaghäufigkeit Materialumschlag -▶Lagerumschlag.

Umweltschutz Die zielbewußte industrielle Entsorgung von Abfällen und Rückständen aus Fertigung und Produktion. Wichtiger Punkt bei der Erstellung von neuen Projekten und Änderungsmaßnahmen im Fertigungsprozeß. Berücksichtigung der Kosten für Entsorgung.

unbrauchbar Verwendungsunfähig, außer Funktion, nicht bedienungsfähig. -▶Fertigungsabweichung.

unfertig Im Rohzustand, in Bearbeitung, unkomplett.

ungültig Aufhebung einer Entscheidung, Ablauf einer befristeten Aktion.

unpaarige Bewegungen Bu-

rebuilding Restyle of products with less- or nil sales effect into salable goods.

rebook Transfer of booking from one account to another.

reclassification Reevaluation of -▶cost classification due to price- or usage alteration.

conversion rate Official rate of exchange.

overturn Total amount of sales earned in a given period of time.

turnover ratio Stock turnover -▶inventory turnover.

environmental safety Systematic industrialized disposal of waste, resulting from production process. Key issue for new project planning and process modification. Consideration of costs for enviromental measurements planning.

useless Of no use, not usable, out of order, -▶out of tolerance.

unfinished In rough condition, in process, uncomplete.

invalid Cancellation of a decission, termination of timely actions.

mismatched items Accounting of

chungsaktionen über Materialbestandsveränderungen bei Verwendung nicht bekannter Referenz. (Unbekannte Teilnummer)

Unteraggregat Kleine Zusammenbaustufe als Teil vom -►Aggregat.

Unterbeschäftigung Das Angebot zur lohnbezogenen Beschäftigung ist aufgrund von geringer Bedarfsgüternachfrage kleiner als die Nachfrage zur lohnbezogenen Beschäftigung.
(Gegensatz: -►Vollbeschäftigung)

Unterbrechung Störung des geordneten Funktionsablaufes.
-►Stillstand

Unterhalt -►Instandhaltung / vorbeugend

Unterlieferant Bezugsquelle des Direktlieferanten zur Beschaffung von Einzelteilen, die zur Herstellung des Bestellgutes dienen.

Unternehmen Organisatorisch-rechtliche Einheit mit dem Zweck der ertragsbringenden Geschäftstätigkeit.

Urlaubsplan Systematische Übersicht über Urlaubstermine der einzelnen Arbeitnehmer als Grundlage für die Fortführung der Geschäftstätigkeit.

Ursache Anlaß, Grund, Motiv, Beweggrund.

Ursprungsangabe -►Kennzeichnung -►Marke

material movement by using unknown reference. (unknown partnumber)

subassembly Smail assembly unit as part of -►aggregate/assembly/end-item.

underemployment Due to lower consumer requirements, the offer of jobs is less than available labour demand for wage related employment. (Opposite: -►full employment)

interruption Stoppage of an orderly functional performance.
-►standstill

maintenance -►preventive maintenance.

subcontractor Source of supply for delivery of initial parts to manufacture ordered product at a direct supplier.

concern Lawful organizational establishment to perform profitable business.

vacation schedule Systematically plan for vacation timing of employee as planning matter for continuation of business performance.

cause Ground, reason, motive.

indication of origin -►identification -►label/brand/identification mark.

Ursprungsland Land, in dem eine Ware hergestellt wird.

country of origin Country in which goods are produced / manufactured.

V

Vakanz Freie, offene, nicht besetzte Stelle.

vacancy Open, not filled position.

Validierung Die Überprüfung von Neuentwicklungen hinsichtlich der Verwendungsfähigkeit durch den Erzeuger.

valididy Checking of new designed products by producer with regard to the feasibility.

Value added Durch Bearbeitung dem -▶Rohmaterial, -▶Rohling hinzugefügter Wert.
-▶Veredelung

value added Added net value to -▶raw material, -▶rough parts by processing to finished condition.
-▶finnishing

Valuta Ausdruck des internationalen Geldhandels für Zahlungsmittel eines Landes.

foreign exchange International term for money dealing for currency of a country.

Veranschlagung Bewertung von Projekten, Erfassung der zu erwartenden Kosten.

estimation Valuation of projected costs, statement of expected expenses.

Verantwortung Verpflichtung und Berechtigung zur Erfüllung einer Aufgabe durch selbständiges Handeln im eigenen Funktionsbereich.

responsibility Commitment and authority to perform job assignment in an independant capacity.

Verarbeitung Umgestaltung vom -▶Zwischenprodukt zum -▶Endprodukt oder Herstellung von neuen Produkten aus -▶Rohmaterial.

processing Changing of -▶semi finished product to -▶end-item /finished product or manufacturing of products from -▶raw material.

Verbesserung Veränderung einer Situation oder Sache zur besseren Gestaltung der Lage oder besseren Nutzung der Ware.

improvement Change of condition to improve current position or modification of products to increase utilization.

Verbesserungsvorschlag Mitarbeit der Beschäftigten zur Steigerung der Produktivität durch geeig-

suggestion scheme Contribution of employees to rise level of productivity by suggestion of appro-

nete Vorschläge, an den Produkten oder in der Fertigung eine -▶Verbesserung herbeizuführen. Zur Realisierung gelangende Vorschläge werden vielfach entsprechend einer betrieblichen Kostenermittlung honoriert.

Verbindlichkeiten Die am Bilanzstichtag bestehenden Schulden eines Unternehmens nach Höhe und Fälligkeit.

Verbrauch Die spezifizierte Verwendung von Gütern und Dienstleistungen für Produktionszwecke. -▶Bedarf/Verbrauch -▶Konsum

Verbraucher Ort, wo Bedarfsgüter zur Verwendung gelangen.
-▶Konsument

Verbrauchsabweichung Mehr- oder Minderverbrauch von Produktionsmaterial gegenüber den Bedarfsvorgaben. -▶Bedarf/Verbrauch -▶Falschverbrauch

Verbrauchsbestimmung Festlegung der zur Produkterzeugung erforderlichen Materialmenge durch die -▶Produktentwicklung -▶Mengeneinheit.

Verdienstausfall Minderung der regulären Einkünfte aus Beschäftigung wegen Arbeitsmangel oder anderer Ursachen.

Veredelung Die Fertigbearbeitung der aus -▶Rohmaterial oder -▶Rohling herzustellenden Teile. -▶Value

Veredelungsstufe Bis zu einer bestimmten Bearbeitungsstufe her-

riate measures for -▶improvement on products or modification of process.
Realization of suggestion are usuly paid according intra company cost finding as payment in return for extra service.

obligations Outstanding debts of a company according to value and date of maturity.

usage Specified utilization of goods and services for product manufacturing -▶requirement/usage -▶consumption

consumer Place where goods consumtion take place. -▶user/-consumer

usage variance Usage of material in excess or minus to schedule.
-▶requirement/usage -▶incorrect usage/misusage

usage determination Determination of producer related material usage by -▶Product development. -▶unit of quantity

loss of wages Suspension of salary - wage reduction due to shortage of work or other reasons.

finishing Processing of products from -▶raw material or rough part to a finished condition. added -▶value added

processing stage Semi-finished product up to a certain point of pro-

gestellte Produkte. -▶Value added

Veredelungsverkehr Zollbegünstigte Be- und Verarbeitung von Waren, die im veredelten Zustand, -▶Veredelungsstufe, ein- und wieder ausgeführt werden.

Vereinheitlichung -▶Standardteile -▶Norm

Verfahrensplanung Planung des kostengünstigsten Verfahrens für eine -▶optimale Produktionsgestaltung auf Basis von -▶Kapazitätsplanungsvolumen. -▶Fertigungsgröße

Verfügbarkeit -▶Bereitstellung

Vergütung Entgelt als Gegenleistung für geleistete Arbeit oder Dienste. -▶Lohn

Verkaufsbedingungen -▶Lieferbedingungen -▶INCOTERMS

Verkaufsorganisation -▶Vertrieb der Produkte im Rahmen der festgelegten Absatzmethoden und Betreuung der Kunden zur Förderung des Absatzes.

Verkehr Austausch von Gütern, -▶Transport.

Verlagerung aus Fremdbezug -▶Integration

Verlagerung nach Fremdbezug -▶De-Integration

Verlustquellen Betriebsinterne Ursachen, die zur Minderung von -▶Erfolg führen. -▶Erfolgslosigkeit

Verpachtung -▶Pacht -▶leasing

cess. -▶value added

improvement trade Preferential tariff or processing and manufacturing of semi finished material,- which is imported and exported. -▶processing stage

standardization -▶standard parts -▶standard

planning of operation method Planning of optimal production process for product manufacturing based on -▶CPV- capacity planning volume, to determ -▶limited quantity and -▶OPT-optimized production timing.

disposibility -▶availability

compensation Payment for labour or services performed. -▶wage

sales condition -▶delivery conditions -▶INCOTERMS

sales organisation -▶Distribution of products based on established methods and customer service to improve sales.

traffic Exchange of goods, -▶transport

integration from outside source -▶integration

outsourcing of make parts -▶de-integration/outsourcing

deficiencies Company internal causes which generate -▶efficiency losses.-▶inefficiency

letting on lease -▶tenancy -▶leasing

Verpackungsart a) -▶Einwegverpackung aus Holz, Pappe, Glas, Kunststoffmaterialien.
(Entsorgungsproblem) b) Mehrwegverpackung, -Standardverpackung, Fässer, -▶Paletten, -▶Behälter, -▶Leihverpackung, -▶Leergut, -▶Dauerverpackung, -▶Sonderverpackung

Versand Lieferung der Bestellungen. -▶Transport

Versandabfertigung Zollmäßige Abwicklung einer zur Ausfuhr bestimmten Warensendung.

Versandanzeige Mitteilung vom Verkäufer an den Käufer, daß die bestellte Ware abgeschickt worden ist.

Versandart Mittel der Versendung, Bahn, Post, Straße, See, Luft.

Versandbedingungen -▶Lieferbedingungen -▶INCOTERMS

Versandbericht Akkumulierte Auflistung der in einem Geschäftsjahr zum Versand gelangenden Güter.

Versanddatum Datum der Warenversendung vom Lieferanten.

Versandkosten Aufwendungen für den Warenversand durch Post, Bahn usw. (-▶Versandart) werden als -▶Vertriebskosten verrechnet.

Versandlager Sammelstelle und Zusammenstellung von Versandaufträgen.

Versandland Land aus der die Warenlieferung kommt.

type of packing a) -▶One-way package made from wood, paper, glas or plastic material.
(Disposal problem) b) Dual-use package, -standard package, barrels,-▶palettes, -▶case, -▶returnable packing, -▶empties, -▶duarable packing, -▶special wrapping

shipping Forwarding of ordered goods. -▶transport

customs clearance Clearance of customs formalities for goods to be exported.

advice note Information from supplier to receiver that ordered goods are in transit.

method of shipping Way of tranportation, rail, mail, road, sea, air.

forwarding terms -▶delivery conditions -▶INCOTERMS

shipping report Accumulative reporting of shippings.

date of dispatch Shipping date ex supplier.

shipping costs Expenses for transportation of goods by mail, rail etc. (-▶method of shipping) are counted as -▶sales costs.

shipping storage Collection point and consolidation of delivery orders.

country of shipment Country from where goods are delivered.

Versandliste Positionen, die zu einer Bestellung gehören; ist maßgebend für die Zusammenstellung der Lieferung.

Versandpapiere Verladepapiere -▶Frachtbrief.

Versandplan Entsprechend Prioritäten der Besteller erstellter Lieferplan, unter Berücksichtigung der -▶Lieferbedingungen -▶INCOTERMS.

Versandreserve Menge an Fertigprodukten, die unter Marketinggesichtspunkten erforderlich ist, um als Hersteller gegenüber der Nachfrage flexibel zu sein. Die -▶Kapitalbindung durch -▶Versandreserve muß in absoluter Relation zur Ertragslage stehen, da im Fertigprodukt der größte Inventurwert gebunden ist. -▶Materialreserve

Versandschein Zollpapier der Abgangszollstelle als Warenbegleitpapier zur Vorlage bei der Zollstelle am Empfangsort.

Versandstation Ort, Stelle, von wo der Materialversand erfolgt.

Versandveranlassung Veranlassung für eine außerordentliche Warensendung zu Lasten des Bestellers.

Versandverzögerung Zeitliche Verzögerung des Versands von vertraglich festgelegten Warensendungen. -▶Versandbedingungen -▶INCOTERMS

Versandzeit -▶Transitzeiten

shipping bill Items related to an order; document for picking and packing of goods to be delivered.

shipping documents Shipping papers -▶consignment note.

forwarding schedule Established schedule of shipment in line with customer priorities under consideration of -▶delivery conditions - ▶INCOTERMS.

shipping bank Stock of finished products held at supplier for reason of flexibility to support unexpected market demand.
The -▶capital binding by stock of -▶shipping bank has to be justified by sales expections, since finished products represent a higher inventory value. -▶production material float

clearance paper Document of home customshouse as goods annexed paper to present at customshouse point of destination.

shipping point Place, location from where material is shipped.

shipping request Request for excess transportation of material on customer expense.

delay in dispatch Delayed transportation of material scheduled for delivery. -▶forwarding terms -▶INCOTERMS

shipping time -▶transit time

verschicken Liefern, zustellen, versenden. -▶Verand

verschieben Verlegung einer geplanten Aktion auf einen neuen Termin.

verschiedene Abgänge Entnahme von Produktionmaterial zur Verwendung an nicht produktionsbezogener Stelle.

Verschiffung Erforderliche Maßnahmen zur Organisation des -▶Seetransports, damit die Ware in der vertraglich festgelegten - ▶Transitzeit den überseeischen Empfänger erreicht. -▶INCOTERMS

Verschlußlager Besondere Lagereinheit zur Lagerung von gefährlichen Stoffen und diebstahlgefährdeter Güter. Die Materialausgabe erfolgt über -▶Bezugsschein.

Verschrottung Die Entwertung von nicht verwertbarem Material. -▶Restbestand

Verschrottungsantrag Die Beantragung zur Verschrottung von nicht betriebsfähigem Material oder Einrichtungen. -▶Schrott

versenden -▶verschicken

Versicherung Die Absicherung der Geschäftätigkeit gegenüber unabwendbaren Gefahren.

Versuchsabteilung Besonders eingerichtete Fabrikstätte zur Durchführung von -▶Einbauprobe/ Funktionsbau, -▶Funktionsprüfung, -▶Erstmuster, aber auch Durchführung von Versuchen bei

send off Dispatching, delivering, mailing, transport. -▶shipping

postpone Deferment of scheduled introduction date for planned action, to a later period.

miscellaneous disbursement Using production material for another purpose.

water carriage Required steps to organize -▶carriage by sea in order that material is received within agreed -▶transit time -▶INCOTERMS

locked store Special store for storage of hazardous goods and items with risk of pilferage. Issuance of material is performed by -▶material requisition slip.

scrapping Treatment to make material useless. -▶remainder of stocks

scrapping request Request for discarding of material or facilities which are not longer being used. -▶scrap

deliver -▶send off

insurance Protection of business transaction to cover unforeseen events.

pilot plant Special equiped manufacturing area to perform -▶functional build, -▶functional test, -▶initial sample, but also trying out new designed products.

Neuentwicklungen.

Versuchsmaterial Eigens hergestellte, bis zur bestimmten Operation vorbearbeitete Teile zum Zweck der Erprobung von neuen Bearbeitungsmaschinen.

Verteiler -▶Linienverteiler

Verteilung Verteilung der hergestellten Güter an die Abnehmer. -▶Verkaufsorganisation

Vertrag Gegenseitig anerkannte Vereinbarung zur Abwicklung der Geschäftstätigkeit, vielfach unter Bezugnahme auf bestehende Richtlinien. -▶INCOTERMS -▶Kaufvertrag

Vertragsablauf Ende einer vertraglichen Vereinbarung.

Vertragsänderung Modifizierung des Vertragsinhaltes.

Vertragsannullierung Die Aufhebung des Vertrages aufgrund nicht Erfüllbarkeit oder Vertragsverstoß.

Vertragsform Art und Formalitäten eines Vertrages. -▶INCOTERMS

Vertrieb -▶Verkaufsorganisation -▶Verteilung

Vertriebskosten Alle beim Absatz von Erzeugnisse anfallenden Kosten, wie Personal-, Fracht-, Verpackungskosten, Werbeausgaben. -▶Versandkosten

Vertriebsleiter Verantwortliche Position in der -▶Verkaufsorganisation für die Absatzkoordination.

tryout material Special manufactured parts, machined up to required operation for the purpose of validation and capability test for new manufacturing machines.

distributor -▶line feeder

distribution Ditribution of manufactured products to customer. -▶selling department

contract Agreement between parties to perform business. In many cases in line with existing rules. -▶INCOTERMS -▶purchase order

determination of a contract Ending of a contract validity.

alteration of a contract Modification of a contract.

avoidance of a contract Ending of a contract due to non compliance.

form of a contract Type and formalities of a contract. -▶INCOTERMS

sales -▶sales organization -▶distribution

sales cost All expenses arising by distribution of products as personnel-, transport-, packing costs, advertising expenses. -▶shipping costs

sales manager Responsible person in -▶sales organization to coordinate distribution of goods.

Verwaltung Die Verwaltung umfaßt alle betrieblichen Tätigkeitsbereiche, die nicht der direkten Produkterstellung zuzuordnen sind. -▶Finanz -▶Materialwirtschaft -▶Personalverwaltung -▶Produktentwicklung -▶Verkaufsorganisation

Verwerfung Durch die -▶Qualitätskontrolle getroffene Entscheidung über Nichtverwendung von Produktionsmaterial bei -▶Toleranzüberschreitung.

Verwertung Die Weiterbehandlung von -▶Verwerfungen durch -▶Nacharbeit, -▶Umbau, -▶Verschrottung, -▶Restmaterialwert

Verzeichnis -▶Index -▶Tabelle -▶Liste

Verzinsung Zahlung von festgelegten Beträgen für die Bereitstellung einer Geldsumme.

Verzollung -▶Versandabfertigung

Verzug Nichteinhaltung der vereinbarten Termine. -▶überfällig

Vollbeschäftigung Situation wo alle Arbeitssuchenden zu gegebenen Lohnbedingungen geeignete Beschäftigung finden. (Gegensatz: -▶Unterbeschäftigung)

vorbeugende Instandhaltung - ▶Instandhaltung/vorbeugend

Vorgabezeit Sollzeit für die Erfüllung eines Auftrages, -▶Richtwert für die Fertigung, -▶Arbeitszeitvorgabe.

administration Administration includes all organization units which are not directly involved with product manufacturing. -▶finance - ▶materials supply -▶IR-industrial relation -▶product design development -▶sales organization

rejection -▶Quality control decision not to use material which is -▶out of tolerance.

disposal Further treatment of -▶rejections by -▶rework, -▶rebuilding, -▶scrapping, -▶scrap value

register -▶index -▶schedule -▶bill

payment of interest Payment of interest rate for the appropriation of funds.

customshouse entry -▶customs clearance

delay Failing to complete within a specified period. -▶overdue

full employment Situation where all people looking for work are being employed to acceptable wage conditions. (Opposite: -▶underemployment

preventive repair keeping -▶preventive maintenance

standard time Nominal work time for performing certain trades -▶production standard -▶work standard

Vorlaufmenge Erforderliche Materialmenge zur Sicherstellung einer kontinuierlichen Fertigung für die Dauer, wo Fertigungseinrichtungen für dieses Material aus Umbaugründen nicht zur Verfügung stehen -▶Fertigungsfrequenz -▶Bevorratung

Vorrat Gesamtheit der Reserve. -▶Lagerbestand -▶Materialbestand -▶Bevorratung

vorrätig Am Lager verfügbar.

Vorratsabbau Reduzierung der Bestände, -▶Materialreserve, -▶Vorrat, durch Rationalisierung der Fertigung und Materialversorgung.

Vorratsproduktion Vorgezogene Produktion im Hinblick auf zukünftige größere Bedarfsnachfrage und zur Nutzung der installierten Kapazität.(Führt zur hohen -▶Kapitalbindung.)

Vorschlagswesen -▶Verbesserungsvorschlag

Vorschrift -▶Richtlinien -▶Instruktionen

Vorserie Einer Produktionsserie vorgelagerten kleinere Fertigungsmenge, zur Erprobung der Fertigungsfähigkeit. -▶Funktionsüberprüfung

Vorstand Geschäftsleitung.

Vorteil Besserstellung gegenüber dem Wettbewerb.

advanced stock Required material to bridge machine-changeover time. -▶manufacturing frequency -▶stock pile

material holding Total amount of -▶production material float. -▶stocks inventory -▶stock on hand -▶stock pile

carried in stock Available on store.

inventory cutting Reduction of -▶material holding, -▶production material float, by methods of rationalization of process and material supply.

stockpiling in advance Advance production to cover future marketing demand as well as utilization of installed capacity. (Leads to high -▶capital binding.)

suggestion programme -▶suggestion scheme

direction -▶directives -▶instructions

pilot run Production of a small amount of products to obtain capability check before bulk supply. -▶functional test

executive board Managing commitee.

advantage Improvement relative to competition.

vorziehen von Bestellungen Vorverlegung der ursprünglich vorgesehenen Liefertermine.

predate of orders Advancing of initial determinate deliveries.

W

Wahlgruppe Zusammenfassung von in der Art unterschiedlichen, jedoch für die gleiche Funktion verwendbaren Teile zu einer gemeinsamen Bestandsgröße.

alternative parts group Subsumption of different designed parts, usable to support same function, to one stock control figure.

Währung Das im Umlauf befindliche Geld eines Landes. -▶Valuta -▶Tabelle: Währungseinheit

currency Money in circulation in any country. -▶foreign exchange -▶Table: Standard currency

Waren -▶Güter

articles -▶goods

Warenabsatz -▶Verkaufsorganisation -▶Verteilung -▶Vertrieb

sale of goods -▶sales organization -▶distribution -▶sales

Warenannahme Betriebsstelle, wo die Anlieferung, Vereinnahmung und Überprüfung der von außen bezogenen Waren erfolgt. -▶Eingang

receiving location Plant location where deliveries are accepted, accounted and checked. -▶receival

Warenausgang Die Veräußerung von Waren oder deren Entnahme. Punkt der Bestandsabmeldung. -▶Versand -▶Warenabsatz

outgoing goods Sales or disposal of goods. Point of inventory relief. -▶shipping -▶sale of goods

Warenbedarf -▶Verbrauch

demand of goods -▶usage

Warenbestand -▶Materialbestand -▶Lagerbestand

material in stock -▶stock on hand -▶stocks inventory

Wareneingangsprüfer Mit der Überprüfung der nach -▶Eingangsschein, -▶Lieferschein avisierten Warenlieferung bauftragter Sachbearbeiter.

receiving checker Clerk responsible for varifying receipts in accordance with -▶delivery document. -▶bill of delivery

Warengruppen Zusammenfassung der nach Art, Herstellung und Beschaffenheit ähnlichen Teile zur

commodity pattern Grouping of like parts, similar design, process and specification, for the purpose

rationellen Gestaltung von Einkauf, Disposition und Qualitätskontrolle.

Warenidentifizierungsmerkmal Auf der Ware angebrachtes Balkendiagramm als verschlüsselte Artikeldaten, um eine -▶Elektronische Warenidentifizierung zu ermöglichen.

Warenlager -▶Lager

Warenpreis -▶Einkaufspreis

Warenprobe -▶Erstmuster

Warensendung Warenlieferung -▶Versand -▶Warenausgang

Warenumsatz -▶Lagerumschlag

Warenzeichen -▶Fabrikmarke / Zeichen

Wartung -▶Instandhaltung /vorbeugend -▶Unterhalt

Wegfall Weglassung von Einzelteilen, die zum Bauumfang eines Produktes gehören. (Kundenwunsch)

Weisung Aufträge des Arbeitgebers an Arbeitnehmer. -▶Richtlinien

Werbung Zielorientierte Ansprache an potentiellen Kundenkreis zur Absatzförderung. -▶Reklame

Werk -▶Fabrik -▶Betrieb

Werkhalle Fabrikationsstätte - ▶Werk

to rationalize purchase, scheduling and quality control matters.

bar coding of goods Bar coded diagram on goods containing article data for -▶bar code reading.

warehouse -▶store / warehouse / depot

price of googs -▶prime cost

trade pattern -▶initial sample

shipment of goods Delivery of goods -▶shipping -▶outgoing goods

sales turnover -▶inventory turnover

trade name -▶trade-mark

servicing -▶preventive maintenance -▶maintenance

omission Omission of details from an assembly content as requested by customer.

direction Instruction of employer to employee. -▶directives

advertising Object orientated address to potential customer for sales promotion. -▶publicity

factory -▶plant/factory -▶operation/shopfloor

shopfloor Manufacturing area -▶factory

Werksanlagen -▶Ausstattung/Anlagen/ Einrichtungen

Werksleitung Koordiniert das Betriebsgeschehen und erstellt -▶Richtlinien zur Erreichung der betrieblichen Erwartungen. -▶Fabrikleiter

Werksleistung -▶Gesamtleistung

Werksschutz Der Personalleitung unterstehende Organisationseinheit mit Verantwortung zur Wahrung der betrieblichen Sicherheit - Ein- und Ausgangskontrolle sowie Objektschutz.

Werkstoff Zusammenfassende Bezeichnung für alle Materialien, die zur Herstellung eines betrieblichen Erzeugnisses bestimmt sind. -▶Fertigteile / Kaufteile -▶Produktionsmaterial -▶Halbfabrikate -▶Rohmaterial -▶Rohling

Werktag -▶Arbeitstag

werktäglich arbeitstäglich

Werktechnik -▶Fabrikationstechnik

Werkzeugausgabe Werkzeuglager

Werkzeugbau Fabrik mit besonderer Ausstattung zur Herstellung von Werkzeugen.

Wertsteigerung -▶Value added

Wettbewerb Konkurrenz - Leistungskampf zwischen Mitanbieter am Markt . -▶Konkurrent

Wiederausfuhr Wiederausfuhr von zuvor eingeführten Produkten,

operating facilities -▶equipment/ facilities

plant management Coordinates plant activities and issues -▶directives to achieve companies objectives. -▶plant manager

operating performance -▶overall efficiency

plant security Organizational unit to perform companies security control on incoming and outgoing as well as object security and personnel control.

material Collectively description of material to be used for product manufacturing.
-▶purchased finished parts -▶production material -▶semi finished production goods -▶raw material -▶rough part

weekday -▶working day

daily daily working

plant engineering -▶manufacturing engineering

tool store Tool outlay

tool shop Factory special equiped for manufacturing of tools.

increased value -▶value added

competition Business rivalry - competition between rivals. -▶competitor

reexport Reshipment of previously imported products, partly as-

zum Teil im -▶Endprodukt/Fertigprodukt gebunden oder weiterverarbeitet. -▶Veredelungsverkehr

Wiedereinfuhr Wiedereinfuhr von zuvor ausgeführten Produkten, zum Teil im montierten Zustand oder weiterverarbeitet. -▶Montage -▶Veredelungsverkehr

Wiederverwertung Verfahren zur Umwandlung von Abfallprodukten in Rückgewinnung der Grundstoffe, die dann zur Neugewinnung dienen. (Papier, Glas, Metalle)

wirtschaftliche Fertigungsgröße -▶Fertigungsgröße -▶optimale Losgröße

wirtschaftliche Lagerhaltung Die permanente Vorratskontrolle durch Vergleich der effektiven Materilbestände gegenüber der autorisierten Bestandsmenge. -▶Materialreserve -▶Bevorratung

Wirtschaftlichkeitsuntersuchung Untersuchung, ob mit der installierten Kapazität oder Veränderungen im Fertigungsablauf eine auf Gewinn ausgerichtete Produktion möglich ist.

Wirtschaftsplan -▶Budget

Woche

wöchentlich

sembled in -▶end-item/ finished product or upgraded by further process. -▶free trade

reimport Reimportation of previously exported products, partly assembled or further processed -▶assembly -▶free trade

recycling Salvage process of waste material to recover raw material to be used subsequently for initial production. (paper, glas, metals)

economical production rate -▶limited quantity -▶optimized production rate

economical stock control Permanent stock control via verification of actual material holdings relative to authorized stock on hand. -▶production material float -▶stock pile

profitability study Economic research to find out whether installed capacity or modified process is sufficient to achieve profitable process result.

economic plan -▶budget

week

weekly

Z

Zahl Nummer, Ziffer

zahlbar - bei Bestellung - bei Lieferung

number Figure, digit

payable - on application - on delivery

zahlen Eine Summe - Forderung begleichen.
Zahlenfolge Zahlenordnung - Zahlenserie.
Zahlenreihe
Zählhäufigkeit -▶Bestandsaufnahmehäufigkeit
Zahltag Tag der Lohnzahlung.

Zählung Zahlenmäßige Erfassung eines Sachverhalts.

Zahlung -▶zahlen -▶Vergütung

Zahlenübersicht -▶statistische Angaben

Zahlungsbedingungen Teil des -▶Kaufvertrages, Vereinbarung zwischen Käufer und Verkäufer über die Bezahlung der gelieferten oder zu beziehenden Ware. -▶Lieferbedingungen

Zählwaage Zählwiegeeinrichtung zur rationellen -▶Bestandsaufnahme von Kleinmaterial, wobei als Gewicht der Dezimalanteil der zur Erfassung anstehenden Menge dient.

Zeichnung Vom -▶Entwicklungsbüro angefertigte Darstellung eines herzustellenden Produktes.

Zeitablauf Fristablauf

zeitgerecht -▶termingemäß

Zeitplan -▶Terminplan -▶Termin -▶Kursbuch

Zeitpunkt - zum jeweiligen - zum frühestmöglchen - zum bestimmten

make payment Liquidation of a claim.
numerical order Numerical series.
column of figures
counting frequency -▶cycle count frequency
day of payment Day of wage payment.

counting Numerical counting of subjected item.

payment -▶make payment -▶remuneration

statistical table -▶statistical data

terms of payment Agreement between buyer and supplier to pay for deliveries or ordered deliveries. Terms of payment are part of -▶purchase order or -▶delivery conditions.

counting scale Counting facility for rational -▶cycle count/stocktaking, whereby as whight, the decimal part of accountable quantity is used.

drawing Illustration of producable product, established and isued by -▶engineering office

expiration of time elapsed time

in time -▶on the agreed time

timing plan -▶time schedule -▶stated time -▶time table

point of time - for the time being -at the earliest possible - at the

Zeitraum Periode - Länge

Zeittafel -▶Tabelle: Welt-Zeit-Tabelle

Zeitverzug -▶Verzug

Zeitvorgabe -▶Vorgabezeit

zeitweilig temporär - gelegentlich

zerlegen Ein Bauumfang zum besseren Versand in Einzelgruppen zerlegen.

Zettel Adressenanhänger an Warenlieferungen.

Zielvorgabe Maßgabe für die Erreichung von Geschäftsergebnissen. -▶Planzahl

Ziffer -▶Zahl

Zinsen Preis für Kapitaldienste.

Zoll -▶Schutzzoll

Zoll und Verkehrsdienste Organisationseinheit der -▶Materialwirtschaft mit Verantwortung für die Zoll- und Transportkoordination im Unternehmen.

Zollabfertigung -▶Versandabfertigung -▶Versandschein

Zollabfertigungsamt Amtsstelle, wo die -▶Verzollung erfolgt - Kann auch im Unternehmen, von wo der Versand erfolgt, durch Zollamtspersonal erfolgen.

Zollager Lagerung von unverzollten Waren unter amtlichem -▶Zoll-

specified date

period of time lenght of time

time indicator board -▶Table: World-Time-Table

loss of time -▶delay

time allowance -▶standard time

temporary provisional - occasional

knock down Dis-assembled material for reason of transport simplification.

slip Label on deliveries.

objective Guideline for achieving companies targets. -▶figure

figure -▶number

interest Payment for capital services

customs -▶protective tariff

customs and traffic Organizational section of -▶materials supply with responsibility to coordinate companies customs and traffic matters.

customs examination -▶customs clearance -▶clearance paper

customs clearinghouse Office where -▶customhouse entry is performed - There are posibilities to clear customs duty at the shipper by customs personnel.

bonded store Storage of unpaid duty goods in -▶customhouse and

231

verschluß und Abwicklung der zollrechtlichen Überführung von Zollagergut in den freien Verkehr.

Zollbehörde Zollamt

zollfrei Befreiung von Zollabgaben für Waren nach -▶Zolltarif oder wo Maßnahmen für -▶Schutzzoll nicht gegeben sind. -▶Veredelungsverkehr

zollpflichtig Waren oder -▶Warengruppen, für die nach -▶Zolltarif Abgaben zu entrichten sind.

Zolltarif Index, geordnet nach -▶Warengruppen mit Tarifbezogenheit für Waren die -▶zollfrei oder -▶zollpflichtig sind.

Zubehör -▶Sonderteile

Zukunftsplanung Marktanalysen zur Ermittlung der -▶Tagesplanungsvolumen /DPV

Zulieferer -▶Unterlieferant

Zuordnung Sachverhalte in Beziehung bringen.

zurückschicken -▶Rückversand

Zurückzahlung Rückzahlung einer Kaufsumme, wenn das Erwerbsgut dem Angebot nicht entspricht.

zusammenklappbare Verpackung Zusammenlegbare Verpackungen zur rationellen Leergutbeförderung.

zusätzliche Operationsreserve

clearance of customs examinations prior transfer of customs goods into free trade.

customs authorities Customs office

free of customs duty Free of duty for goods according -▶customs tariff or where subject for collecting -▶protective tariff does not exist. -▶free trade

liable to pay customs duty Products or -▶commodity pattern, for which duty is required as stated in -▶customs tariff.

customs tariff Index in -▶commodity pattern order with tariff related indication of goods,-▶free of customs duty- or -▶liable to pay customs duty.

accessory -▶options / accessory

forward planning Market analysis to develop -▶DPV-daily planning volume.

component supplier -▶subcontractor

allocation Putting in relation of associated items.

send back -▶return shipment

repayment Return payment of sales price, in case that bought product does not meet specification.

collapsible package Collapsible package for rational empty returnshipments.

additional operational reserve

Materialmenge, die vorübergehend nach individuellen Notwendigkeiten eingelagert wird. Kriterien, die eine zusätzliche Operationsreserve erlauben, sind Gegenstand der -▶Prinzipien zur Bestimmung der Materialreserve. -▶Materialreserve -▶Bevorratung -▶Überbrückung

Zusatzlieferung -▶Nachbestellung -▶Nachlieferung

Zuschuß/Subvention -▶staatliche Zuschüsse

Zustellung / Lieferung Die Materialanlieferung. -▶Warensendung

Zweigbetrieb -▶Filiale

Zwischenlösung -▶Interimsmaßnahmen

Zwischenprodukt Teile, die im vorbearbeiteten Zustand bezogen werden und deren -▶Verarbeitung beim Bezieher erfolgt.

Additional material demand as temporarely increase to normal operational reserve, as protection for expected supply interruption. Criterias are subject of -▶principles of float allocation. -▶production material float -▶stock pile -▶bridge over

supplementary delivery -▶reorder -▶additional delivery

grants/investment -▶govermental grants

delivery Material delivery. -▶shipment of goods

affiliated organization -▶subsidiary

interims solution -▶provisional measure

semi finished product Parts received in pre-manufactured condition for further -▶processing at receiver plant.

Anhang

Zur Gestaltung der Tabellen: Maße und Gewichte, Zahlwörter, Ordnungszahlen und Wochentage / Monate, diente als Referenz, Cassels Wörterbuch S.630 /31 Fischer Weltalmanach 1989 S.1047 / 52 Gablers Wirtschaftslexikon Band 4 S.255 /56

Zur Erstellung der Tabelle: Währungseinheit und Nationalitätskennzeichen dienten länderbezogene Angaben aus der Chronik 1987 und Gabler Wirtschafts - Lexikon, Angaben zu den Nationen. ISO-Codes, (International Standards Organization) zur Klassifizierung der nationalen Währungen, wurden aus dem SWIFT-Handbuch (Society for Worldwide Interbank Financial Tele-communication) entnommen. Aktuelle Daten über Kursverhältnisse der wichtigsten Währungen zum ECU (European Currency Unit) sind nach Börsennotierung vom 08.01.90, veröffentlicht durch die Tageszeitung DIE WELT Nr.7 vom 09.01.1990 S.17. Wertanteil der einzelnen EG-Staaten am ECU (Währungskorb) wurden nach der Neuwichtung am 19.06.89, durch die Tageszeitung HANDELSBLATT Nr.116 vom 20.06.89 S.9 und Bundesfinanznachrichten Nr.51/89 vom 22.09.89 veröffentlicht. Der Durchschnittswert der ECU zur Deutschen Mark (DM) wird entsprechend Bundesfinanznachrichten 2/90 vom 05.01.90 auf DM 2,03 festgestellt.

Die Welt Zeit-Tabelle wurde auf Vorlage der Zeitzonenkarte, RECTA FOLDEX - Levallois - France erstellt.

INCOTERMS (International Commercial Terms) Auflage 1984, war Vorlage zur Stichwortbeschreibung INCOTERMS.

Appendix

The tables for measures and weights, numerals, numeral-figures and weekdays/months were taken from Cassel's German & English Dictionary, page 630/31; Fischer Weltalmanach 1989, page 1047/52; Gablers Wirtschaftslexikon volume 4, page 255/56.

Data for standard currency and nationality symbols were taken from Chronik 1987 and Gabler Wirtschaftslexikon. ISO Codes (International Standard Organization) for classification of national currencies are from the SWIFT-Handbook (Society for Worldwide Interbank Financial Tele-communication). Actual currency data in relation to the ECU (European Currency Unit) were taken from the exchange section of the newspaper DIE WELT No. 7, of 9. Jan. 1990, page 17.

The monetary value of the EG Countries share of the ECU (based of available commodities) were after the re-valuation on 19. June 1989, published by the newspaper HANDELSBLATT, No. 116, dated 30. June 1989, page 9 and the Bundesfinanznachrichten No. 51/89 dated 22. June 1989. The average value of the ECU to the Deutsche Mark (DM) of DM 2,03 was established according to the Bundesfinanznachrichten No. 2/90, dated 5. Jan. 1990.

The World Time Table was taken from RECTA FOLDEX - Levallois -France.

INCOTERMS (International Commercial Terms), edition 1984, was used for the index of INCOTERMS.

Anmerkungen des Autors

Das Buch entstand durch Vermittlung und Unterstützung von Ernst Knott, der durch seine langjährige Erfahrung auf dem Gebiet der Logistik Anregungen und Erfahrungswerte zur Gestaltung eingebracht hat.

Weitere Unterstützung wurde mir zuteil durch die Mitarbeit von Hubert Garding, der durch seine hervorragenden betriebs-wirtschaftlichen Sachkenntnissen, an der inhaltlichen Gestaltung großen Anteil hat.

Mein Dank gilt auch Robert Schreyer, der durch manche Gespräche zur Erweiterung durch Aufnahme von logistischen Zusammenhängen beigetragen hat.

Notes of the Author

The glossary was initiated by the kind mediation and Support of Ernst Knott who helped in shaping this glossary with his long-time experience in the field of logistics.

I received additional support from Hubert Garding who helped me with his specific knowledge of material management in formulating this glossary.

Finaly I would like to thank Robert Schreyer for his recommendations to include special aspects of logistics.

Literatur- und Quellennachweis
Biographical Data - Reference

1. Gabler Wirtschafts - Lexikon
   11. Auflage
   Verlag: Dr. Th. Gabler GmbH Wiesbaden
2. H. C. Recktenwald
   Wörterbuch der Wirtschaft
   Verlag: A. Körner Stuttgart
3. Der Kleine Eichborn
   Wirtschaft und Wirtschaftsrecht
   Deutsch - Englisch
   Englisch - Deutsch
   Verlag: Siebenpunkt Burscheid
4. Cassels Wörterbuch
   Deutsch - Englisch
   Englisch - Deutsch
   Verlag: Compact G m b H München
   Neuausgaben: Harold T. Betteridge
5. Langenscheidts Universal - Wörterbuch
   Englisch - Deutsch
   Deutsch - Englisch
   Verlag: Langenscheidt
   Berlin - München - Zürich
6. Chronik - Verlag
   Horenberg Kommunikation Verlag und Mediengesellschaft mbH & Co.KG Dortmund 1987
7. DIE WELT Tageszeitung Nr.7 1990
   Verlag: Axel Springer AG. Hamburg
8. HANDELSBATT Tageszeitung Nr.116 1989
   Verlag: Düsseldorf
10. Der Fischer Weltalmanach 1989
    Verlag: Fischer Taschenbuch
11. INCOTERMS ICC Services S.A.R.L.
    38 Cours Albert Paris
    Ausgabe: 1984

Verteilerdienst der internationalen
Handelskammer Köln
12. Recta - Foldex
Verlag: Realisations Etudes Cartographiques
Touristiques et Administratives
Levallois - France
13. BMF Finanznachrichten
Bundesministerium der Finanzen
Ausgabe: Nr. 51/89 22.09.1989
14. SWIFT-Handbuch Society for Worldwide
Interbank Financial Telecommunication
(ISO-Codes Währungskennzeichen)

Franz J. Linden, Jahrg. 1931, war 25 Jahre im Bereich der Materialwirtschaft in einem international organisierten Industrieunternehmen, in verschiedenen Funktionen - und hiervon 15 Jahre in leitenden Positionen tätig.

Franz J. Linden, born, 1931, was active for 25 years in Materials Supply of a multi national company, covering several functions in Material Planning, and thereof for 15 years in management positions.